PRAISE FOR
Lincoln and Whitman

"A revealing character study."
—*The Washington Post*

"Deftly written and carefully researched, this book uncovers fresh and often surprising connections between America's greatest poet and its greatest statesman. Daniel Mark Epstein reveals a political side to Whitman and a literary side to Lincoln, finding new subtleties of character and skill in each of these towering figures. Along the way, he re-creates nineteenth-century life in fascinating ways."
—David S. Reynolds, author of *Walt Whitman's America* and *Beneath the American Renaissance*

"Epstein presents a compelling affinity of ideas."
—*Newsday*

"Epstein offers a revealing character study of Whitman and a penetrating analysis of his wartime poetry. . . . [He] expertly paints the worlds in which Whitman moved, from Pfaff's saloon, where the poet enjoyed the bohemian camaraderie of the New York literati, to the military hospitals in Washington where he tended wounded soldiers."
—*The Ann Arbor News*

"Powerful and evocative."
—*Kirkus Reviews* (starred review)

"Epstein has yoked Lincoln and Whitman in a detailed narrative sure to please the vast audience both men justly command. The book is a fine combination of biography, history, and literary criticism, with several quirky excursions into the mysteries of the two men's lives and loves."

—*The Philadelphia Inquirer*

"An illuminating, elegant book. The scholarship is excellent, the ideas provocative, and the writing simply sublime. Both Lincoln and Whitman—together with the long-vanished culture in which they lived—come vividly, sometimes startlingly, alive in Daniel Mark Epstein's luminous prose."

—Harold Holzer, author of *The Lincoln Image*

"Cuts back and forth as compellingly as a good novel between evocative accounts of each man. The book places its two subjects in a uniquely sharp perspective."

—*The Burlington Free Press*

"Epstein memorably evokes the look and feel of Washington during the Civil War, the eerily adjacent lives there of Walt Whitman and Abraham Lincoln, and the frantic events that issued in the murder of our greatest president and the writing of our greatest poem, 'When Lilacs Last in the Dooryard Bloom'd.' Combining biography and history, his ingeniously constructed double narrative of personal development and national tragedy radiates humor, wonderment, and terror."

—Kenneth Silverman, author of
Lightning Man: The Accursed Life of Samuel F. B. Morse

DANIEL MARK EPSTEIN is the author of highly acclaimed biographies of Aimee Semple McPherson, Nat King Cole, and Edna St. Vincent Millay, as well as seven volumes of poetry. His verse has appeared in *The Atlantic*, *The New Yorker*, and *The Paris Review*, among other national publications. He lives in Baltimore.

Lincoln and *Whitman*

PARALLEL LIVES *in* CIVIL WAR WASHINGTON

DANIEL MARK EPSTEIN

RANDOM HOUSE TRADE PAPERBACKS
NEW YORK

For Neil Olson

2005 Random House Trade Paperback Edition
Copyright © 2004 by Daniel Mark Epstein

This work was originally published in hardcover by Ballantine Books, an imprint of
The Random House Publishing Group, a division of Random House, Inc., in 2004

LIBRARY OF CONGRESS CATALOGING-IN-PUBLICATION DATA
Epstein, Daniel Mark.
Lincoln and Whitman : parallel lives in Civil War Washington /
Daniel Mark Epstein.
p.   cm.
ISBN 0-345-45800-1
1. Lincoln, Abraham, 1809–1865.   2. Presidents—United States—Biography.
3. Whitman, Walt, 1819–1892.   4. Poets, American—Biography.   5. United
States—Politics and government—1857–1861.   6. United States—Politics and
government—1861–1865.   7. Political culture—United States—History—
19th century.   8. Political culture—Washington (D.C.)—History—19th century.
9. Washington (D.C.)—History—Civil War, 1861–1865.   I. Title.
E457.2.E67 2004
973.7'092'2—dc22
[B]   2003045141

Random House website address: www.atrandom.com

Printed in the United States of America

2   4   6   8   9   7   5   3

Book design by Casey Hampton

CONTENTS

PREFACE

𝒯wo visionaries, Abraham Lincoln and Walt Whitman, dominated the American scene from 1855 until 1865 in their respective fields of politics and literature. Their works, unique but analogous, have continued to affect our lives and thoughts, down to the present generation.

Therefore, any influence of the one genius upon the other and the slightest personal encounters between them have been subjects of intense scholarly and public interest since October 1865, when Whitman published his elegy for the President, "When Lilacs Last in the Dooryard Bloom'd." In 1875 Whitman brought out his *Memoranda During the War,* which included his detailed recollections of Lincoln. And in February 1876, in the New York *Sun,* Whitman published an account of the assassination in Ford's Theatre, which he expanded into a lecture incorporating his personal memories of Lincoln. Whitman's delivery of that speech a dozen times between 1879 and 1890 forged an unbreakable link between the President and the poet in the public mind. This book reexamines the actual connection.

The present narrative begins in a dusty law office in 1857, where Lincoln was first heard reading aloud from *Leaves of Grass,* and it ends in a "jewel box" theater in 1887, where Whitman delivered his Lincoln lecture to an audience that included Mark Twain, Andrew Carnegie, Frances Hodgson Burnett, and General and Mrs. William Tecumseh Sherman. But the story has deeper roots in the political turmoil of the 1850s.

During this decade when Abraham Lincoln became a power in national politics, and Walt Whitman was changing the medium of poetry by writing and publishing *Leaves of Grass,* America was rushing toward civil war with a momentum horrifying to those who were aware that war was inevitable, and unsettling to others who believed that the calamity might be avoided. There was hardly a facet of civil or political life that was not affected by the controversy over slavery. The failure to ban slavery from the territories inspired Whitman to write and publish his first free-verse poem, "Blood Money," in 1850. In 1852 Harriet Beecher Stowe published *Uncle Tom's Cabin,* a fictional critique of the "peculiar institution." It sold three million copies, and abolition became an unavoidable topic of conversation.

In those days, most people agreed that a transcontinental railroad would be the nation's best investment, since the frontier had reached the west coast. But whether the track would be laid along a northern or a southern route was a hotly debated question, in which the rivalry between the slaveholders and the free-soilers insinuated itself. The railroad would give economic advantage to the section it crossed, and it would decisively influence the politics of the yet unformed West. In 1853 the Pierce administration showed its intention to route the railroad south, from New Orleans to San Diego, by purchasing from Mexico a strip of land along the Gila River (the Gadsden Purchase). Northerners favoring a route from Chicago or St. Louis to San Francisco would have to act swiftly and forcefully. If the northern route was chosen, a long stretch of track needed to pass through the Great Plains—Indian country west of the Missouri River—which had not yet been received into the Union. Whether slavery would be legal in the territories depended entirely upon congressional legislation.

In the thick of this fateful controversy toiled a highly ambitious, leonine, charismatic orator from Illinois, Senator Stephen A. Douglas, the Little Giant. As chairman of the Committee on Territories, the forty-year-old presidential hopeful had shaped policy in the West. It was Douglas's contribution to the Great Compromise of 1850 that the territorial governments of Utah and New Mexico were given the power to decide the slavery question for themselves, by voting on it. Thus to the vexed question of slavery's future came the concept of "popular sovereignty." This idea was loathsome to patriots like Abraham Lincoln, who believed the Founding Fathers and the Constitution itself were fundamentally opposed to the spread of slavery.

Douglas had his dreams and ambitions, and he also held railroad investments. As an Illinois Democrat, he was expected to advance the St. Louis and Chicago interests in the northern route. This required an organization of the Nebraska Territory, which Douglas contrived to accomplish by a bill introduced on January 4, 1854. Trusting that what worked for Utah and New Mexico would suit the Great Plains, Douglas put together a bill that provided that Nebraska (and Kansas) would be accepted into the Union *with or without slavery,* as its constitution, yet to be written, might allow.

No one has ever quite understood why Douglas—who was in

many ways a worthy statesman, and by no means an advocate or apologist for slavery—took the spectacularly bold position he did in early 1854, abandoning the slavery question to the legislatures of unformed states. This is not the place to repeat Douglas's arguments, famously dashed by Lincoln. The Senator's actions may be attributed to political expedience: by allowing slaveholders the hope of taking their slaves west, he briefly gained popularity among Southern Democrats and support for the northern railroad route. Yet there is a more illuminating determinant, one that casts increasing light as Lincoln emerges from obscurity to oppose the Little Giant. Douglas lacked a guiding moral principle, a sense of vision. This put him at a severe disadvantage in debate against the political visionary who would topple him, Abraham Lincoln.

The drafted bill was illegal, as it violated the Missouri Compromise of 1820, which outlawed slavery north of the 36°30′ latitude. When colleagues pointed this out, Douglas irrationally explained that a careless clerk had left out the section of the bill referring questions concerning slavery to the territory's residents, i.e., to "popular sovereignty." Southern lawmakers complained that as long as the Missouri Compromise held sway the residents could not vote for slavery even if they wanted it, so Douglas obligingly added two amendments to the bill. First, the 36°30′ provision of the Missouri Compromise was to be repealed. Second, the area was to be split into two territories, Kansas and Nebraska, the southernmost of which, Kansas, seemed favored to become a slave state.

Abolitionists and liberal Yankees were enraged. Lincoln later said, "We were thunderstruck and stunned." Prominent liberal senators Charles Sumner of Massachusetts and Salmon Portland Chase of Ohio tried to rally the public against the outrageous bill by issuing the exposé "Appeal of the Independent Democrats" on

January 24, before the legislation was passed. It decried "a gross violation of a sacred pledge . . . a criminal betrayal of precious rights." These protesters were no match for the ferocious Douglas, the Southern Democrats, and the charming President Franklin Pierce. Although Douglas was burned in effigy from Maine to Wisconsin, and some women in Ohio solemnly awarded this latter-day Judas thirty pieces of silver, the bill became law, and American politics were changed forever. The simmer of abolitionism came to a boil. The Whig Party (to which Lincoln had belonged) lost its vestiges of relevance and soon vanished. The Democratic Party cracked wide open, sundered by the slavery dispute. Editor Horace Greeley called for the formation of a new antislavery party in his *New-York Tribune* on June 15. And that autumn, the fledgling party he called "Republican" won seats in the U.S. Congress and captured the legislatures of seven Northern states.

The concentration of Republicans in the industrial North, united by the single cause of free soil, hastened the slide of the Democratic Party into the agrarian culture of the South. The party system became sectionalized.

Popular sovereignty, which Stephen Douglas argued was the obvious solution to the devilish question, allowing settlers to decide for or against slavery—in the American way—by voting, turned out to be a ticking bomb.

William Seward of New York rose up in the Senate in righteous defiance. "Come on then, Gentlemen of the slave States; since there is no escaping your challenge, I accept it in behalf of the cause of freedom. We will engage in competition for the virgin soil of Kansas, and God give the victory to the side which is

stronger in numbers as it is in right." Fellow New Yorker Walt
Whitman greatly admired Seward for his defense of freedom.

The competition rapidly escalated from a war of words and
ballots to one of guns and swords. By 1855 there were two governments in Kansas, one proslavery, the other Free State. In May 1856
the proslavery government sent a gang to cannonade the free-soil
town of Lawrence, Kansas. The men wrecked the presses of the
Herald of Freedom, burned down the Free State Hotel, and looted
some shops. A few days later, fifty-six-year-old John Brown, with
his four sons and two other men, set out to avenge the "sack of
Lawrence." Believing himself to be an instrument of God's wrath,
the abolitionist led his band against a proslavery settlement on Pot-
tawatomie Creek. They broke into three cabins, hacked five men
to pieces with broadswords, and stole their horses.

Sentiments in the nation's capital ran so high that congressmen
began carrying pistols. On May 19 and 20, 1856, Charles Sumner
delivered his speech on "the Crime against Kansas," a blistering
indictment that not only censured the legislation that had led to
"Bleeding Kansas" but took aim at Douglas and Senator Andrew
P. Butler of South Carolina. The sharp-tongued Sumner ridiculed
Butler for his affection for his "mistress . . . the harlot slavery"; in
those bitter times this was taken as a slur against the Southern gentleman's character. Two days later, as Senator Sumner sat alone,
working at his desk after hours in the Senate chamber, a congressman from South Carolina, Butler's nephew Preston Brooks,
approached Sumner and rebuked him for his insults against Butler.
Not satisfied with the conversation, Brooks cracked Sumner's skull
with a gutta-percha cane. As Sumner turned and raised his arms in
defense Brooks continued to rain blows upon his victim's head and
spine until the weapon broke into pieces. His passion spent, Brooks

turned and left Sumner lying in his own blood, nearly dead on the floor of the great hall.

Charles Sumner, the most powerful voice against slavery in Washington, was so critically wounded that he could not return to his seat until 1859. His empty desk in the Senate became a symbol of the conflict that words could not mediate. Civil war had broken out in Kansas, and there was internecine combat between Northern and Southern lawmakers on Capitol Hill.

This, then, is the America in which Walt Whitman wrote *Leaves of Grass* and Abraham Lincoln sought his voice in the tumultuous discourse that was reshaping party politics. This is the troubled decade in which our story begins.

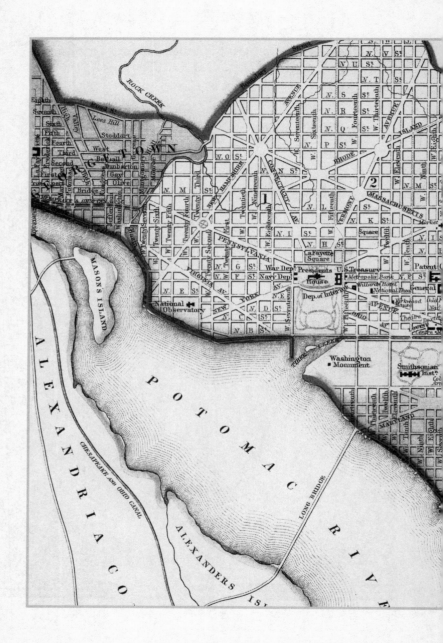

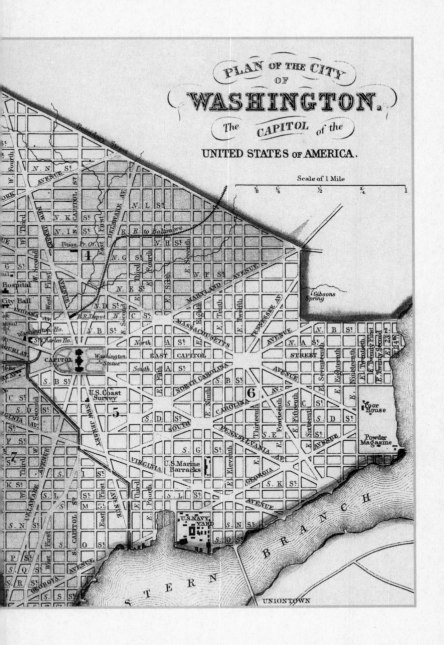

part one

**DISCOVERIES AND
INVENTIONS**

SPRINGFIELD, 1857

*A*braham Lincoln's law partner William "Billy" Herndon, thirty-nine, loved the birds and wildflowers of the prairie, pretty women, and corn liquor. He also had an immoderate passion for new books, and for the transcendental philosophizing of pastor Theodore Parker and poet Ralph Waldo Emerson. By his own accounting he had spent four thousand dollars on his collection of poetry, philosophy, and belles lettres—a fortune in those days, when a good wood-frame house in Springfield, Illinois, cost half as much. Journalist George Alfred Townsend called Herndon's library the finest in the West.

Herndon's narrow, earnest-looking face was fringed with whiskers in the Scots manner, and his eyes were close-set, intense. His favorite philosopher-poet was Emerson. Herndon so admired the Sage of Concord that he purchased Emerson's books by the carton and gave them away to friends and strangers with the zeal of an evangelist. A backwoods philosopher, Herndon even solicited

Emerson's endorsement for his tract "Some Hints on the Mind," in which he claimed to have discovered the mind's fundamental principle, "if not its law."

So when Emerson espoused a new book of poetry, calling it "the most extraordinary piece of wit and wisdom that America has yet contributed," Herndon wasted no time in locating a copy, which could be found on the shelves of R. Blanchard's, Booksellers, in Chicago, where he frequently traveled on business.

Having held the olive-green book, its cover blind-stamped with leaves and berries; having regarded with a twinge of envy the salutation "I Greet You at the / Beginning of A / Great Career / R W Emerson," gold-stamped on the spine, the bibliophile-lawyer plunked down his golden dollar for the second edition of Whitman's *Leaves of Grass*. And knowing the storm the book had caused in more sophisticated circles, Herndon brought the brickbat-shaped volume to the office he shared with Lincoln and set it in clear view on the table, where anyone might pick up the book and thumb through it. *Leaves of Grass* was exactly the length of a man's hand. He laid it down on the baize-covered table with the complacence of an anarchist waiting for a bomb to explode.

The Lincoln-Herndon law office was on the second floor of a brick building on the west side of Springfield's main square, across from the courthouse. Visitors mounted a flight of stairs and passed down a dark hallway to a medium-sized room in the rear of the building. The upper half of the door had a pane of beveled glass, with a curtain hanging from a wire, on brass rings. Lincoln would unlock the door, open it, and draw the curtain as he closed the door behind him. Two dusty windows overlooked the alley.

Herndon's biographer David Donald describes the office as "a center of political activity, of gossip and friendly banter, and of such remote problems as the merits of Walt Whitman's poetry."

The office was untidy and cobwebbed. Once, after Lincoln had come home from Congress with the customary dole of seeds to distribute to farmers, John Littlefield, a law student, discovered while sweeping that some of the stray wheat seeds had sprouted in the cracks between the floorboards. A long pine table that divided the room, and met with a shorter table to make a T, was scored by the jackknives of absent-minded clerks and clients. In one corner stood a secretary desk, its many pigeonholes and drawers stuffed with letters and memoranda, its besieged surface sustaining a spattered earthenware inkwell and a few gold pens. Bookcases rose between the tall windows. A spidery black stain blotted one wall, at the height of a man's head, where an ink bottle had exploded—the memento, according to Lincoln, of a disagreement between law students over a point of jurisprudence that would not yield to cold logic.

Papers were strewn everywhere, as if by a prairie wind: on the table, on the floor, on the five scattered cane-bottomed chairs and the ragged sofa where the senior partner of the firm liked to stretch out his full length, his head on the arm of the sofa. His legs were too long to fit the settee, so Lincoln would rest his feet on the raveling cane seat of a chair. There he reclined every morning, after arriving at nine, clean-shaven. And he would read, aloud. He read newspapers and books, always aloud, much to the annoyance of his partner, who found the high, tuneful voice, with its chuckling interludes and asides, a distraction from the warrants and writs and invoices. Herndon once asked Lincoln why he had to read aloud, and the forty-eight-year-old ex-Congressman explained: "Two senses catch the idea: first I see what I read; second I hear it, and therefore I can remember it better." Lincoln—not boasting—said that his mind was like steel: the gray matter was difficult to scratch, but once engraved on it, information was nearly impossible to efface. According to Herndon, Lincoln did not read many books, but whatever he did read he absorbed completely.

The law students got to Whitman first. Perhaps they had read about *Leaves of Grass* in *Putnam's Monthly Magazine*, where the eminent Charles Eliot Norton had announced that words "banished from polite society are here employed without reserve" and called the book a curious mixture of "Yankee Transcendentalism and New York rowdyism"; or they might have caught notice of it in the New York *Criterion*, where the dyspeptic Rufus Griswold referred to it as "this gathering of muck." In America's most influential literary journal, the *North American Review*, Edward Everett Hale rhapsodized about *Leaves of Grass*. And in May 1856 no less an authority than Fanny Fern—the highest-paid columnist in the country—referred to Whitman in the New York *Ledger* as "this glorious Native American." The book was widely praised and condemned, much discussed, if not much purchased or read.

According to Henry Bascom Rankin, who was a student in the Lincoln-Herndon office in 1857, "discussions hot and extreme sprung up between office students and Mr. Herndon concerning its poetic merit." A few verses:

> *I mind how we lay in June, such a transparent summer morning,*
> *You settled your head athwart my hips and gently turned over upon*
>   *me,*
> *And parted the shirt from my bosom-bone, and plunged your tongue*
>   *to my bare-stript heart . . .*

> *I turn the bridegroom out of bed and stay with the bride myself,*
> *I tighten her all night to my thighs and lips.*

Poetry indeed! These long, racy, unrhymed verses did not look like any poetry the provincial law students had ever seen, no matter what Emerson or the bluestocking Fanny Fern wrote.

The talk of Whitman that animated the law office during the unseasonably warm spring of 1857 relieved the furious, anguished discussion of the Supreme Court's recent decision about Dred Scott, which aroused Lincoln from a spell of political torpor. Yet even Scott's fate led them back to *Leaves of Grass:*

> *I am the hounded slave, I wince at the bite of the dogs,*
> *Hell and despair are upon me, crack and again crack the marksmen,*
> *I clutch the rails of the fence, my gore dribs, thinned with the ooze of*
>   *my skin . . .*

The argument over Whitman did not differ much in Springfield from the dispute in Boston and New York. Was this poetry? Then there arose the livelier controversy over the book's brazen immodesty. Was *Leaves of Grass* indecent? Many of the verses sounded shameless, unfit for mixed company. Take for example the anonymous woman watching twenty-eight young men bathing by the shore, who comes "Dancing and laughing along the beach" to caress their naked bellies:

> *They do not know who puffs and declines with pendant and bending*
>   *arch,*
> *They do not think whom they souse with spray.*

Was this Walt Whitman actually depicting a sexual act outlawed everywhere but in the debaters' dreams? It was shocking, pornographic. The men wondered whether such a book should be allowed on library shelves, or in homes where women and children might casually be seduced by it. Who was responsible for the corruption of morals: the author, the printer, the Chicago bookseller, or buyers of *Leaves of Grass* like Billy Herndon?

The students wrangled, and read the poems aloud, with Herndon sometimes acting as Whitman's advocate, other times as an impartial referee. Visitors dropping by, such as Dr. Newton Bateman, superintendent of schools, would join in the discussion provoked by lines such as:

> *A woman waits for me—she contains all, nothing is lacking,*
> *Yet all were lacking if sex were lacking, or if the moisture of the*
> *right man were lacking.*

Lincoln worked quietly at his desk, raking his coarse hair with his long fingers, or he came and went, apparently oblivious to the disturbance the new book was causing in the workplace. Having lost a year to politics, stumping for the Republican John Frémont during the presidential campaign of 1856, advocating "free soil, free labor and free men," he had a lot of catching up to do in his neglected law practice. He was also having a spell of depression, "the hypochondria," as it was called in those days. This mood afflicted him periodically, often between periods of intense business or creative work. So he turned his back on the students, and Herndon and Dr. Bateman, as they challenged one another's taste in literature and questioned one another's morals, reading passages of *Leaves of Grass* and attacking or defending Whitman as the spirit, or the letter, moved them. The poet was utterly uninhibited, whether he was describing himself, or addressing the President:

> *Walt Whitman, an American, one of the roughs, a kosmos,*
> *Disorderly, fleshy, sensual, eating, drinking, breeding,*

No sentimentalist, no stander above men and women, or apart from
*   them—no more modest than immodest*
* . . .*

I speak the pass-word primeval, I give the sign of democracy,
By God! I will accept nothing which all cannot have their counterpart
*   of on the same terms.*

Have you outstript the rest? Are you the President?
It is a trifle—they will more than arrive there every one, and still
*   pass on.*

One day, after the debaters had departed, a few clerks, including Henry Rankin, remained, copying documents. Lincoln rose from his desk. This was always a sight because sitting down Lincoln appeared to be of average height, but his limbs were so disproportionately long that when he unfolded and stretched them it was as if a giant had sprung up out of a common man.

"Quite a surprise occurred," Rankin recalled, in a memoir written years later. Lincoln picked up the book of poems that had been disturbing the peace and began to read, as he rarely did, in devoted silence, for more than half an hour by the Regulator clock. When the pressure of perusing the poetry silently became more than Lincoln could endure, he thumbed back to the first pages of *Leaves of Grass* and began reading aloud, in that tenderly expressive voice with the Kentucky accent and continual undercurrent of whimsical humor.

I celebrate myself,
And what I assume you shall assume,
For every atom belonging to me as good belongs to you.

I loafe and invite my soul,
I lean and loafe at my ease, observing a spear of summer grass.

The light of afternoon streamed through the office windows, gilding the dust motes.

Houses and rooms are full of perfumes—the shelves are crowded
   with perfumes,
I breathe the fragrance myself, and know it and like it,
The distillation would intoxicate me also, but I shall not let it.

The atmosphere is not a perfume, it has no taste of the distillation, it
   is odorless,
It is for my mouth forever, I am in love with it,
I will go to the bank by the wood, and become undisguised and
   naked,
I am mad for it to be in contact with me.

The smoke of my own breath,
Echos, ripples, buzzed whispers, love-root, silk-thread, crotch, vine
My respiration and inspiration, the beating of my heart . . .

"His rendering," Rankin remembered, "revealed a charm of new life in Whitman's versification." Here and there Lincoln found a verse too coarse, a line or phrase he felt the poet might have avoided. But on the whole he "commended the new poet's verses for their virility, freshness, unconventional sentiments, and unique forms of expression."

Lincoln put the book back down on the office table, desiring Herndon to leave Whitman there where he might not get lost in the tide of books, newspapers, and documents. "Time and again, when Lincoln came in, or was leaving, he would pick it up, as if to glance at it for only a moment, but instead he would often settle down in a chair and never stop reading aloud such verses or pages as he fancied."

Once Lincoln made the mistake of taking *Leaves of Grass* home. The next morning he brought the book back, grimly remarking that he "had barely saved it from being purified in fire by the women." This anecdote goes a long way toward explaining the politician's lifelong reticence about the poet and his book. Of course, by "the women" he meant his wife, Mary Todd Lincoln, who controlled nearly everything that went on inside the big, two-story house at the corner of Eighth and Jackson where they lived with their three boys.

It is uncertain what verses or pages Lincoln fancied. The feuds among Lincoln's early biographers, struggling over the soul of the martyred President, have few parallels in American letters. In 1928 a rival biographer, Reverend William E. Barton, in a popular book that took pains to disassociate Lincoln from Whitman, challenged Rankin's memory. As early as 1932, however, the scholar Charles Glicksberg, in *Whitman and the Civil War*, declared that Barton's book was "marked throughout by a hostile spirit toward Whitman" and discredited Barton's premise that Lincoln was unaware of Whitman's existence. Modern scholars, such as Whitman biographers Gay Wilson Allen and Jerome Loving, and David Herbert Donald, who wrote books on both Herndon and Lincoln, likewise have accepted Rankin's story in spite of Reverend Barton.

One of the points that authenticate Rankin's account is his dating of Lincoln's encounter with *Leaves of Grass*. Only in that year, two years after the first publication of Whitman's poems in 1855, would the ex-Congressman and future President Lincoln have had the freedom and inclination to study such a literary curiosity. Only

☞ The Poems of
LEAVES OF GRASS,

PUBLISHED BY THE AUTHOR,

May be ordered at any Book-Store or Newspaper Depot, or especially of

FOWLER & WELLS, 308 Broadway, New York.

Their place of business is the principal Agency for the Work, wholesale and retail. A note written to them, giving the writer's address, and enclosing $1 00, will procure a bound copy, post-paid, by return mail.

They supply Booksellers at a liberal discount.

'LEAVES OF GRASS' may also be purchased or ordered by mail, or the country-trade supplied, from the following *Agencies :*

BOSTON, . . . Fowler, Wells & Co., 142 Washington St.
PHILADELPHIA, Fowler, Wells & Co., 231 Arch street.
BALTIMORE, . . J. W. Bond & Co.
TORONTO, (Ca.,) Maclear & Co.
BUFFALO, . . . T. S. Hawks.
    "   . . . A. Burke, Jr.
CINCINNATI, . . F. Bly.
CHICAGO, . . . R. Blanchard.
ST. LOUIS . . . E. K. Woodward.
NEW ORLEANS, J. C. Morgan.
SAN FRANCISCO, George M. Bourne, M.D.

FOREIGN AGENCIES.

LONDON, . . . Horsell & Co., Oxford St.
PARIS, ... H. Bailliere & Co.
BRUSSELS, . . . William Good, Antwerp.

☞ Any communication by mail, for the author of Leaves **of** Grass, can be directed to him, namely,

WALT WHITMAN, care of

FOWLER & WELLS, 308 Broadway, New York.

in 1857 could the reading of Whitman have produced such an impact on his oratory.

Billy Herndon, who knew Lincoln better perhaps than any man in Lincoln's day, said he was the rare man without vices, but with a flagrant disregard for propriety, "the appropriateness of things." He was so heedless of his appearance that he forgot to comb his coarse black hair. He cared so little about clothing that sometimes he wouldn't wear this piece or that. After all, he was raised on a farm in Kentucky, barefoot. "He never could see the harm in wearing a sack-coat instead of a swallowtail to an evening party, nor could he realize the offense of telling a vulgar yarn if a preacher happened to be present."

Abraham Lincoln was, therefore, the last man in Illinois who would have dismissed Walt Whitman's verse on the grounds of its being vulgar or unseemly. Lincoln had a single-minded interest in the truth. Herndon wrote: "No lurking illusion or other error, false in itself and clad for the moment in robes of splendor, ever passed undetected or unchallenged over the threshold of his mind . . . He threw his whole mental light around the object, and, after a time, substance and quality stood apart, form and color took their appropriate places, and all was clear and exact in his mind . . . He crushed the unreal, the inexact, the hollow, and the sham."

Whitman's Adamic nakedness in itself would have appealed to the lawyer's "perfect mental lens." Lincoln's favorite author was not Shakespeare, Burns, or Byron, though he loved them all. It was the Greek geometer Euclid; Herndon marveled during their circuit-riding days how Lincoln could lie awake concentrating until 2:00 A.M., memorizing the propositions of Euclid by candlelight while the other lawyers snored in the hotel room. The Greek formed Lincoln's style of debate. Now Lincoln was searching for a still center of the turning world of human nature, a diamond-hard pivot on which he might set his compass to draw the circle of an American civilization. "I am the poet of commonsense and the demonstrable and of immortality," said Whitman. "Only what proves itself to every man and woman is so, / Only what nobody denies is so."

The new world ideal appeared in *Leaves of Grass*, this naked poet, this "body electric." Whitman boldly identified not only with every other human being—black, white, or red; slave or master—but with every atom of the universe, in every moment of history since Creation, and with God Himself! The poet had even distinguished between the accidents of his birth, upbringing, and present circumstances, and the essential man that underlay all those trappings.

W

Trippers and askers surround me,
People I meet—the effect upon me of my early life, of the ward and
city I live in, of the nation,
The latest news, discoveries, inventions . . .
My dinner, dress, associates, looks, work, compliments, dues,

. . .

. . . loss or lack of money, or depressions or exaltations,
They come to me days and nights and go from me again,
But they are not the Me myself.
Apart from the pulling and hauling stands what I am,
Stands amused, complacent, compassionating, idle, unitary . . .

. . .

I believe in you, my soul—the other I am must not abase itself to
you,
And you must not be abased to the other.

Lincoln never completely overcame his embarrassment over his humble origins, particularly the question of his mother's illegitimacy. This fueled his ambition even as it colored his abiding melancholy. Now came this personification of democracy, this unencumbered, free-spirited poet, demonstrating to him the soul's liberty from breeding and class. Everything in Whitman's philosophy and point of view appealed to Lincoln's powers of reason, passion for democracy, vigilant conscience, and what Herndon called "his intense veneration of the true and the good."

In Lincoln's study the 1856 edition of *Leaves of Grass* had fallen upon rich and fertile ground. Whether Lincoln read all 384 pages of the book is uncertain. But the poetry of Whitman Lincoln did read left its mark upon him in 1857. In that transitional year a change came over Lincoln. The change is evident in his speeches, an alteration in idiom that has never been thoroughly explained. Lincoln's early successes in debating, in the courtroom, and "on the stump"—campaigning for himself or his colleagues—resulted from his spellbinding powers as a storyteller and his mastery of logical demonstration and analysis. The "rail-splitter" was a first-class logic-chopper. Again Herndon bears witness: "He reasoned from well-chosen principles with such clearness, force, and directness that the tallest intellects in the land bowed to him. He was the strongest man I ever saw, looking at him from the elevated standpoint of reason and logic."

Here is an excerpt from an early speech protesting the repeal of the Missouri Compromise:

> Equal justice to the south, it is said, requires us to consent to the extending of slavery to new countries. That is to say, inasmuch as you do not object to my taking my hog to Nebraska, therefore I must not object to you taking your slave. Now, I

admit this is perfectly logical, if there is no difference between hogs and negroes. But while you thus require me to deny the humanity of the negro, I wish to ask whether you of the south yourselves, have ever been willing to do as much? It is kindly provided that of all those who come into the world, only a small percentage are natural tyrants. That percentage is no larger in the slave States than in the free. The great majority, south as well as north, have human sympathies, of which they can no more divest themselves than they can of their sensibility to physical pain.

The combination of wit, common sense, and juridical reasoning is practically irresistible. Yet for all his passion for truth and justice, for all the folksy humor of Lincoln's early speeches, and his exceptional powers of persuasion, we can find nothing in the first thousand pages of Lincoln's prose to call sublime—little that we can rightly call literature. His discourse is the analytic, clear medium of an advocate, leavened by barnyard metaphors, tall tales, biblical parables, and fables modeled upon Aesop.

One can begin to see the change coming in 1854, as Lincoln lashed out against the Kansas-Nebraska Act sponsored by Senator Stephen A. Douglas. This act, permitting settlers in new territories to decide for themselves for or against slavery, spelled the "end of the Missouri Compromise," which for thirty-four years had banned slavery above latitude 36°30'. Lincoln was grudgingly tolerant of slavery as a necessary evil—where it already existed— but he fiercely opposed the extension of the peculiar institution in the West, which the new law would make inevitable.

The speeches he gave that year in Bloomington, Springfield, and Peoria, dismantling Douglas's arguments for the Kansas-Nebraska Act, are models of classical rhetoric invigorated by Lin-

coln's belief that the new law was unjust. In their way, these talks
are quite convincing. Yet they do not seize the imagination; they
do not resonate. Like his stump speeches for the free-soil presidential candidate John Frémont, these were not rousing, for all their
righteous indignation. Lincoln had learned to draw up a clear
demonstration of a just principle, and the slavery controversy had
motivated him. But he had yet to develop that lyric eloquence for
which he is now remembered.

It would take a touch of the poet to move Abraham Lincoln's
oratory from the cold light of rhetoric into the warm iridescence
of dramatic literature, with its multicolored rays, its distinct shad-
ings. He had it in him. In his youth he wanted to be a poet. He was
familiar with Edgar Allan Poe's poetry, and memorized "The
Raven," as well as many verses of Oliver Wendell Holmes. He
admired the poem "Mortality," by the Scot William Knox, and also
got it by heart.

> 'Tis the wink of an eye, 'tis the draught of a breath,
> From the blossoms of health, to the paleness of death.
> From the gilded saloon, to the bier and the shroud.
> Oh, why should the spirit of mortal be proud!

He wrote to a friend, in 1846, "I would give all I am worth, and go
in debt, to be able to write so fine a piece as I think that is."

As late as 1846 Lincoln was writing skillful imitations of
Augustan English poetry, showing the influence of Thomas Gray.

> As distant mountains please the eye,
>   When twilight chases day—
> As bugle-tones, that, passing by
>   In distance die away—

As leaving some grand water-fall
  We ling'ring list its roar,
So memory will hallow all
  We've known, but know no more.

These verses and others were inspired by a visit in 1844 to his childhood home in Perry County, Indiana, where his mother and sister were buried. During that visit he saw his old schoolmate Matthew Gentry, who, "At the age of nineteen . . . unaccountably became furiously mad, from which condition he gradually settled down into harmless insanity." Lincoln wrote of him:

But here's an object more of dread
  Than ought the grave contains—
A human form with reason fled,
  While wretched life remains.

Poor Matthew! Once of genius bright,
  A fortune-favored child—
Now locked for aye, in mental night,
  A haggard mad-man wild.

  .   .   .

And when at length, tho' drear and long,
  Time soothed thy fiercer woes,
How plaintively thy mournful song
  Upon the still night rose.

I've heard it oft, as if I dreamed,
  Far distant, sweet and lone—
The funeral dirge, it ever seemed
  Of reason dead and gone.

These tuneful stanzas, charged with pathos, come from a long narrative poem called "The Maniac," published anonymously in the *Quincy Whig* on May 5, 1847. The story behind the poem helps to explain Lincoln's lifelong obsession with madness, as well as its antithesis, rational thought. Eight months later the poet took a seat in the U.S. House of Representatives. While no one nowadays wishes Lincoln had given up politics, the critics Jacques Barzun and Edmund Wilson have both proposed that Lincoln—alone among our presidents—could have made a lasting contribution to American letters if he had preferred a literary career.

In 1849 Lincoln returned from his rather clumsy if high-minded term in Congress with the new awareness that he lacked literary culture. His two years in Washington among college graduates had exposed this fault, and so, according to Herndon, Lincoln "extended somewhat his research in that direction." The trauma of losing a child might have led him to seek solace among books—Eddie Lincoln, age four, died of tuberculosis on February 1, 1850. During the next seven years, as Lincoln built up his law practice and worked behind the scenes in Illinois politics, he spent his leisure hours reading Shakespeare, Pope, Holmes, and Francis Bacon, as well as the occasional book Herndon recommended, such as his favorites Parker and Emerson, and the poems of Walt Whitman.

Lincoln was fatefully drawn into the crucial controversy of those years: the fight over slavery in the territories, which led to armed conflict ("Bleeding Kansas") in 1856, and finally the argument over the Dred Scott decision in 1857. His opinions launched him into the front ranks of the fledgling Republican Party. This was the Free-Soil Party that nominated John Frémont to run for the presidency in 1856 against the Democrat James Buchanan. Lincoln, incensed over Stephen A. Douglas's concept of popular sovereignty, spoke out. This is not the place to recount Lincoln's rise in the Republican Party on the tide of free-soil sentiment, his combination of calculation and insouciance, cold-blooded ambition and reckless idealism. Others have told it often and well. Here we are concerned with Lincoln's literary development—how words transformed him from a local politician into a national figure, a statesman who, some said, might make a good presidential candidate in 1860.

First Lincoln would have to lose an election, the nationally publicized battle with Douglas for a seat in the U.S. Senate in 1858. Walt Whitman's earliest mention of Lincoln came in a brief newspaper notice of Lincoln's debates with Douglas in that year. Lincoln, upon his nomination in Springfield on June 16, 1858, delivered a speech, now called the "House Divided" speech, that rocked the Republican convention. Published in the *Illinois State Journal* on June 18 and the *Chicago Tribune* on June 19, it was quoted, and attacked or defended, by everyone concerned about the future of slavery and the Union. Quoting St. Mark, Lincoln proclaimed: " 'A house divided against itself cannot stand.' I believe this government cannot endure, permanently half *slave* and half *free*." The speech sounded so radical that some feared it might cost him the Senate seat; the message was so resonant others believed it would win him a presidential nomination. This is the first of Lincoln's speeches to be widely regarded as a work of literature.

Lincoln had used the figure of the "house divided" in an 1843 campaign circular he wrote for the Whig Party, urging the party to adopt a convention system; and that figure was taken up by abolitionists and Southern apologists alike during the early 1850s. The draft of a similar speech discovered after Lincoln's death indicates that the candidate also employed the figure in a talk given on May 18, 1858, in Edwardsville, Illinois.

The "House Divided" message arose from Lincoln's fury over the Dred Scott decision. On March 6, 1857, the Supreme Court under Chief Justice Roger B. Taney ruled that Congress had no right to prohibit slavery in the territories, that the Missouri Compromise was unconstitutional, and that Dred Scott's residence in Minnesota did not make him a free man because Minnesota had never been free soil. Furthermore, as a slave and a Negro, Scott had no legal rights under the Constitution—he could not sue for his freedom in the U.S. courts even if he lived in a "free" state. Dred Scott returned to his master.

The Dred Scott decision, handed down only days after Buchanan's inaugural address (in which Taney's opinion was blatantly foreshadowed) and so soon after blood was shed in Kansas over the slavery issue, made Lincoln suspect a conspiracy was afoot among the proslavery Democrats. While Lincoln was not an abolitionist, he hated slavery. He knew Taney's ruling was not only an attack on the Declaration of Independence and the Constitution—it opened the door to slavery of all kinds, in every state of the Union.

Stephen A. Douglas was the chief spokesman for the administration's policy in Kansas. He visited Springfield in mid-June of 1857, speaking on several topics, including Kansas and Dred Scott. Lincoln sat in the audience, fuming over Douglas's defense of the Court's decision. The day Douglas left town, Lincoln started formulating his response. He labored over it for two weeks; then he delivered the message in the Illinois statehouse on June 26. Taken paragraph by paragraph, this hour-long argument contains more poetic tropes than any speech Lincoln had ever given. And it is poetry of surprises, challenges, and brazen disregard for propriety and convention. It is Whitmanesque. Lincoln appears to be under the poet's spell.

In the first twenty minutes or so of the speech he is the old familiar Lincoln, quoting Douglas's popular-sovereignty beliefs and sarcastically reducing them to absurdity: "If there should be one real living free state Democrat in Kansas, I suggest it might be well to catch him, and stuff and preserve his skin, as an interesting specimen of that soon to be extinct variety of the genus, Democrat." But when he comes to the topic of Judge Taney's decision against Dred Scott, Lincoln adopts a new tone; from this point on the language is charged with naked passion and frank sexuality. Every paragraph ends in a poetic flourish—a figure of speech or a metrical coup. Contrasting the old reverence for the Declaration of Independence—its insistence upon inclusiveness and equality— with the outrage of Taney's decision, Lincoln says:

> In those days, our Declaration of Independence was held sacred by all, and thought to include all; but now, to aid in making the bondage of the negro universal and eternal, it is assailed, and sneered at, and construed, and hawked at, and torn, till, if its framers could rise from their graves, they would not at all recognize it. All the powers on earth seem rapidly combining against him. Mammon is after him; ambition follows, and philosophy follows, and the Theology of the day is fast joining the cry.

His description of the imprisoned Negro is the most sophisticated extended metaphor Lincoln has ever drawn:

> They have him in his prison house; they have searched his person, and left no prying instrument with him. One after

another they have closed the heavy iron doors upon him, and now they have him, as it were, bolted in with a lock of a hundred keys, which can never be unlocked without the concurrence of every key; the keys in the hands of a hundred different men, and they scattered to a hundred different and distant places . . .

This little-known speech given in midsummer of 1857 is the work of a seasoned orator in control of a rich battery of figures and metrical rhythms—an orator who grasps the charm of poetry and its power to unleash the emotions of both speaker and audience.

Douglas had long played upon the "natural disgust in the minds of nearly all white people, to the idea of an indiscriminate amalgamation of the white and black races;" hoping to "fasten the odium of that idea upon his adversaries . . . he therefore clings to this hope," said Lincoln, "as a drowning man to the last plank." Until this moment both Douglas and Lincoln had handled the subject gingerly, with due respect for the explosive—unspeakable— sexual content that lay just under the surface of their polite controversy. But from here on out, Lincoln, like a true "camerado" of Walt Whitman, lays the subject bare:

Now I protest against that counterfeit logic which concludes that, because I do not want a black woman for a *slave* I must necessarily want her for a *wife*. I need not have her for either, I can just leave her alone.

This was so shocking, Lincoln would never need to express himself more boldly on the subject. *I can just leave her alone.* A short time later, toward the end of his speech, Lincoln uses understatement to establish that a number of slave masters *could not* resist the allure of the captive female. He devotes a paragraph of statistics to the proportion of mulattos to blacks—far greater in the slave states than in the free. In 1850 there were 405,751 mulattos in the United States. "Nearly all have sprung from black slaves and white masters," he observes. Then, driving his point home, he demurely adds: "Of course, I state this case [Dred Scott's] as an illustration only, not meaning to intimate that the master of Dred Scott and his family, or any more than a per centage of masters generally, are inclined to exercize this particular power which they hold over their female slaves." The numbers show the percentage is large. The politician stops short of condemning the slavemasters and miscegenation, although he himself would prefer to keep the races separate, were it possible. It is not possible. And slavery does not discourage miscegenation, it abets it.

There are white men enough to marry all the white women, and black men enough to marry all the black women, and so let them be married . . .

The plainest print cannot be read through a gold eagle; and it will be ever hard to find many men who will send a slave to Liberia, and pay his passage while they can send him to a new country, Kansas for instance, and sell him for fifteen hundred dollars, and the rise.

So ends Abraham Lincoln's explosive reply to Stephen Douglas on June 26, 1857, with the stunning metaphor of blinding greed, and capped with a perfect verse of iambic pentameter. This was the beginning of his bid for Douglas's Senate seat. Because Illinois, and Lincoln, were wielding more and more influence on the national political scene, the *New York Times* printed the speech word for word, where Whitman himself could read it.

W

*Now I am curious what sight can ever be more stately and admirable
to me than my mast-hemm'd Manhatta, my river and sun-set,
and my scallop-edged waves of flood-tide, the sea-gulls
oscillating their bodies, the hay-boat in the twilight, and the
belated lighter . . .*

—WHITMAN, "SUN-DOWN POEM"

On July 22 Lincoln brought his wife with him to New York via
Niagara Falls, where they enjoyed a belated honeymoon. Because
his work took him away from home for weeks at a time, they treas-
ured these days alone together. Mary wanted to shop for dresses.
Lincoln hoped to collect an overdue fee from the Illinois Central
Railroad, whose company headquarters was in Manhattan. He fig-
ured on better luck dunning them in person, but found the railroad
on the verge of bankruptcy.

The Lincolns arrived in New York on the eve of the financial
panic of 1857. Banks and businesses were closing their doors.
Forty thousand workers out of jobs would soon march through the
streets to City Hall bearing banners reading WE WANT WORK and
HUNGER IS A SHARP THORN. Manufacturers blamed the depression
on the Democrats, who had steadily reduced protective tariffs.
The industrial East, as well as the Middle West, reeling from bank
failures and unemployment, would turn toward the new Republican Party in 1860.

*Burn high your fires, foundry chimneys! Cast black shadows at night-
fall! Cast red and yellow light over the tops of the houses . . .*

While Abraham and Mary Lincoln walked arm in arm along
the Manhattan wharves, watching the gulls float on the wind and

the smoke plume from the ferry, Lincoln marveled at the vast potential of the metropolis. This was the city Walt Whitman had celebrated in his "Sun-Down Poem."

> Crowds of men and women attired in the usual costumes, how curious you are to me!
> On the ferry-boats the hundreds and hundreds that cross are more curious to me than you suppose . . .

Yearning to match humankind with the golden hour, in this poem (which would later become "Crossing Brooklyn Ferry") Whitman sometimes seems to be looking out at his reader from the pages of his book:

> Who was to know what should come home to me?
> Who knows but I am enjoying this?
> Who knows but I am as good as looking at you now, for all you cannot see me?

As self-conscious as any tourist, Lincoln looked all around him.

> Consider, you who peruse me, whether I may not in unknown ways be looking upon you!

Only months earlier Whitman had written a political tract called "The Eighteenth Presidency!" He said he would be "much pleased to see some heroic, shrewd, fully-informed, healthy-bodied, middle-aged, beard-faced American blacksmith or boatman come down from the West across the Alleghenies, and walk into the Presidency, dressed in a clean suit of working attire, and with the tan all over his face, breast, and arms." Whitman called for this "Redeemer President of These States" to come out of "the real West, the log hut, the clearing, the woods, the prairie, the hill-side." Now here was Abraham Lincoln, lacking only the beard, standing on the shores of Whitman's beloved Manhattan. And at his side was Mary, with her moon face, her narrow eyes, plump cheeks, and pointed nose, as happy as she would ever be in her sad life.

Mary dreamed of visiting Europe. But she told her husband it was not to be, because "poverty was my position." She teased him—a lawyer who was very prosperous—with the joke "I am determined my next husband *shall be rich.*" Meanwhile, across the East River, in a crowded house in Brooklyn, the author of *Leaves of Grass* was in the throes of a financial panic of his own that was no laughing matter.

Walt Whitman may have been famous in Lincoln's law office, but neither he nor his publisher was making any money from his books. The thirty-eight-year-old poet was sharing an attic bedroom with his crippled, mentally retarded brother Eddie, twenty-two, in their mother's brownstone on Classon Avenue in Brooklyn. Two other brothers lived there: George, twenty-seven, a cabinetmaker who was soon to join the army, and Jeff, twenty-four, a civil engi-neer. To make ends meet, Louisa Whitman took in boarders. But since the death of her husband two years earlier, she and the rest of the family had depended upon Walt, more for his kindness and loy-alty as "pater familias" than for his erratic income as a writer, printer, and editor. Hard times had come, and though Whitman was writing a little for the *Brooklyn Daily Times,* he was in debt.

In 1856, deciding to take matters into his own hands, he had accepted a two-hundred-dollar loan from Fanny Fern's husband, James Parton, on a short-term note, to purchase the plates of *Leaves* from his old booksellers, Fowler & Wells. He hoped to find a more enterprising publisher, who might make more profit from the text.

When the note fell due in the spring, Whitman had no money to pay it off. In late June, a knock came at the door. It was Oliver Dyer, Fanny Fern's friend and editor, acting as counsel for James Parton, and come to collect the plaintiff's two hundred dollars. When Whitman pleaded poverty, pointing to his cramped quarters under the eaves, Dyer carried away what little the poet had that might fetch ready money, including his books and a beloved oil painting by his friend the eminent Jesse Talbot illustrating a scene from *Pilgrim's Progress*. Fern, a.k.a. Sara Parton, had been more than a little bit in love with the handsome, gray-eyed poet. And when, at length, she discovered that the object of her passion did not return it in kind, she decided to demand payment on her loan. Dyer later told Whitman that James Parton had accepted his belongings as full payment of the debt. But this was a lie. Dyer probably kept the painting for himself, and the Partons ever after condemned Walt Whitman as a deadbeat and a "bill-jumper."

If Abraham and Mary Lincoln, on holiday in New York during the summer of 1857, had passed Walt Whitman as he strolled along Broadway, south past the Tremont Hotel toward Bleecker Street, a premier shopping district (Mary bought the finest bonnets and dresses), the happy, prosperous Western couple would have beheld a perfect specimen of midcentury bohemia. Walt—in the words of a contemporary—was "broad-shouldered, rouge-fleshed, Bacchus-browed, bearded like a satyr, and rank." He wore pants of a very full cut ("bloomers") tucked into his cowhide boots, and a red undershirt unbuttoned to the sternum, exposing his brawny neck. Over this he wore a short "roundabout" jacket, striped calico with oversized pockets and large buttons. Gray eyes, cautious yet wise and full of a tender sympathy, looked out from under a broad-brimmed slouch hat.

W

If you meet some stranger in the street, and love him or her,
    do I not often meet strangers in the street and love them?
If you see a good deal remarkable in me, I see just as much, perhaps
    more, in you.

. . . what is more subtle than this which ties me to the woman or man
    that looks in my face,
Which fuses me into you now, and pours my meaning into you.

We understand, then, do we not?
What I promised without mentioning it, have you not accepted?
What the study could not teach . . .
What the push of reading could not start is started by me personally,
    is it not?

The bohemian poet, flat broke, down on his luck, his mind
teeming with unwritten poems, was on his way to the basement
saloon called Pfaff's, to drink a beer he could not afford, in company where his gifts and style were certain to be appreciated. His
thoughts for the respectably attired men and women he had passed
along the way, headed for the Tremont or the St. Nicholas Hotel,
may be summed up in his verses:

You will hardly know who I am, or what I mean,
But I shall be good health to you nevertheless,
And filter and fibre your blood.

W

Failing to fetch me at first, keep encouraged,
Missing me one place, search another,
I stop some where waiting for you.

Whitman's poetry was elusive, and so was he. But sooner or later he would inspire—with his verse or in person—the people who needed him.

———

For the rest of the year 1857, despite the nation's increasing curiosity about the eloquent politician from Illinois, Lincoln avoided controversy, while practicing law. Some of his cases, such as the Rock Island Bridge case in Chicago in September, got him a great deal more publicity than he expected. At that moment, he preferred to work behind the scenes for the Republican Party.

In the spring the Chicago *Journal* had described him as "the successor of Stephen A. Douglas in the U.S. Senate." On October 24, the editor of the Urbana *Constitution* wrote: "Among the notables who have attended our Court the past week, the Hon. A. Lincoln stuck up prominently. We regret to say that his eyesight is failing him seriously: tall as he is, he appears to be entirely unable to see far enough to get a glimpse of that U.S. Senatorship." Toward the end of the year, he quietly hired John O. Johnson as his political organizer.

Yet Lincoln made no public gesture to confirm this ambition. In fact, after his powerful speech in Springfield against slavery and Senator Douglas's opinion on Dred Scott, nearly a year passed before Lincoln chose to address any audience outside of a courtroom.

When he finally did speak, in Bloomington on April 6, 1858, for the Young Men's Association, the lecture was such an eccentric piece of work, in manner and substance, so removed from current events and popular concerns, that it was received coolly. Cosmic in scope, ironical and poetical in style, the discourse has left biographers bewildered ever since. Many have dismissed the "First Lecture on Discoveries and Inventions," which is a historical ode to human ingenuity since Adam invented the fig-leaf apron. Many have explained it away as a caprice, an indulgence of Lincoln's zany, nonconformist streak. But one distinguished biographer, J. G. Randall, in his *Lincoln the President,* decided the speech deserved a closer look. "In its flow of sentences it marks Lincoln as something of a stylist, but that is secondary," according to Randall. "The main point is that in lecturing on discoveries and inventions he was thinking of enlightenment, of progress down the centuries, of the emancipation of the mind . . ." In a footnote, Randall adds, "Despite its unfavorable reception the lecture has meaning to one who would study the trends of Lincoln's thought on the eve of his nomination to the presidency."

Indeed, for anyone interested in Lincoln's intellectual progress, all three of these speeches—the speech answering Douglas on June 26, 1857; the "First Lecture on Discoveries and Inventions," delivered on April 6, 1858; and finally the "House Divided" speech of June 16, 1858—are crucial. For nearly two years the intriguing orator gave only these few addresses, and each shows us a different aspect of his mind. The "Lecture on Discoveries and Inventions" begins:

> *All creation is a mine, and every man, a miner.*
> *The whole earth, and all within it, upon it, and* round about *it*
>   *including* himself, *in his physical, moral, and intellectual*
>   *nature, and his susceptabilities [*sic*] are the infinitely*
>   *various "leads" from which man, from the first, was to*
>   *dig out his destiny.*
> *In the beginning, the mine was unopened, and the miner stood naked*
>   *and knowledgeless, upon it.*

In 1858 only one other writer in America was spinning lines like these: the author of *Leaves of Grass*. Like Whitman, Lincoln echoed the King James Bible; like Whitman, Lincoln was making a bible of his own, where the will of God gave way before man's motives and ingenuity. Lincoln's prose poem is a historical catalogue of discoveries and inventions, beginning with the invention of spinning and weaving, the discovery of iron, and the fashioning of tools like the hammer. "How could the 'gopher wood' for the Ark have been gotten out without an axe? It seems to me an axe, or a miracle, was indispensible [*sic*]," Lincoln writes. He celebrates the powers of locomotion, "wheel-carriages, and water-crafts— wagons and boats," as well as food and agriculture, the plow, and reaping and threshing machines. He sings the motive power of sailing vessels, windmills, pumps and waterwheels, and that very modern discovery, steam power. Whitman, in "A Song for Occupations" (published in the 1856 version as "Poem of The Daily Work of The Workmen and Workwomen of These States"), exhorted, "All doctrines, all politics and civilization, exurge from you," and he wrote of the meanings to be found in

> *Manufactures, commerce, engineering, the building of cities, every*
>   *trade carried on there, the implements of every trade,*
> *The anvil, tongs, hammer, the axe and wedge, the square, mitre,*
>   *jointer . . .*
>   . . .
> *The steam-engine, lever, crank, axle, piston, shaft, air-pump,*
>   *boiler . . .*
>   . . .
> *The pump, the pile-driver, the great derrick, the coal-kiln and brick-*
>   *kiln,*
> *Coal-mines, all that is down there, the lamps in the darkness . . .*

S P eech

More than half of Whitman's fifteen-page poem is taken up with a catalogue of the same discoveries and inventions (including elaborate mining imagery) that Lincoln celebrates.

What, to Lincoln, is the ultimate Divine discovery and invention? The Divine gift, or invention, is speech, "articulate sounds rattled off from the tongue."

> We shall find the capacities of the tongue, in the utterance of articulate sounds, absolutely wonderful. You can count from one to one hundred, quite distinctly in about forty seconds. In doing this two hundred and eighty-three distinct sounds or syllables are uttered, being seven to each second; and yet there shall be enough difference between every two, to be easily recognized by the ear of the hearer . . .

And how convenient, because "One always has the tongue with him [unlike pen and paper], and the breath of his life is the ever-ready material with which it works."

Speech may be God's gift, but "*writing*—the art of communicating thoughts to the mind, through the eye—is the great invention of the world. Great in the astonishing range of analysis and combination . . . great in enabling us to converse with the dead, the absent, and the unborn, at all distances of time and of space . . ."

Finally, Lincoln ranks the arts of writing and of printing with the discovery of America. In a humorous aside, he includes "the introduction of Patent-laws" among the greatest of human inventions. America, in the new religion of Whitman and Lincoln, has received a special dispensation in the history of the human family. "A new country is most favorable—almost necessary—to the immancipation [*sic*] of civilization and the arts."

Readers of *Leaves of Grass,* in the 1856 edition, will recognize in Lincoln's "Lecture on Discoveries and Inventions" the ideas and images, as well as the tone, expressed in four of Whitman's poems: "A Song for Occupations," "Poem of Many In One," "Poem of a Few Greatnesses," and "Sun-Down Poem." The main theme of the "Poem of Many In One" is that America is the greatest hope for the future of all civilizations.

> *America, curious toward foreign characters, stands sternly by its own,*
> *Stands removed, spacious, composite, sound,*
> *Sees itself promulger of men and women, initiates the true use of*
> *   precedents . . .*
>
> .   .   .
>
> *Any period, one nation must lead,*
> *One land must be the promise and reliance of the future.*

And after describing a panorama of American life and industry, Whitman declares:

> *Language-using controls the rest;*
> *Wonderful is language!*
> *Wondrous the English language, language of live men,*
> *Language of ensemble, powerful language of resistance,*
> *Language of a proud and melancholy stock, and of all who*
> *   aspire . . .*
>
> .   .   .
>
> *Language to well-nigh express the inexpressible,*
> *Language for the modern, language for America.*

In "Poem of a Few Greatnesses" we find a precise blueprint for Lincoln's speech, from the first lines:

Great are the myths, I too delight in them,
   Great are Adam and Eve, I too look back and accept them,
Great the risen and fallen nations, and their poets, women, sages,
   inventors, rulers, warriors, priests.

W

And after a litany of praise for all things American—liberty, democracy, youth, old age, and science—Whitman sings another hymn to language:

Great is language—it is the mightiest of the sciences,
It is the fulness, color, form, diversity of the earth, and of men and
   women, and of all qualities and processes . . .
. . .
Great is the English speech—what speech is so great as the English?

W

SHOCK

Leaves of Grass introduced several ideas to Western civilization, ideas so boldly expressed that readers in England, France, and America were shocked by them. These include the equality of all things and beings, the sacredness and supremacy of personality (the "Self"), and the belief that the poet was "commensurate" with his people, incarnating the sexual and working life of America as well as its geography. Whitman's verses continue to surprise us today, a century and a half after they were written. And perhaps no idea of his is more startling and eerie than his insistence that his words and his personal presence transcend time and space.

W

It avails not, neither time or place—distance avails not,
I am with you, you men and women of a generation, or ever so many
   generations hence,
I project myself, also I return—I am with you, and know how it is.

So it is a notable and significant fact that Abraham Lincoln paraphrases Whitman's singular concept in this line from a speech given in 1858: "Great [is writing] in enabling us *to converse with the dead, the absent, the unborn, at all distances of time and space . . .*" This congruity, along with the similarity in tone, is not mere coincidence. The two men were not drawing upon a common source. Lincoln was neither a major poet nor a philosopher, and Whitman's ideas and style were remarkable—if for no other reason—in that they were not to be found elsewhere. What is evident here is a distinct literary influence. It may not have been conscious. I do not mean to suggest that Lincoln wrote any speech with *Leaves of Grass* at his elbow. But Whitman's thoughts are infectious, and they infuse the whole of his book, as he repeats them tirelessly in artful variations. Lincoln, whose memory was famously retentive, had read Whitman's poetry, and the poet's fingerprints are all over the "Lecture on Discoveries and Inventions." The very title of the lecture echoes the "Poem of Walt Whitman, American," on page 9 of the edition Billy Herndon placed upon the pine table in the law office. "Trippers and askers surround me, / . . . [ask] The latest news, discoveries, inventions . . ."

And this was the last public oration Lincoln delivered before the "House Divided" speech, which he gave upon being chosen as Republican candidate for the U.S. Senate in June 1858.

———

On May 31, 1858, his thirty-ninth birthday, Whitman wrote an appeal for "a revolution in American oratory" and "a great leading representative man, with perfect power, perfect confidence in his power . . . who will make free the American soul."

The diamond-bright head of Donati's comet, trailing its splendid triple plume, burst forth in the night sky in early June as Lincoln worked on his new speech. The comet would blazon its omens upon the heavens the rest of the year, as Lincoln campaigned against Stephen A. Douglas for his seat in the Senate. The long-tailed luminary was visible overhead to the tens of thousands of farmers, mechanics, and merchants who heard the seven debates that summer and autumn, as the two candidates argued the questions of slavery and freedom, the rights of Negroes, and the meaning of the Constitution. The comet became a focus of wonder and a subject of speculation to millions of readers while they followed the lively debates in newspapers in Boston, New York, Chicago, Richmond, Charleston, and San Francisco. For the first time, editors employed stenographers so they could print the Great Debates word for word. Slavery threatened to divide the Union, North and South, Republican and Democrat. Lincoln and Douglas were battling over far more than a Senate seat; they were fighting for the future of the Republic. The comet, many believed, portended war.

The debates, which began in August and closed in October, take up more than three hundred pages of Lincoln's *Collected Works*. They are considered fine examples of American oratory, and they won Lincoln national fame. But the spark that ignited the seven confrontations was the oration Lincoln delivered at the close of the Republican convention that June, a speech that would be remembered long after the thronged and noisy debates were forgotten.

According to his law partner, Lincoln wrote the "House Divided" speech over a period of several weeks, "on stray envelopes and scraps of paper, as ideas suggested themselves, putting them into that miscellaneous and convenient receptacle, his hat." The stovepipe hat, size 7⅛, stood about 6½ inches from brim to crown. The brim was 1¾ inches wide, and the inside band, where Lincoln tucked his notes and letters, measured 2¾ inches. On the heavy silk lining he had written "A. Lincoln, Springfield, Illinois," in case the stovepipe, with its precious cargo, should be left on a wall peg or newel-post, and be mistaken for another man's hat.

Let us consider what was going on under Lincoln's hat. One short line of Whitman might have lodged there: "What is prudence, is indivisible." As we have noted, the central image of the house divided, originating in the Gospels, had been used by Lincoln and others to illuminate the slavery controversy. The line "I believe this government cannot endure, permanently half *slave* and half *free*" was not new either, having appeared in slightly different forms in an 1855 letter and in several of Lincoln's speeches during the Frémont campaign. What made the new speech so electrifying was the personal passion with which Lincoln seized upon the "house divided" metaphor, and the poetry that grows out of it in the second half of the argument.

Lincoln knew the Bible better than any other book. The proverb "A house divided against itself cannot stand" appears in Matthew, Luke, and Mark (though never exactly in the words Lincoln used). All three refer to the same incident, in which Christ is suspected of calling upon the aid of Beelzebub, the prince of devils, in the course of working miracles of healing and casting out devils from the afflicted and possessed. Lincoln had wrestled with his own demons, chiefly his overweening ambition. He had warned in his 1838 address to the Young Men's Lyceum in Springfield: "Towering genius disdains a beaten path . . . It denies that it is glory enough to serve under any chief . . . It thirsts and burns for distinction; and if possible, it will have it, whether at the expense of emancipating slaves or enslaving freemen." He was cautioning the young men against "the loftiest genius, coupled with ambition sufficient to push it to its utmost stretch," in other words, a person just like himself. Lincoln had been born with the makings of a tyrant or a rebel angel. If such a man has any conscience, he faces agonizing moral choices.

So this particular Bible story held a special significance for Lincoln. Christ tells the scribes that Satan cannot cast out Satan, because "if Satan rise up against himself, and be divided, he cannot stand, but hath an end" (Mark 3:26). Only good can drive out evil, and injustice must sooner or later sink of its own weight. Embracing the parable, Lincoln had dedicated himself to truth and justice, refusing to use deceit even in championing a good cause, even under the pressure of ambition to advance his career or increase his personal fortune. "Honest Abe" was not a myth or a publicist's gimmick; it was a model of American folk virtue in tireless action.

The candidate saw how the metaphor of the house divided could figure in his battle with Douglas and the slavemasters. Knowing that slavery is wrong, Lincoln understood that defending it would not preserve the Union. Knowing that the Founding Fathers had intended to halt the proliferation of human bondage, Lincoln was sure that the Democratic Party, which had opened the territories to slavery with its support of the Dred Scott decision, would sooner or later collapse from within.

"Great is justice!" Whitman sings in "Poem of a Few Greatnesses."

Justice is not settled by legislators and laws—it is in the soul,
It cannot be varied by statutes, any more than love, pride, the
*   attraction of gravity, can*

It is immutable—it does not depend on majorities—majorities or
what not come at last before the same passionless and exact
tribunal.

Every poem in the 1856 edition of *Leaves of Grass* is luminous with
the passion for justice, liberty, and truth.

There is one flagrant exception. The most outrageous, obscene
poem in the book Lincoln read in 1857 bears the seductive Euclid-
ean title "Poem of The Propositions of Nakedness." The fifty-six
"propositions" ironically invite the reader to turn the world upside
down, to desecrate the spiritual laws that rule the ideal republic
Whitman has proposed in the preceding three hundred pages of
Leaves, his "new Bible."

Let the crust of hell be neared and trod on! Let the days be darker
than the nights!
. . .

Let freedom prove no man's inalienable right!
Every one who can tyrannize, let him tyrannize to his satisfaction!
Let none but infidels be countenanced!
. . .

Let there be no God!
Let there be money, business, railroads, imports, exports, custom,
authority, precedents, pallor, dyspepsia, smut, ignorance, unbelief!
Let judges and criminals be transposed! Let the prison-keepers be put
in prison! . . .
. . .

Let the slaves be masters! Let the masters become slaves!
. . .

Let shadows be furnished with genitals! Let substances be deprived of
their genitals!

. . .

Let the she-harlots and the he-harlots be prudent! Let them dance on,
   while seeming lasts! . . .

. . .

Let the white person tread the black person under his heel!

Although the opening lines of this invitation to a nightmare
("Respondez! Respondez! / Let every one answer!") indicate that
Whitman was calling for a protest, it appears that the poet's strategy failed, and his audience was simply appalled by the horrible
lines that followed. In a rare instance of self-censorship, he
removed the verses from future editions. The only man in America
who responded in a way that might have pleased him was Lincoln.
Whitman's mad poem perfectly described the chaos of a nation
divided against itself, the dark side of the American psyche, which
the candidate attacked. The "House Divided" speech is a kind of
exorcism.

The first few minutes of Lincoln's great speech, with its sharp
architectural imagery and its hint of a coming conflict, would
never be forgotten.

If we could first know *where* we are, and *whither* we are tending, we could then better judge *what* to do, and *how* to do it.

   We are now far into a *fifth* year, since a policy was initiated, with the *avowed* object, and *confident* promise, of putting
an end to slavery agitation.

   Under the operation of that policy, that agitation has not
only, *not ceased,* but has *constantly augmented.*

   In my opinion, it *will* not cease, until a *crisis* shall have been
reached and passed.

   "A house divided against itself cannot stand."

I believe this government cannot endure, permanently half *slave* and half *free*.

I do not expect the Union to be *dissolved*—I do not expect the house to *fall*—but I *do* expect it will cease to be divided.

Like the opening bars of Beethoven's "Eroica" Symphony, these sentences boldly stake their ground and point their direction. Lincoln proposes a conspiracy theory: that leaders of all three branches of government—the President, the Congress, and the Court—colluded in revoking the Missouri Compromise and depriving the Negro of his rights under the Constitution. The orator begins by vividly likening the "complete legal combination" to a "piece of machinery." But as he gathers momentum in narrating the skullduggery of presidents, senators, and judges, he returns to the dominant architectural figure. In the middle of the speech he exclaims: "Under the Dred Scott decision, 'squatter sovereignty' squatted out of existence, tumbled down like temporary scaffolding—like the mould at the foundry served through one blast and fell back into loose sand—helped to carry an election, and then was kicked to the winds."

This is powerful poetry, and an hour of such concentrated imagery would not do. Lincoln eases into a straightforward story of events leading up to the Dred Scott decision. The speech is almost operatic in its balance of lyricism and narration. When it comes time to nail the lid on his argument, the "rail-splitter" echoes Whitman's "Broad-Axe Poem," which contains the lines

The house-builder at work in cities or anywhere,
The preparatory jointing, squaring, sawing, mortising,
The hoist-up of beams, the push of them in their places, laying them
    regular,

*Setting the studs by their tenons in the mortises, according as they
    were prepared . . .*

No one can "absolutely *know*" the Dred Scott decision was a
conspiracy, Lincoln admits. "But when we see a lot of framed timbers, different portions of which we know have been gotten out at
different times and places by different workmen—Stephen [Dou-
glas], Franklin [Pierce], Roger [Taney] and James [Buchanan], for
instance—and when we see these timbers joined together, and see
they exactly make the frame of a house . . . all the tenons and mor-
tices exactly fitting . . . and not a piece too many or too few . . . in
such a case, we find it impossible to not *believe* that Stephen and
Franklin and Roger and James all understood one another from
the beginning . . ." Lincoln's use of their Christian names is
rhetorically masterful, as he reduces the enormity of the men's
crime to the misguided foolery of a few mischievous boys.

There is much more poetry in this speech, but I will cite only
Lincoln's variation on the proverb "A living dog is better than a
dead lion" (Ecclesiastes 9:4), because when Lincoln pinned this on
Stephen Douglas it stuck. Like the image of the house divided, it
was something neither the newsmen nor the two candidates ever
let rest. Douglas, with his mane of thick, wavy hair, his short neck
and broad features, *looked* a little bit like a lion. Lincoln said:
"Judge Douglas, if not a *dead* lion *for this work*, is at least a caged
and *toothless* one. How can he oppose the advances of slavery? He
don't *care* about it. His avowed *mission is impressing* the 'public
heart' to *care* nothing about it."

Lincoln had turned a corner back in 1857. He had developed
the power to raise his oratory to the level of dramatic poetry
whenever the occasion called for it.

When Lincoln had emptied his hat of notes, then stitched the notes together into a first draft—which he laboriously revised into a second, third, then a fourth draft—when at last he had finished the final draft of the speech under the watchful eye of his law partner Herndon, he got up and closed the office door. He turned the key in the lock and drew the curtain across the glass.

Lincoln read the speech aloud to Herndon, pausing at the end of each paragraph for his friend's comments and questions. After the first seven sentences Herndon said, "It is true, but is it wise or politic to say so?" And Lincoln replied that he would rather be defeated with the "house divided" expression in his address than win the election without it.

On June 16, the day before the convention, Lincoln invited a dozen friends to the statehouse library so that he could try the speech out on them. When he had read the last lines—"If we stand firm, we shall not fail. Wise councils may accelerate or mistakes delay it, but, sooner or later the victory is sure to come"—he asked for everybody's opinion. One man called it "a damned fool utterance"; one said the doctrine was "way ahead of its time," while another claimed it would drive away voters who had recently left the Democratic Party. Not a man present had a good word for the speech but Billy Herndon. He agreed with the others that it was "rank," but he confessed it suited his own views.

"Lincoln," said Herndon, "deliver that speech as read and it will make you President."

2

NEW YORK, 1861

Omnibuses—white, red, black, and yellow horsecars drawn by teams of Cleveland bays—plodded up and down Broadway from the Battery to Union Square, their shouting drivers sometimes making a traffic jam at the lower end of Manhattan. Everybody in New York rode in a Broadway horsecar—rich merchants, bankers, lawyers, and mechanics; young ladies, actresses, matrons, and harlots; and noisy boys—all jostled and bounced together on long benches in the open-air Knickerbocker coaches. Along the Broadway and Fifth Avenue line, the Broadway and Twenty-third Street line, the Yellow Bird, the Madison Avenue–Bleecker Street, from four o'clock in the morning until midnight the drivers raced their teams and reined them in to gather up the fares.

"Everything appertaining to them is a study, perhaps even a fascination, if once you begin to see it. One lounging man appears to think so, at any rate," says Walt Whitman. He cannot resist "as the driver of that handsome Fifth Avenue pulls up, casting at the lounger a friendly and inquiring glance, as much as to say, Come take a ride Walt Whitman?" He turns from the thoroughfare where beautiful women, celebrities, fops, "any well-dressed nobodies" are window-shopping, seizes the handle by the driver's box, and swings up gracefully. He calls himself the "pet and pride of the Broadway stage-drivers," and he says: "As onward speeds the stage, mark his nonchalant air, seated aslant and quite at home. Our million-hued ever-changing panorama of Broadway moves steadily down; he, going up, sees it all, as in a kind of half dream." The drivers southward bound salute the poet in recognition; silently he returns their salutations, "the raised arm, and upright hand."

"Every blade of grass is a study," Abraham Lincoln told a crowd of Wisconsin farmers late in 1859. "And not grass alone; but soils, seeds, and seasons . . . the thousand things of which these are specimens—each a world of study within itself." Walt Whitman was a collector of human specimens, each one a leaf of grass that would enrich the luxuriating field of his "New American Bible." Many pages of Whitman's diaries and notebooks are simply lists of names and addresses, along with thumbnail sketches of men that he found engaging. "Bill Guess—aged 22. A thoughtless, strong, generous animal nature, fond of direct pleasures . . . Taken sick with the small-pox . . . a large, blond fellow, weighed over 200; Peter—— ——, large, strong-boned young fellow, driver. Should weigh 180. Free and candid to me the first time he saw me. Man of strong self-will, powerful coarse feelings and appetites. Had a quarrel, borrowed $300, left his father . . . ; December 28—Saturday night Mike Ellis—wandering at the corner of Lexington Av & 32nd St.—took him home to 150 37th Street— 4th Story back room—bitter cold night—works in Stevenson's Carriage factory." He mentions "Dan'l Spencer . . . somewhat

feminine—5th av (44) (May 29)—told me he had never been in a
fight and did not drink at all . . . Slept with me September 3rd" and
the stage driver George Marler, "driving No. 8 on 4th Ave. large-
nosed, tallish fellow—Western, is from Ohio—has traveled with a
show as 'candy butcher.' "

Riding the side-wheel ferries across the Hudson River, prowl-
ing the wharves and lumberyards along the water, strolling along
Broadway, riding on the omnibuses, where he helped this or that
driver collect fares in exchange for a free ticket and a chance to chat
with passengers, Whitman was looking for love, "Picking out here
one that I love, to go with on brotherly terms." It was the kind of
love that he had known and lost, the kind that had inspired the
erotic cluster of forty-five poems he called "Calamus" after the
aromatic marsh plant with its phallus-shaped spadix. He had had
good luck on the omnibuses. Whitman was fond of the type of
man who drove the horses—strong, skillful and intelligent (if
sometimes illiterate), usually country-bred. In fact, the man he had
loved in the late 1850s, Fred Vaughan, a younger man from Brooklyn who inspired the "Calamus" poems, was himself a stage
driver. For a while they had stayed together in the Whitman house
on Classon Avenue.

He and Fred Vaughan had parted. Now Whitman had the
poetry to console him, free-verse poems he called his "sonnets," to
record that manly love he named "adhesiveness" (a term borrowed from phrenology, where it refers to our propensity to bond
with one another) to distinguish it from the "amative love"
between men and women, which the poet found less appealing to
him personally. In his day Whitman was considered an authority
on erotic love, to his greater glory and notoriety among the general public.

A new, enlarged edition of *Leaves of Grass* bound in orange cloth was available in the Astor Place bookstores. Blind-stamped with symbolic devices—the Western hemisphere nestled in clouds, a rising sun with nine spokes of light, a pointing hand with a butterfly perched on its index finger—the 456-page crown octavo was enriched by more than a hundred new poems. These included the "Calamus" cluster, as well as what are now known as "Starting from Paumanok" and "Out of the Cradle Endlessly Rocking." "Calamus" was now counterbalanced by a sequence called "Enfans d'Adam," erotic poems about heterosexual love so explicit that Ralph Waldo Emerson begged his friend to delete them. Whitman told Emerson that expurgation of "Enfans d'Adam" would be "apology," "surrender," and "an admission that something or other was wrong."

"The dirtiest book in all the world is the expurgated book," Whitman told his friend Horace Traubel.

The 1860 edition of *Leaves* was a rich, handsome volume. Whitman's new publishers, the young partners W. R. Thayer and Charles W. Eldridge, out of Boston, promised, "We can and will sell a large number of copies." The poet was proud of the new edition and hoped Thayer & Eldridge would deliver upon that promise. But despite the firm's expensive promotional brochures, display ads, and puffery, this edition fared only a little better than its predecessors, selling a couple of thousand copies. And by the end of 1860 the publishers were bankrupt. Their plan to create for Whitman "an overwhelming demand among the mass public" had failed.

As if in anticipation of failure, the new poems in the reddish-brown colored book are tinged with melancholy and dread. The joyous, optimistic speaker of the poems Lincoln once read in his office now sang in sorrowful tones of a bird that has lost its mate:

O darkness! O in vain!
O I am very sick and sorrowful

O brown halo in the sky, near the moon, drooping upon the sea!
O troubled reflection in the sea!
O throat! O throbbing heart!
O all—And I singing uselessly all the night!

. . . .

O past! O joy!
In the air—in the woods—over fields,
Loved! Loved! Loved! Loved! Loved!
Loved—but no more with me,
We two together no more.

The many poems of love and lost love, which were certainly personal, Whitman insisted were political. In the "Calamus" cluster, as in the "Enfans d'Adam," the Dionysian Whitman imagined erotic love, especially the "love of comrades," to be the true foundation of democracy and the Union. In an open letter to Emerson included in the book, he explained that his poetry was meant to unify the nation, "for the union of the parts of the body is not more necessary to this life than the union of These States is to their life." In this effort, too, the poet realized he had fallen short, when South Carolina seceded from the Union six weeks after Abraham Lincoln was elected president. By January 26, 1861, Mississippi, Florida, Alabama, Georgia, and Louisiana had joined South Carolina. Now it would take something more than poetry to unify the nation.

Most of the finest poetry Whitman would ever write was now printed and bound in the 1860 edition—all but a few poems he would later compose about the war and Abraham Lincoln. His great work had been done in the seven years previous. Writers are mercifully spared such knowledge, yet a poet's power of prophecy is often most acute in telling his own fortune. Whitman may have sensed that his creative power was waning.

The poet was in low spirits at the turn of the year 1860–1861, a dark period he called a "slough" or "stagnation." In a draft of verses, he wrote of "Years that whirl I know not whither / Schemes, politics fail—all is shaken—all gives way / Nothing is sure." The domestic situation in the Brooklyn home where he lived with his mother, four brothers, and the brothers' wives and children was wretched. The oldest brother, Jesse, a laborer and sailor who came and went erratically, was in the tertiary stage of syphilis. His madness ranged from catatonia to fits of violence in which he threatened even his ailing mother, sixty-six-year-old Louisa. The family had moved to a house on Portland Avenue in 1859, and there Walt, Jesse, Eddie, George, and Louisa were joined by Jeff (Walt's favorite brother); his wife, Martha; and their daughter Mannahatta (Hattie). Nearby lived the thirty-four-year-old brother Andrew, dying of alcoholism and T.B.; his slatternly wife, Nancy; and their two children. The two babies were so pathetically neglected that Walt and his mother were constantly concerned for their welfare.

Whitman's self-spun legend of the happy, robust poet, and the exuberance of many of his poems, might persuade us he was exceptionally fortunate. His greatest good fortune was his temperament. The full-scale biographies of Whitman by Gay Wilson Allen, Justin Kaplan, Jerome Loving, and others tell the story of Whitman's troubled family, his compassion for them, and his unfailing loyalty. Whitman's household—the rooms and lives that surrounded the table where he wrote—was, in 1861, not a place where a man would go for peace, comfort, or even a good night's sleep. Little is known about Whitman's work habits, but we do know he was a late riser; doubtless he wrote much of his poetry while the rest of the clan slept or tried to sleep. The house on Portland Avenue was a place to be avoided at any opportunity.

That winter Walt Whitman was not writing much. He was loafing and worrying. The face that looks out from the frontispiece of the 1860 *Leaves* is not the lean, defiant young man ("a hundred and sixty-five or thereabouts"), his hat cocked to one side, that Lincoln saw in the 1856 edition. [The 1860 engraving Whitman called "characteristic" portrays a wavy-haired Byronic figure sporting an elaborate bow tie dangling low from an open collar that shows plenty of breastbone. "I was in full bloom then: weighed two hundred and ten pounds . . ." This later engraving, based on a painting by Charles Hine, shows signs of dissipation: pouches under the eyes, premature wrinkles in the brow and over the eyelids. Whitman had grown fond of the beer they served in Pfaff's Cellar, not to mention the *Frankfurter Wurst*, the *Schwarzbrot*, and the *Schweizer Käse*. But it was the lager that added the forty-five pounds and made the graying poet look so much older than his forty-one years. Nobody ever reported Walt Whitman drunk, although he could be seen sipping beer at his table against the wall at Pfaff's every evening.

His days were spent on the Fulton Ferry, for two cents a ride; on the driver's seat of a horsecar, where he rode for free up and down Broadway; and in the wards and house doctor's office of the old New York Hospital. The dark stone building with its Gothic cupola lay beyond a green lawn a hundred yards back from Broadway, facing Pearl Street. Whitman would stroll the serpentine pavement of Pearl Street, pass through the iron gates, cross the yard, and enter the hospital.

He had come to visit the stage drivers, injured in the line of

duty. Driving an omnibus was dangerous. If you drove one long
enough the odds were that sooner or later you would crash, turn
over the coach, or fall off and be trampled by horses' hooves, if
you were not blackjacked by thieves.

Dr. John Roosa, who knew him there, recalled: "We were
interested in the man, and hardly any one could fail to be. Whatever might be the truth about the literary merit and good taste of
his poems, his personality was extremely pleasing. Why this was
so it would be hard to say. It must have been from the gentle and
refined cast of his features, which were rather rude, but noble." He
remembered Whitman dressed in a woolen shirt with a white collar open at the neck, blue flannel coat and vest, and baggy gray
trousers. "His face and neck were bronzed by exposure to the sun
and air . . . He was scrupulously careful of his simple attire, and
his hands were soft and hairy." A large man, Whitman gave the
impression of great vigor, though he moved slowly.

"No one could see him sitting by the bedside of a suffering
stage driver without soon learning that he had a sincere and profound sympathy for this order of man," Roosa wrote. "Close
observation of their lives would convince one that they had
endured hardship, which naturally invited the sympathy of a great
nature."

Whitman went to check on his stage drivers, men with names
like Broadway Jack and Yellow Joe, drivers beaten senseless by
bandits, knifed by other drivers in rage, or breathless with consumption. He stayed to comfort total strangers with pneumonia,
palsy, typhoid fever, or gunshot wounds, and men whose gangrened limbs were about to be amputated. Whitman was fascinated by all the diseases he saw: malnutrition, "wolverine
paralysis," and especially the cases of delirium tremens: "Robust,
brown sailor seven days ashore—monkeys after him dogs biting

him—men & women beat him." The poet admired "the romance of surgery and medicine."

The house staff let him come and go as he pleased. He was even welcome in the house doctor's office, the little room over the hospital entrance that served as "wicket of the house," where all visitors had to pass—policemen with injured felons, wives and mothers fretting over their menfolk, journalists, the novelist Anthony Trollope, even President Franklin Pierce. This was "the hiding place of many a secret," though few were kept from Whitman, who always found out what he wanted to know. The doctor recalled that Whitman was "always very glad, when our time and his permitted, to stop and have a chat, in which he managed to get pretty complete details of the case of his friend, the stage driver . . .

"He seemed to live above the ordinary affairs of life. I do not remember—and I saw him at least fifty times—ever having heard him laugh aloud, although he smiled with benignancy. He did not make jokes or tell funny stories . . ." When the time came for laughter Whitman would laugh out loud until he cried, but the hospital was no place for levity. The sick ward was an outpost he visited to bring comfort and peace, and to learn.

That winter, by day, he was a student of life: of human nature and illness and suffering. By night he was an idler, a peripatetic philosopher, a boulevardier. What money he had to spend came from his occasional journalism and $250 in royalties that trickled in from his book. But every night, at the end of his omnibus route, or his self-appointed rounds at the hospital, Whitman would retire to the subterranean warmth and bohemian camaraderie of Pfaff's, across from the little St. Charles Hotel and the immense corner tabernacle of the Manhattan Savings Bank.

Charley Pfaff had opened his restaurant-saloon just months

after Whitman first published *Leaves of Grass*. The place soon became the prime watering hole for "bohemians," where Whitman served as unofficial poet-in-residence. (Actually, he shared that honor with the late but still scandalous Edgar Allan Poe, Pfaff's guardian spirit.)

From the west side of Broadway just above Bleecker, a stairwell descended to the small, dingy rathskeller—Whitman once compared the place in size to his bedroom on Portland Avenue. Pfaff's had fewer than a dozen little round tables, with rush-bottomed wooden armchairs clustered around, three or four to a table. A few triple-branched gas chandeliers lighted the white-painted walls, the bar at the far end, the bartender, and the drinkers. From novelist William Dean Howells to naturalist John Burroughs, editor Horace Greeley, and the actresses Adah Isaacs Mencken and Ada Clare, anybody in town who wanted to see Walt Whitman in 1861 knew he could be found nightly at Pfaff's.

Whitman was the dangerous literary lion of New York's bohemia. The beautiful actress and novelist Ada Clare, known as "the Queen of Bohemia," had borne a child out of wedlock to the pianist Louis Moreau Gottschalk, without notable embarrassment. She was rumored to be Whitman's mistress. This is unlikely, although they were intimate friends and she championed his poetry in reviews published in the *Saturday Press*. The company of Ada Clare and other women at Pfaff's, in the days when ladies were not usually welcome in taverns, was one of the reasons folks considered the atmosphere bohemian. Another was the presence of the one-eyed Polish Count Adam Gurowski, who wore a cape, and blue-tinted glasses to protect his good eye. The brilliant, explosive exile wrote for Greeley's *Tribune,* and he brought with him an air of romance and intellectual arrogance.

The saloon lasted hardly a decade, but during that period it provided Walt Whitman with a home away from home and the society of writers, actors, painters, and patrons and amateurs of the arts, many of whom admired him. Howells said that the poet was practically the object of a cult. Gurowski idolized Whitman, and praised him aloud in Pfaff's. It was there, in the smoky light of the saloon, that Whitman would often meet Fred Vaughan, and there that Whitman enjoyed the bonhomie of the group of anonymous young men he called the "Fred Gray Association."

Henry Clapp

"The King of Bohemia," by common consent, was the reckless editor of the *Saturday Press,* the diminutive Henry Clapp—witty, daring, and hard-drinking. He called rival editor Greeley "a self-made man, who worshipped his creator." He also counseled, in his piping voice: "Never tell secrets to your relatives. Blood will tell."

Nowadays Pfaff's is remembered, if at all, because Whitman drank there. In its day the saloon was famous for hosting a crowded roundtable of now forgotten literati, the Pfaffians—Ada Clare, Fitz-James O'Brien, Artemus Ward, Frank Wood, Charles Shanley, George Arnold. The powerful, arch, and often caustic Clapp presided over this colorful crew. The editor was way ahead of his time, grasping the potential of marketing in democratizing commerce—even in literature and the arts. "Everything succeeds if money enough is spent on it," he said. An abolitionist and free-love advocate, five years older than his poet, Clapp may once have been Whitman's lover. Be that as it may, Whitman recalled, "Henry was my friend . . . Henry Clapp stepped out of the crowd of hooters." Clapp became Walt Whitman's most skillful and devoted publicist.

Henry Clapp and his marketing theory bolstered Whitman's constant self-promotion, paid advertising, and stirring of controversy. Clapp would make hay out of scandal. "Better to have people stirred against you if they can't be stirred for you."

The editor was happy to publish almost any review or notice of Whitman in the *Saturday Press,* from adoring Pfaffian tributes to the most scathing indictments. He ran columns that hailed Whitman as a prophet alongside invitations for the poet to hang himself and charges that he was a "sexual predator." One wrote: "Walt Whitman on earth is immortal as well as beyond it"; another said his morals were best fit "for a stock breeder." In the 1859 Christmas issue Clapp printed the first version of "Out of the Cradle Endlessly Rocking." Then, during 1860, when the third edition of *Leaves* was issued, *Saturday Press* ran more than twenty-five items by and about the poet—reviews, advertisements, and parodies of Whitman's style.

William Dean Howells recalled that, of all the magazines then published, only the *Atlantic* was seen by young writers as a more desirable showcase than the *Saturday Press,* "and for the time there was no other literary comparison." He admired the magazine so much that he came down from Boston to pay his respects to the editor. Clapp twitted Howells for being respectable and from Boston. In search of bohemia, Howells ended up in Pfaff's Cellar, but not until he was leaving did he realize that Whitman was there in the gloom. Someone took the novelist by the arm and led him to Whitman's table. "He leaned back in his chair, and reached out his great hand to me, as if he were going to give it to me for good and all. He had a fine head, with a cloud of Jovian hair upon it . . ."

Whitman looked into the young man's eyes "most kindly," and although the writers exchanged only a few words, Howells would remember: "our acquaintance was summed up in that glance and the grasp of his mighty fist upon my hand." Howells said that meeting Whitman was "the chief fact of my experience" of New York literary culture.

Whitman was in his element at Pfaff's, and more than that: he *was* Jovian, mighty, sipping the ambrosia of his hard-earned fame, surrounded by poets, novelists, editors, one-eyed counts, actresses, and adoring young men.

> *The vault at Pfaffs where the drinkers meet to eat and drink and*
>   *carouse*
> *While on the walk immediately overhead pass the myriad feet of*
>   *Broadway*
> *As the dead in their graves, are underfoot hidden*
> *And the living pass over them, recking not of them,*
> *Laugh on laughers! Drink on drinkers!*
> *Beam up—Brighten up bright eyes of beautiful young men!*

Politics, the gross tides of popular consensus and low intrigues in quest of power that shaped parties and statesmen in a democracy, had not always interested Whitman. But these were times when no man who loved his country dared ignore politics. In two years the conflict between Democrats and Republicans over slavery, as expressed by Lincoln and Douglas in their debates, had escalated to the verge of civil war. Though Whitman was not an abolitionist like Henry Clapp and other bohemians, he loathed slavery. He believed, as did Abraham Lincoln, that as long as slavery was not allowed to grow it would inevitably perish in the South. It would sink under its own dire weight because such bondage involved too many human contradictions to survive. But like Lincoln, Whitman opposed the radical abolitionists whose policies would scare the South into secession.

Whitman admired the antislavery senator from New York, William Henry Seward, and once wrote to him, "I too have at heart Freedom, and the amelioration of the people." He hoped

Seward might become president. But a slip of the tongue, the phrase "irrepressible conflict," made in a speech similar in content to Lincoln's "House Divided" message, had imperiled Seward's status as front-runner. The party was longing for a standard-bearer.

Then in February 1860, a tall, gaunt "stump-orator" arrived from Illinois, in a new frock coat of black alpaca, a bit long in the sleeves. He had just bought new boots and they hurt him. He usually walked with a swift flat-footed stride and bounded up steps two or three at a time. But now he limped up the staircase of the Astor House on Broadway to his lonely room, where he would put the finishing touches on a speech he had been invited to give in New York. Five blocks from Pfaff's, where Whitman had come in out of a snowstorm to drink beer, Abraham Lincoln stood before a crowd of fifteen hundred elite New Yorkers, some Pfaffians among them, at the Cooper Union.

The crowd of well-dressed men and women had purchased seats to see "this Lincoln person" who had held his own against Stephen A. Douglas, long considered the nation's greatest orator, in the seven debates everyone had read in the *Times* and *Tribune*. Poet William Cullen Bryant, editor of the *Evening Post*, introduced him. As the crowd applauded, Lincoln put his left hand in the lapel of his coat and smiled broadly, gratefully, and with winning good humor, showing two rows of large white teeth.

Lincoln's craggy features are well known. Their animation is not. He froze in front of the camera, so photographs convey only the intelligence and kindness, qualities so salient in Lincoln that even his adversaries did not dispute them. Fortunately we have many descriptions of his expressions for a variety of moods and emotions dating back to his days on the Illinois court circuit. As a boy, the homely Lincoln had mastered the art of mimicry of

Mimicry

voices, mannerisms, and physical defects. Herndon remembered "whole crowds lifted off their seats by his unequaled powers of mimicry . . . It was only on rare occasions that he resorted to this method of killing off . . . an enemy."

A friend noted that when animated, Lincoln's face brightened like a lantern. "His dull eyes would fairly sparkle with fun, or express as kindly a look as I ever saw, when moved by some matter of human interest."

Great stage actors are not always classic beauties, but their faces have one thing in common: their features are prominent and generously spaced. Large eyes, set well apart, high cheekbones, and long nose and chin are typical. Without such equipment one cannot carry emotions beyond the footlights. Lincoln was not handsome. But he had the features of a professional actor, and they responded with maximum mobility to inner and outer stimuli, delight, sorrow, or subtle wit. He could raise and lower his bushy eyebrows in mock surprise or deadly menace, or lift one eyebrow in doubt or before delivering the punch line of a joke. The mouth was beautifully shaped, the full underlip conveying his compassion, the firm upper lip his strength of purpose. His smile was famous, incandescent, a Frans Hals smile that lit up the gray eyes and drew up the cheeks, drawing back the deep-cut lines that flared from his nose to the corners of his mouth and bracketed his chin. And this grin seemed all the more brilliant when it suddenly broke from behind the clouds of gloom for which the man was equally known.

"Mr. President and fellow-citizens of New York," he began, smiling, "the facts with which I shall deal this evening are mainly old and familiar." Standing square on his feet, his arms at his sides, he proceeded to demonstrate how the framers of the Constitution meant for the federal government to control slavery in its territories. However, "wrong as we think slavery is, we can yet afford to let it alone where it is, because that much is due to necessity arising from its actual presence . . ."

Herndon recalled, "He used his head a great deal in speaking, throwing or jerking or moving it now here and now there . . . to drive the idea home." Lincoln was cool, calm, self-possessed, very natural, and pleasing. He did not gesticulate much, but sometimes he would raise his right hand, "shooting out that long boney forefinger of his to dot an idea or to enforce a thought, resting his thumb on his middle finger."

"His face lights with an inward fire," wrote Noah Brooks of the *New-York Tribune,* while a New York *World* reporter noted: "His voice was soft and sympathetic as a girl's . . . not lifted above a tone of average conversation . . . a peculiar naïveté in his manner and voice produced a strange effect on his audience . . . hushed for a moment to a silence like that of the dead." Now and then the audience, spread in a broad semicircle before the speaker, burst forth with applause or laughter or ringing cheers. And after the thunder of the final ovation, as hats and handkerchiefs flew into the air, Brooks would remark: "The tones, the gestures, the kindling eye, and the mirth-provoking look defy the reporter's skill. No man ever before made such an impression on his first appeal to a New York audience."

Brooks's editor, Horace Greeley, was present. He would soon report to his fellow Pfaffians that Lincoln's was "the ablest, the greatest, the wisest speech that had yet been made; it would reassure the conservative Northerner; it was just what was wanted to conciliate the excited Southerner; it was conclusive in its argument, and would assure the overthrow of Douglas."

Greeley, editor of the most influential papers in America, eventually threw his support to Lincoln, doing everything in his considerable power to see that Lincoln won the Republican nomination for president.

A year later, on February 19, 1861, a mild, clear afternoon, Whitman was perched on his seat next to a young, brawny omnibus driver on a Knickerbocker trundling down Broadway toward City Hall. The traffic thickened and the horsecars slowed for the gathering crowd. People hurried from every direction: carpenters, mechanics, mothers with children, clerks in their frock coats and top hats, lawyers and merchants leaving their offices, "untold and perhaps thousands of idle and starving workmen," according to the *Times*. They had come to try and catch a glimpse of President-elect Lincoln on his way to the Astor House. A suite of adjoining rooms, second-floor front, was awaiting him in the city's finest hotel.

Mounted police were curbing all buses, drays, and buckboards up and down Broadway, Barclay Street, and Vesey Street to clear the way for the carriages of the presidential party. The cortege would be coming down from the new depot of the Hudson River Railroad on Thirtieth Street between Ninth and Tenth Avenues. Whitman's omnibus fetched up against the curbstone on Broadway somewhere between Barnum's Museum and the City Hall Park. The passengers got off. There was nothing to do but hold the horses and wait for Lincoln to show up.

The three cars of the presidential train had pulled into the station at 3:00 P.M. sharp. Lincoln's chest was sore and his voice hoarse from the fifty-three speeches he had given during the week it had taken him, his family, and his Negro house servant (known simply as William) to travel the sixteen hundred miles from Springfield. He had wished for the people to become acquainted

with him, and so he had chosen a roundabout route on a dozen railroads.

His entourage included the two boys, Tad and Willie, and
young Robert, dubbed "the Prince of Rails"; Lincoln's brother-
in-law and personal physician W. S. Wallace; Lincoln's young private secretaries, John G. Nicolay and John Hay; the Illinois judges
N. B. Judd and David Davis, old friends who had advised Lincoln
during his campaign; half a dozen army officers including Colonel
Ward Hill Lamon, an old friend intensely concerned for Lincoln's
safety; editor Horace Greeley; and a separate carload of newsmen.

At whistle-stops where he had no time for a full speech he
would stand before the crowd at the back of the train and repeat
the formulaic phrases:

> I see that you have provided a platform, but I shall have to
> decline standing on it . . . (Laughter and applause) The
> Superintendent tells me I have not time . . . I come only to see
> you and give you the opportunity to see me; and I say to you,
> as I have said before to crowds where there were so many
> handsome ladies as there are here, I have decidedly the best of
> the bargain . . . With your aid, as the people, I think we shall
> be able to preserve—not the country, for the country will pre-
> serve itself, (cheers), but the institutions of the country—
> (great cheering) . . . If I can only be as generously and
> unanimously sustained as the demonstrations I have witnessed
> indicate I shall be, I shall not fail . . .

The snow had been deep at Batavia and Utica, so Lincoln was
grateful for milder weather in Manhattan. A *Times* reporter complained that during the entire trip Mr. Lincoln had worn a "shock-

ing bad hat" and a thin, threadbare overcoat. After leaving Utica, Mary Lincoln ordered William to bring Mr. Lincoln's new coat and hat out of the boxes he had not thought to unwrap. In his new stovepipe topper and black broadcloth overcoat Lincoln looked "fifty percent improved," the newsman allowed, and "the country may congratulate itself that its President-elect is a man who does not reject, even in important matters, the advice and counsel of his wife."

The superintendent of police had detailed thirteen hundred of New York's finest "to keep the enthusiasm of the crowd within the bounds of good manners." One hundred and fifty, in shiny new belts and yellow calf gloves, awaited the party at the depot, which was decorated with flags. Thirty-five carriages were drawn up outside the station on Thirtieth Street. Mary kissed her husband and smoothed his hair. Lincoln and his party advanced through the passenger room behind police and bodyguards. Outside, the President-elect bowed gracefully to the cheering crowd.

As the *New York Times* reported, "Amid cheers and the waving of handkerchiefs he entered his carriage—the same in which the Prince of Wales rode, drawn by six black horses." The procession of eleven barouches followed a squad of mounted policemen. First came a four-horse carriage bearing the reception committees of the Common Council, next the President-elect's barouche flanked by a platoon of policemen, and then nine more carriages followed; bringing up the rear was the express wagon, drawn by four plumed steeds, which carried the party's baggage. "Both sides of Thirtieth Street were packed with people, who cheered lustily as Mr. Lincoln passed—and he returned the compliment by raising his hat and bowing," the *Baltimore Sun* noted.

The parade turned down Ninth Avenue to Twenty-third

Street, rolled along Twenty-third to Fifth Avenue, then down Fifth to Fourteenth Street and along Fourteenth to Broadway. Flags were flying almost everywhere, and the streets were lined with people waving and cheering, the crowd swelling as the procession moved downtown. Across Twenty-third Street at Eighth Avenue stretched a banner, WELCOME LINCOLN, and over it the Stars and Stripes. A group of boys dressed in military coats and caps waved flags inscribed LINCOLN AND HAMLIN.

Another banner spanning the street bore the words from Genesis FEAR NOT, ABRAHAM, I AM THY SHIELD AND THY EXCEEDING GREAT REWARD. From hotel balconies and windows, ladies waved their handkerchiefs. "Mr. Lincoln bowed and smiled constantly, and seemed vastly delighted with the spectacle."

Putnam, the publishing house at 532 Broadway, had hung out a placard with the famous words from Lincoln's Cooper Union speech RIGHT MAKES MIGHT! A merchant two blocks south displayed the message WELCOME ABRAHAM LINCOLN, WE BEG FOR COMPROMISE. This gave Lincoln pause. He was not about to compromise his principles regarding the spread of slavery.

The crowd in front of the Astor House was packed at 4:30 P.M. when the presidential cavalcade arrived, and it was only with great firmness that the police were able to make way for them. Walt Whitman stood on the top of the omnibus hoping to glimpse the man who had won his vote.

The five-story Greek Revival–style hotel had a four-columned portico, surmounted by an ornate triangular gable and cornice. According to reporters the President-elect and his escort alighted immediately, went up the steps between the Doric columns, and entered the hotel. At the crowd's deafening command, and after much coaxing of aldermen, Lincoln was prevailed upon to mount the coping of the hotel doorway by climbing out the window, so that he might say a few words to the crowd, estimated at 250,000, that had thronged to see him. He was hoarse. "After bowing his acknowledgments for his enthusiastic reception," he said:

> Fellow Citizens—I have stepped before you merely in compli-
> ance with what appeared to be your wish, and with no purpose
> of making a speech. In fact, I do not propose making a speech
> this afternoon. I could not be heard by any but a very small
> fraction of you at best; but what is still worse than that is, that
> I have nothing just now worth your hearing. (Loud applause.)
> I beg you to believe that I do not now refuse to address you
> through any disposition to disoblige you, but the contrary. But
> at the same time I beg of you to excuse me for the present.

There was vibrant applause. A Councilman Barney called to the crowd, "That's enough," and he and Alderman Cornell handed the weary President-elect back through the window of the hotel.

Eighteen years later Whitman would recall that from the top of the omnibus he had "a capital view of it all, and especially of Mr. Lincoln, his look and gait—his perfect composure and coolness—his unusual and uncouth height, his dress of complete black, stovepipe hat push'd back on the head, dark-brown complexion, seam'd and wrinkled yet canny-looking face, black, bushy head of hair, dis-proportionately long neck, and his hands held behind as he stood observing the people. He look'd with curiosity upon that immense sea of faces, and the sea of faces return'd the look with similar curiosity." Whitman did not recall any speech.

Press reports of Lincoln's New York reception differ somewhat—from that of the Republican *New York Times,* which
describes "an immeasurable outpouring of the people [that]
flooded the avenues and streets" and says, "the harmony of inces-
sant cheers was unbroken by indecent language or gesture . . .
Certainly no welcome could have been more cordial or respectful," to that of a Democratic newspaper that called the crowd subdued and small compared to the recent turnout for the Prince of
Wales. There is little mention of assassination plots or potential
violence.

After his election Lincoln had begun to appear in Whitman's
dreams, and there is much that is dreamlike in the poet's memory
of that February afternoon in 1861. Although Whitman had been
an acutely observant journalist, his account, written in 1879, is suffused with dread, as if he is anticipating the tragedy to come. And
it differs so sharply from the news reports we must suspect that the
poet has imposed upon this thrilling moment the memories and
impressions of later years, when he would see the President much
more closely.

Two or three shabby hack barouches made their way with
some difficulty through the crowd, and drew up at the Astor
House entrance. A tall figure stepp'd out of the center of these
barouches, paus'd leisurely on the sidewalk, look'd up at the
granite walls and looming architecture of the grand old
hotel—then, after a relieving stretch of arms and legs, turn'd
around for over a minute to slowly and good-humoredly scan
the appearance of the vast and silent crowds. There were no
speeches, no compliments—no welcome—as far as I could
hear, not a word said. Still much anxiety was conceal'd in that
quiet.

This is a vivid, accurate portrait of Lincoln getting out of a hackney cab, rather than of the President-elect descending from the regal barouche whose six black steeds had transported the Prince of Wales. The silent, sullen crowd was not the cheering multitude described in the *Times, Tribune,* and *Herald.* And the long minute the poet beheld the President-elect for the first time seems to exist nowhere in history but in Whitman's recollection. His "capital view of it all" from the top of the omnibus was at once much better and far worse than others', if he saw Lincoln so plainly for so long a time and yet did not see him stretch his leg over the windowsill and climb onto the coping to address the crowd. Whitman seems to have been deaf to their applause, too.

"Cautious persons had fear'd some mark'd insult or indignity to the President-elect," Whitman recalled, and this is true. The *Times* observed: "mischief makers have been feverishly busy all Winter . . . impressing upon the masses the conviction that the responsibility for their woes rests mediately upon the Republican Party, but directly upon Mr. Lincoln for not announcing the programme of his Administration, and so giving peace to the country. Acts of outrage and violence have been counseled and justified." But Whitman's 1879 account claims that Lincoln then "possess'd no personal popularity at all in New York City, and very little political," and this is far from true. Of course, Lincoln had his enemies in New York. While most of the ships harbored in the East River displayed bunting of red, white, and blue, the American ensign, or the English Jack—the *Texas* and *New Orleans* hoisted no colors, nor did any other Southern vessel. All the hotels displayed the American flag excepting the Democrat-owned New York Hotel uptown, and so did every newspaper office but the Democratic *Day-Book.* Even among Republicans, Lincoln had his critics. Men like the spurned candidate Salmon Chase were exasperated by the President-elect's stubborn silence about the Secession crisis. Some, like Seward, feared that Lincoln would not compromise with the seceding states, and many more Republicans felt he was insufficiently "radical" in his stand against slavery.

But ever since the Cooper Union speech had sent shock waves through the intellectual community, Lincoln had enjoyed mounting popularity in New York. With the help of Greeley's paper, and the political muscle of Seward and ward boss Thurlow Weed, Lincoln had carried New York on election day, along with the rest of the Northeastern states—all but New Jersey, which he split with Douglas. Whitman's impression of "a sulky, unbroken silence" caused by "the few political supporters of Mr. Lincoln" being bullied by "the immense majority, who were anything but supporters," is false. Yet historians have echoed Whitman's story until it has become part of the legend of Lincoln's harrowing journey to Washington, which was mostly joyful, though not without peril. "I have no doubt," said the poet, "many an assassin's knife and pistol lurk'd in hip or breast pocket there, ready, soon as break and riot came."

Subsequent events account for the melodrama of Whitman's vision. It is meant to distinguish the poet's affection from the mob's—though they were probably not so different. The gaunt man with the sweet smile, from beyond the Alleghenies, had rare charisma, and Whitman felt it immediately. During that moment, fixed forever in the poet's memory, the real crowd milled into a blur and fell silent, and there was no one left but Lincoln and Whitman.

News from Washington and the Southern states grew more worrisome by the hour, yet Lincoln's two days in New York City had a

52yrold

holiday air. His boys visited Barnum's Museum across the street; in the evening the Lincolns went to the opera to hear Verdi's *Un Ballo in Maschera*. At midnight the National Guard band and a German quartet appeared outside the hotel to serenade them.

The fifty-two-year-old President-elect charmed everyone from New York's Mayor Fernando Wood to ninety-four-year-old Joshua Dewey, who had voted in every election since George Washington's. Lincoln would stand back-to-back with any man the crowd pushed forward to challenge his height of six feet three inches. Few did. He accepted hats from competing haberdashers, and when asked which hat he favored Lincoln drawled, "They mutually surpassed each other." He shook hands with thirty veterans of the War of 1812.

"His style of shaking hands and chatting with people is prepossessing," wrote a reporter, "frank, genial, unassuming, and in a word—Western." According to the *Times*, "The brief remarks of Mr. Lincoln, in reply to the courtesies tendered to him, were in exceeding good taste . . . We know enough of Mr. Lincoln to appreciate his entire sincerity and patriotism . . . He is an earnest man, but not an obstinate or impracticable one. His speech gives us the assurance of a vigorous and firm, but conciliatory Administration." Lincoln told his audience at City Hall: "There is nothing that can ever bring me willingly to consent to the destruction of this Union, under which . . . the whole country has acquired its greatness, unless it were to be that thing for which the Union itself was made." The statement is afloat in ambiguity.

These details and more were available in the daily newspapers Walt Whitman perused, with increasing fascination, since he had seen the President-elect climb down from a barouche and survey the crowd in front of the Astor House. Now Whitman was keenly interested in presidents, and in the president's symbolic role in the life of the democratic republic. The word "President" appears sixteen times in the 1856 *Leaves of Grass* and many more times in the later editions. In his youth he hated presidents, by and large, with an oedipal enthusiasm, feeling that none of them did justice to that sacred office. In his pamphlet "The Eighteenth Presidency!" he railed against Millard Fillmore and James Buchanan, called them disunionists and political corpses that had been lifted out of putrid graves, painted, and stuffed by "electioneers, body snatchers, bawlers, bribers, compromisers . . . blind men, deaf men, pimpled men, scarred inside with the vile disorder, gaudy outside with gold chains made from the people's money and harlot's money twisted together." In the White House, said Whitman, Franklin Pierce "eats dirt and excrement for his daily meals, likes it, and tries to force it on The States."

The new President was obviously cut out of different cloth. He looked remarkably like the Redeemer President that Whitman had envisioned in that same vehement pamphlet, "heroic, shrewd, fully-informed, healthy-bodied, middle-aged, beard-faced" (at last the beard was growing!), who had "come down from the West across the Alleghenies . . . with the tan all over his face, breast and arms." Of course he was not yet "heroic" and might not be "fully-informed," but he might have the makings of a hero if he *could* be properly informed . . .

Whitman began dreaming of Lincoln, jotting in his notebook: "Two characters as of a dialogue between A. L——n and W. Whitman—as in a dream / or better? Lessons for a President elect / Dialogue between WW and 'President elect.'" He imagined talking to the future President. He imagined the man from Illinois talking back to him. The questions he would ask Lincoln had been worked out years before:

Who are you that would talk to America?

Have you studied out my land, its idioms and men?

Have you learned the physiology, phrenology, politics, geography,
    pride, freedom, friendship, of my land? its substratums and
    objects?

Have you considered the organic compact of the first day of the first
    year of the independence of The States?

Have you possessed yourself of the Federal Constitution?

Do you acknowledge liberty with audible and absolute
    acknowledgment, and set slavery at naught for life and death?

. . .

Can you hold your hand against all seductions, follies, whirls, fierce
    contentions?

Are you not of some coterie? some school or religion?

All of these questions had been put to the future President in the
1856 *Leaves of Grass*. No man who ever ran for the office could
have answered them more to the poet's satisfaction than this "rail-
splitter" who was on his way to the White House.

part two

THE WAR OF
THE REBELLION

3

THE FEDERAL CITY,
NEW YEAR'S DAY, 1863

The last night of the year had been a restless one for the President: he went to bed after twelve and rose before dawn. At midnight all around the crowded city soldiers and civilians fired their guns over the grave of the Departed Year. The New Year was welcomed by the prayers and thanksgiving of preachers and the fanfare of bands, "the boisterous laugh of the gay and thoughtless," the whirl of dancers, "the flowing bumpers of worshippers at the shrine of Bacchus, and the rattle of musketry by ever hopeful and happy 'Young America,'" the *Morning Chronicle* observed. The merrymaking that flowed up Pennsylvania Avenue and Fifteenth Street past the Willard Hotel, and down Vermont Avenue past St. John's Church on Lafayette Square, went on in the light of the swelling moon. But it stopped at the gates of the President's House.

The fireworks thundered all night. Then as the sun rose, the streets around the White House began to fill with citizens who had

come from far and wide to greet Mr. Lincoln at the president's customary New Year's levee.

Lincoln did not drink, and in any case this was not a night for
him to celebrate. Military dispatches from Murfreesboro, Tennessee, were appalling. On December 31 the Rebels, led by General
Braxton Bragg, had attacked General William Starke Rosecrans's
Federal Army of the Cumberland. "Our entire line suffered terribly this morning," said Anson Stager's telegram. "Four regiments
of regulars lost half of their men, and all of their commanding
officers . . . Majors Rosengarten and Ward were killed, Generals
Stanley, Rousseau and Palmer were wounded . . . The Fifteenth
Wisconsin lost seven captains. General Negley's artillery is still
mowing the rebels in the center." In his third dispatch the telegraph
superintendent admitted, "the greatest carnage of the war has
occurred." Soon the President, then the country, would learn that
there were twenty-four thousand casualties at Murfreesboro. Two
weeks earlier, at Fredericksburg, eighteen thousand soldiers had
been killed and wounded, and the President had said, "If there is a
worse place than Hell, I am in it."

Walt Whitman's brother George, a first lieutenant under General Ambrose Burnside's command, survived the Union disaster at
Fredericksburg in December, advancing over a narrow turf the
Rebels had so perfectly enfiladed that one gunner remarked, "a
chicken could not live in that field when we opened on it." Walt
called Burnside's charge "the most complete piece of mismanagement perhaps ever known in the earth's wars." Public confidence
in the Commander-in-Chief collapsed, and his cabinet was at log-
gerheads, so that he was able to hold it together only by the most
ingenious diplomacy.

"I am heartsick," lamented Senator William Pitt Fessenden of
Maine, "when I think of the mismanagement of our army . . .

There never was such a shambling, half-and-half set of incapables collected in one government before or since the world began." The New York lawyer George Templeton Strong wrote in his famous diary: "Even Lincoln himself has gone down at last. Nobody believes in him any more."

The tempest in the cabinet stirred by Secretary of the Treasury Salmon Chase's jealousy and hatred of Secretary of State William H. Seward briefly distracted the public and the press from the epic, pathetic slaughter at Fredericksburg. Radical Republican senators called for Seward to resign; as the President defended the Secretary of State, Seward's and Chase's indignant, reciprocal resignations descended into comic opera. Lincoln's ingenuity in resolving the conflict in his official family "to entire satisfaction"—in his words—impressed the whole Republican Party and bought him some time to win back the confidence of the American people.

But now there was the carnage at the Battle of Stone's River, Murfreesboro, known at the moment only to the men fighting and dying there, to Secretary of War Edwin M. Stanton, to General-in-Chief Henry Halleck, and to President Abraham Lincoln. All evening, December 31, Lincoln had been working on the final draft of his Emancipation Proclamation, which had been the subject of a cabinet meeting that same morning at ten o'clock when Lincoln presented the document for final approval. The changes Chase and others suggested were slight. The major disagreements had been resolved by September 22, when Lincoln announced that the emancipation of slaves would be effective January 1, 1863. But the President had to write a fair copy of the document during the night and into the early morning of New Year's Day.

Lincoln wrote slowly and painstakingly, with little facility in his fingers and wrist. An inkblot or a misspelled word would cause him to discard the paper and begin again. The pistol-cracks and rifle-volleys outside his window mocked the shots fired in fury and terror a thousand miles away in Tennessee. And for every shot, a young soldier—losing a life or a limb. It was not a night conducive to sleep or concentration. The very document under his hand seemed to waver and tremble, disturbed by the sounds of gunfire.

Horace Greeley, Republican Radicals, and abolitionists had been begging Lincoln to free the slaves for as long as he had been in office. As much as he wished to oblige them and suit his own conscience, he had to wait for a military victory, an impression of superiority in the war, if the Proclamation were not to seem an act of desperation. In September the Battle of Antietam—an ambiguous victory—had provided the occasion for Lincoln to act. But since then nothing had gone right. The London *Times* called emancipation "the wretched makeshift of a pettifogging lawyer" who had stooped to "the execrable expedient of a servile insurrection." A bloody defeat in Tennessee would make freeing the slaves appear, more than ever, a desperate act rather than a conscientious change in policy.

Lincoln sat in a large armchair, his legs crossed, writing beneath the glass-globed jets of a chandelier, at a desk between two high windows in his office. The silk braid of a bell cord hung to the right of the desk. A fire was burning on the hearth, with its high brass fender and andirons. The chamber Lincoln called his "shop" took up the southeast corner of the second floor. It was large enough to accommodate, on one wall, a sofa flanked by matching button-and-roll armchairs, and across the room the long oak table where the cabinet met. From above the Victorian marble mantelpiece a portrait of Andrew Jackson overlooked the meeting table toward the military maps hanging on the opposite wall: Maryland, Virginia, Tennessee, Georgia. The table, desks, chairs, the slant-top escritoire with its pigeonholes and bookshelves in the southeast corner, all were as cluttered as in the Springfield office of Lincoln and Herndon, although here the maids swept and dusted. There was plenty of room to pace.

As the light of day dawned upon the south lawn, Lincoln could see the red sandstone Gothic towers and battlements of the Smithsonian Institution through the barren trees, and the stump of the unfinished Washington Monument surrounded by cattle sheds, stockyards, and slaughterhouses. Over the Potomac loomed the lavender hills of Virginia. He put down his pen. A block away stood the Decatur House, a mansion with an auction block in its courtyard where for years anyone with enough money could buy a man, woman, or child. Near the Capitol traveling slave dealers lodged at the posh St. Charles Hotel, where the management advertised "roomy underground cells for confining slaves for safe-keeping . . . in case of escape, full value of the negro will be paid by the proprietor." With a stroke of the pen he would put an end to this. He picked up the pen, and wrote, and put it down again.

He could not stop thinking about the woman who had come to call on him the day before. "Yesterday, a piteous appeal was made to me by an old lady of genteel appearance, saying she had, with what she thought sufficient assurance she would not be disturbed by the government, fitted up the two South Divisions of the old 'Duff Green' building in order to take boarders . . ." The woman might be the same age as his stepmother Sarah, the only member of that family he ever really loved after his sister died. He had made a long pilgrimage from Springfield to Farmington to visit Sarah weeks before his inauguration, and the parting had been difficult, tearful.

Now this lady (whose identity remains a mystery), dressed in formal black, as forlorn as Sarah, arrived on a day when Lincoln's duties included admitting West Virginia into the Union as an independent state and trying to persuade a frustrated General Burnside not to resign his command of the Army of the Potomac. She sat outside the President's office with hands folded primly in her lap. On a day when senators and colonels were being turned away from the anteroom where secretary John Nicolay scanned *cartes de visites* and petitions, guarding Lincoln from all but the most distinguished suitors, the old lady would not move before the President had heard her. She would wait in dignified silence until he agreed to see her. And at last he did.

His unvarying approach to such calls was a pleasant nod and smile, and the query "What can I do for you?" Rising from his chair he would, in the case of "an old lady of genteel appearance," have inquired, "How do you do?" before asking the more direct question.

The lady was not well. She was probably in tears over her predicament, in order to have wrung such a response from the busy President. She was likely a well-bred woman who had fallen upon hard times, suffering the fate of so many other wealthy families with Southern roots.

Duff Green, seventy-two, was a railroad and newspaper magnate, a secessionist who had lived in Washington before Lincoln's election, after which he moved south to serve the Confederacy. Green still owned a mansion on Tenth and E and a group of houses on East Capitol Street between Second and Third Streets, which had become known as "Duff Green's Row." The old lady had gotten a lease on the two south divisions and fitted them out for a boarding house. Housing in Washington was scarce, so she quickly acquired boarders, including some congressmen. After being assured that her lease was secure, she had suddenly been ordered by the government to vacate Green's Row by Saturday, January 3.

"Independently of the ruin it brings on her, by her lost out-lay, she neither has, nor can find another shelter for her own head," Lincoln wrote to Secretary of War Edwin M. Stanton. "I know nothing about it myself, but promised to bring it to your notice."

This was Lincoln's way of channeling suits and suitors. The fact that he addressed this appeal to the Secretary of War on January 1, a day when he would hardly have time to visit the water closet between social and military obligations, proves that he knew more about the woman's plight than he was revealing. He wanted Stanton to do something about it immediately.

Nothing, it seemed, occurred separately. The woman's fate was connected to the document Lincoln was finishing, as gray dawn became golden morning and he could hear servants' footsteps in the corridor. Duff Green's buildings had been appropriated by the city's military governor, James Wadsworth. An abolitionist, Wadsworth planned to use the entire block to house "contrabands"—curious term for the runaway slaves from the South who had been flooding the city, destitute, in rags, homeless. Their tents and piteous shanties would soon litter the Ellipse, visible from Lincoln's window. After the President had issued his Proclamation, there would be not just thousands but tens of thousands of freed Negroes in the Federal City. And General James Wadsworth wanted to shelter as many of them as he could.

General Wadsworth reported directly to the Secretary of War, an earnest, bespectacled man whose long black beard had a distinctive silver streak at the chin. Day and night Stanton stood in the musty barrack of the War Department building, at a high desk facing the entrance to his room, scowling and barking orders. He was rarely seen anywhere else. Lincoln said Stanton was "the rock upon which are beating the waves of this conflict," and newsmen dubbed him "Mars." Everyone feared Stanton except Lincoln, and even the President was slow to contradict the Secretary or give him direct orders. But at the moment Lincoln could do no more for the sad lady of genteel appearance than alert the frightful, unsentimental Secretary of War. Her fate was in his hands.

Returning to the Proclamation, the President wrote: "And upon this act, sincerely believed to be an act of justice, warranted by the Constitution, upon military necessity, I invoke the considerate judgment of mankind, and the gracious favor of Almighty God." He was finished. He pulled the bell cord next to his desk to summon a courier, who would carry the manuscript to the Secretary of State's office. There William Seward would review the document and have it copied for the press before midday, when both men would sign it. A clerk would pen the formal close, "In witness whereof . . . ," while Lincoln had his breakfast: one egg and a cup of coffee.

When he had dressed for the formal reception, Lincoln went to fetch Mary. She wore a black velvet dress with lozenge trimming at the waist, diamond earrings and necklace, and around her head a black shawl. This would be her first public reception since the burial of their eleven-year-old son Willie, who had died of typhoid in February 1862. The Lincolns were racked by guilt that the foul air of the canal that flowed behind the White House had killed the boy. Of all their four sons (Robert, Eddie, Willie, and Tad), Willie had been the favorite, and Mary had not recovered from the shock. She took comfort in the company of spirit mediums, whose séances held in the darkened Red Room brought her in touch with Willie's sensitive, poetic ghost. Lincoln was concerned about his wife this morning, doubting she could hold up under the pressure of receiving a thousand visitors, who began arriving at nine-thirty.

The gorgeous parade of the diplomats came first, ambassadors and their wives from India, Japan, Spain, and elsewhere in their colorful costumes and headdresses—red and blue saris with gold thread; fiery kimonos; the fez, the veil, the mantilla. The distinguished representatives of foreign courts, in their carriages, drove rapidly up the semicircular drive, alighted, and advanced through a screen of Ionic columns to the audience room, where they met the President and First Lady standing together. Marshal Ward Hill Lamon, chief of protocol, made the introductions. Meanwhile the army and navy officers in full parade dress were gathering at the War Department. They marched to the White House at ten o'clock and the Lincolns, standing side by side, smiling and bowing, received them in the order of their rank.

At noon the gates were opened to the public, an overwhelming, if well dressed and orderly, crowd. Men wore formal black; women came in silks and lace, satins and feathers, but unbonnetted. "With the stirring events of the times and our largely increased community," said the *Washington Chronicle*, "the desire this year was greater than ever to call on the patriotic Chief Magistrate ... Aware of the public sentiment, and anticipating the extreme pressure on New Year's morning, every arrangement was made at the mansion to facilitate the general movements of the people ..."

The threat of assassination was constant. A detachment from a Pennsylvania regiment plus most of the metropolitan police were on hand to supervise the crowd. Officers stood guard under the portico, behind the projecting semicircular colonnade, forming a line up the two flights of steps, ushering people into the vestibule in installments. Canvas had been spread over the new carpeting in the East Room to protect it from muddy boots.

The crowd pressed forward in columns, first to the Red Room, where Mrs. Lincoln greeted them. The short, plump First Lady stood under the full-length portrait of George Washington, which

Dolly Madison had rescued from the English invaders in 1814 by clipping it from the frame with her sewing scissors. Mary knew the story. The White House still showed the scorch marks from the day British General Robert Ross had set it afire. The copper roof, lapped instead of grooved, leaked; yet Mrs. Lincoln had quickly spent more than twenty thousand dollars on carpets, damask curtains, gold-fringed tapestries for the Green Room, a Limoges dining service, French wallpaper, drapes, ornately carved armchairs and sofas, and new gasoliers of brass with milk-glass globes.

From Mrs. Lincoln's parlor the visitors passed into the Blue Room. There the President stood smiling, his little boy Tad at his side, while Marshal Lamon performed the ceremony of introduction. Vigilant, protective, the burly, mustachioed marshal was almost as tall as Lincoln—they made an imposing pair. Noah Brooks, a correspondent for the *Sacramento Union*, recalled a tumultuous scene as the crowd filled the reception rooms. "It required no little engineering to steer the throng, after it met and engaged the President, out of a great window from which a temporary bridge had been constructed for an exit."

The President stood serenely, "availing himself of every opportunity to drop a pleasant word or remark," the *Chronicle* reported. Noah Brooks, who was also a friend of Lincoln's, knew that after a couple of hours of hand-shaking the President's fingers would be so swollen he could hardly write; the white kid glove on Lincoln's busy right hand looked as if it had been dropped in the dustbin. Brooks noticed that Lincoln "often looked over the heads of the multitudinous strangers who shook his hand with fervor and affection." The President's thoughts "were far away on the bloody and snowy field" in Tennessee, where men were dying to save the Union, or destroy it.

Walt Whitman had recently arrived in the Federal City from a battlefield in Virginia where he had spent Christmas with the troops. "My place in Washington was a peculiar one—my reasons for being there, my doing there what I did do. I do not think I quite had my match . . . No one—at least no one that I met—went just from my own reasons—from a profound conviction of necessity, affinity—coming into closest relations—relations oh! so close and dear!—with the whole strange welter of life gathered to that mad focus."

New Year's Day, William O'Connor took Whitman from their rooming house on L Street on a stroll down Vermont Avenue toward Lafayette Square to see the hoi polloi jostling to shake Lincoln's hand. The morning was brilliant, clear and not too cold. O'Connor was a writer—Thayer & Eldridge had published his antislavery novel *Harrington*. Slender and blue-eyed, he was well-favored, said to resemble the "Chandos" portrait of young Shakespeare. O'Connor first met Whitman in the Boston office of their bold new publisher. After the firm's bankruptcy, both Charlie Eldridge and his novelist landed in the civil service: Eldridge in the Army Paymaster's Office, and O'Connor as a clerk at the Light-House Board. Whitman liked the "gallant, handsome, fine-voiced, glowing-eyed man" and his wife, Nellie, a wise woman whose austere features belied her generous nature. She adored the visitor even more than did her husband, who wrote of Whitman: "He is so large and strong—so pure, proud and tender, with such an ineffable bonhomie and wholesome sweetness of presence; all the young men and women are in love with him."

Whitman was lucky to find such friends in Washington. He had left New York after the Battle of Fredericksburg because the *Tri-bune* had listed his brother among the wounded. Walt had come hoping to find George in one of the hospitals and to take care of him. He arrived on December 16, 1862, flat broke, having had his pocket picked while changing trains in Philadelphia. When he couldn't find George in Washington, he decided to search in Virginia, but first he looked up his old friend O'Connor. The novelist loaned him money; Eldridge inquired at the Paymaster's Office about a job for him; Nellie O'Connor fed him and made him up a bed.

The next day, the seventeenth, Whitman took the boat down to Falmouth, Virginia. After reaching the front, near Falmouth Station, he came to Lucy Mansion, a makeshift field hospital where Clara Barton was bandaging and feeding hundreds of soldiers. Whitman studied a heap of amputated arms, legs, and feet piled under a tree in front of the building, wondering if any of them had belonged to his brother. In a nearby garden he glimpsed a row of corpses, "each covered with its brown woolen blanket," and in the dooryard fresh graves, mostly of officers, each marked by a barrel stave with name and rank hastily carved.

George was not there. He had lost neither life nor limb. Two days later, when Walt finally located him in one of the scattered tents of New York's Fifty-first Regiment, George was recovering from a bullet wound in his cheek. He said you could push a stick all the way through it. George was hearty and cheerful, and was preparing to return to active duty as a newly promoted captain.

Walt spent Christmas with his brother and the Army of the Potomac in a campground near the Rappahannock. By the bivouac fires he heard stories of men at war, "more wonderful than all the romances ever written"; of bravery and cowardice, folly and suffering; "of a dead man sitting on the top rail of a fence . . . shot there at sundown, mortally wounded, clung with desperate nerves, and was found sitting there, dead, staring with fixed eyes in the morning."

He shared a tent with George and three other men; ate their green corn, hard crackers, chicken, and potatoes; and drank their whiskey-spiked coffee. He watched the artillery drill to the sounds of a bugle, and heard the hooves of cavalry, the clatter of sabers. Once, under a flag of truce, he helped bury the dead lying on the battlefield. He listened to the growling of the men in the ranks. "Even the good fellows would burst if they couldn't grumble," he wrote. Whitman was amazed at how young they were. So many boys and youths were fighting—"and only a sprinkling of elderly men."

He spent most of his time that week with the sick and wounded in the drafty tents that had been pitched for "division hospitals." He wrote, "I go around from one case to another," soldiers lying on the frozen ground, their blankets spread on pine twigs. "I do not see that I do much good to these wounded and dying; but I cannot leave them. Once in a while some youngster holds on to me convulsively, and I do what I can for him; at any rate, stop with him and sit with him for hours, if he wishes it."

He wrote to his old friend from Pfaff's, Fred Gray, of a nineteen-year-old Mississippi captain who had lost his leg at Fredericksburg. He was taken as prisoner to the Lacy Mansion hospital where Whitman "cheered him up . . . our affection is quite an affair, quite romantic . . ."

The poet had found a new vocation; or rather, he renewed the passion that he had first discovered among the wounded stage drivers in New York Hospital. As Gay Wilson Allen has written, "This work of bolstering the morale of the sick and discouraged was the one thing that Walt Whitman seemed especially created to do." At dawn on December 28, when Whitman left Falmouth, he found himself in charge of a trainload of sick and wounded men bound for the Federal City. One of these was the Rebel captain

with whom he had developed such an intense bond. Federal soldiers and Rebels were not treated separately. They were all loaded
on flatbed cars and hauled ten miles to Aquia Creek, which flows
into the Potomac; there they boarded a steamer bound north. Walt
moved from stretcher to stretcher, consoling and encouraging the
men. There was no one else to do this, no one else to take messages
assuring their wives and mothers that they were alive. As the boat
steamed toward Washington, Whitman took dictation, ladled water, and rearranged aching limbs and stumps, all the while gently
talking to the soldiers. When the ship reached the Sixth Street
wharves where the ambulances were waiting, only one of Whitman's patients had died.

George Whitman did not need his brother's help, but many
other men did, especially in the Federal City. So Walt decided to
stay a while and visit the hospitals there.

On that sunny New Year's Day, Walt and his young friend, the
lithe William O'Connor, stood across from the White House, a little removed from the surge of the crowd, the "welter of life gathered to that mad focus." The writers had no intention of getting in
line under the colonnade. In his shabby country clothes, his open
collar, Whitman was not properly attired to meet the President
(might in fact never be properly dressed for it). Besides, there
would be plenty of time to meet Mr. Lincoln, years and years, and
much better occasions than a New Year's levee, when one had to
wait in line with so many other people for the privilege of five sec-
onds of the President's attention.

"A profound conviction of necessity, *affinity*" had drawn Whitman to the capital, focus of the Union's administration and the

ELECT

MAGNET

nation's suffering. "America, already brought to Hospital in her fair youth," is how he put it in an often-quoted letter to Emerson.

Electricity was in the air, Whitman believed, quite literally; and in the words of Justin Kaplan, "Whitman was a sort of storage battery or accumulator for charged particles of the contemporary." In his thirties the poet studied phrenology, the popular "Science of Mind" as practiced by his friend Orson Fowler in a studio in lower Manhattan. Fowler, a proponent of animal magnetism—a theory that also interested Nathaniel Hawthorne—imagined the universe as an enormous battery of "irradiating power" or "nervous force" whose workings resembled the magnetic telegraph. "Men and women, horses, cows . . . even rocks and puddles, were all part of a network of sending and receiving stations relaying an invisible electric fluid."

Such notions were common at the time. Goethe popularized the idea of "elective affinities," in his 1809 novel of that title. The term refers to a phenomenon that occurs when certain chemical compounds meet: their component elements "change partners," so to speak. Goethe's fictional lovers are mysteriously in tune, and "magnetically" drawn to each other. Animal magnetism, along with elective affinities, hydropathy, and phrenology, were "sciences" that informed Whitman's actions. The poet believed in the force of his own animal magnetism, and many of his war letters speak of his healing others by this gift.

Years after the war, Whitman would recall the long hospital wards, "the clank of crutches on the pavements of the floors of Washington," the Grand Review of veterans bound for home, a dying Irish boy in the corner of a ward with a Catholic priest and a makeshift altar—these and a thousand other "first class pictures, tempests of life and death . . . and looking over all, in my remembrance, the tall form of President Lincoln, with his face of deep-cut lines, with the large, canny eyes, the complexion of dark brown, and the tinge of weird melancholy saturating all."

In 1863, as the poet rents rooms near the White House, takes his walks in view of the mansion, and learns the President's schedule so well he can watch him come and go daily in his carriage, it becomes clear that Lincoln himself has drawn the poet to the Federal City, as magnet to magnet. At first Walt told his family he would return in a week after checking up on some wounded Brooklyn soldiers, to make sure his friends from home were properly cared for. Yet he stayed, long after his Mississippi captain had gone. There were many hospitals from Falmouth to Manhattan where Whitman might have found more suffering soldiers than he could comfort, and cheaper rent. But he wanted to live in Washington because Lincoln was there. They were Elective Affinities—the poet as public servant, the President as dramatic poet. The compounds of the two personalities had "exchanged" essential elements.

Whitman went to Washington to heal and console the men in the hospitals. But his actions during that year indicate he had other things in mind, more complex, inchoate, and incommunicable urges and schemes. "Lincoln is particularly my man—particularly belongs to me; yes, and by the same token, I am Lincoln's man: I guess I particularly belong to him; we are afloat on the same stream—we are rooted in the same ground."

In the years to come a rich literature would spring from the connection between the President and the poet. But on this New Year's Day, Lincoln had no idea of the poet's proximity, and Whitman knew little of Lincoln. In a few hours the President would leave the crowd, slip upstairs to his office, and, with his swollen, trembling fingers, sign a paper that would free slaves.

Whitman and O'Connor, having seen enough of the holiday crowd, turned the corner and walked south on Fifteenth Street, past the two-story State Department building and the thirty colossal Ionic columns of the Treasury building, with its portico at the south corner. Across the street rose the five-story red-brick edifice of the Army Paymaster's Office, where Charlie Eldridge had already gotten Whitman a job. Throughout January, February, and March Whitman spent a few hours each day in Major Lyman Hapgood's office on the fifth floor, copying pay documents. From his desk at the southeast window, Whitman shared Lincoln's view of the Potomac River and the wooded hills of Arlington.

The two writers headed up the avenue toward the Capitol, passing the fashionable Willard Hotel on the northwest corner of Fourteenth and Pennsylvania. The four-story hotel, with its graceful balcony on the second floor curving around the four-columned portico of the corner entrance, was the social and political nerve center of the Union. The Lincolns had stayed there before his inauguration. Its dining rooms, lounges, and barbershop were a hive of conviviality for affable politicians, journalists, lobbyists, contractors, generals, and spies; the saloons were hubs for deal making, focal points for rumors and reports.

The newsman and poet John James Piatt, from Indiana, twenty-eight, and his pretty wife, Sarah, likewise a published author of rhymed, sentimental verses, had breakfasted at the Willard. Dressed formally—he in swallowtail coat, black tie, and wing-collar; she in silk and lace, a wicker-birdcage skirt and crinolines—they were on their way to pay their respects not only to the President and First Lady, but also to secretary John Hay. The Piatts knew Hay through Hay's close friend, William Dean Howells. In 1860 Howells and Piatt had published a book together called *Poems of Two Friends,* and Hay had stopped in Columbus,

Ohio—en route to Lincoln's inauguration—to congratulate Howells and his friend on the new volume.

Mr. and Mrs. Piatt exited the hotel. As they crossed the street, they hailed William O'Connor, "then a friend of two years standing, accompanied by a large, gray-haired, gray-bearded man, dressed rather shabbily, in what might be called 'country clothes,' " Piatt recalled. Since returning from Falmouth, where he had slept on the campground, the poet had not refurbished his wardrobe.

Piatt recalled that O'Connor "at once introduced his companion to us. I did not need to be told who Whitman was." Indeed, the intimate friend of William Dean Howells (who idolized Whitman) did not need to be told who Whitman was any more than did John Hay, who would soon learn that the writer had moved into the neighborhood. By 1863, few literary people in America were unaware of Walt Whitman's name. Although the exchange was brief, "our greeting was cordial;" Piatt was glad to meet the renowned poet, if only briefly. The stylish couple had to hurry to arrive at the White House in time to join the receiving line. They must have made a good impression. In a letter to Secretary Seward, Lincoln later recommended John J. Piatt for a "moderate sized consulate," one of those "which facilitate artists a little in their profession."

Meanwhile the artist who created *Leaves of Grass* was moving in the other direction along the muddy thoroughfare of Pennsylvania Avenue, past the cupola of the Central Guard House and the Hay Market at Ninth Street, heading toward Armory Square Hospital on the Mall, in front of the Capitol. A crane slanted above the Capitol's unfinished dome. At the hospital pavilion, and in the frescoed halls of the Capitol, Whitman would seek his fortune in public service.

According to John Hay and John Nicolay, the President did not return to his office from the public reception until mid-afternoon, as "the rigid laws of etiquette held him to this duty for the space of three hours." Mary had gone up to her bedroom long before, grieving over her lost son, her fragile nerves unequal to the occasion.

Lincoln's right hand was so wrung out that he found it difficult to hold the pen steady. He sat at the long table where William Seward and his son Frederick had spread the broad parchment. Fewer than a dozen people had dropped by to witness the official signing of the Emancipation Proclamation, "merely from the personal impulse of curiosity joined to momentary convenience."

Lincoln is supposed to have said: "If my name ever goes into history it will be for this act." But the source is suspect, and the line sounds too self-conscious for this President. Assistant Secretary of State Frederick Seward quotes Lincoln as saying, "this signature is one that will be closely examined, and if they find my hand trembled they will say 'he had some compunctions.' " The President carefully wrote his name at the bottom of the paper. "The signature proved to be unusually clear, bold, and firm, even for him, and a laugh followed at his apprehension." William Seward signed beneath, the great seal was affixed, and handwritten copies quickly went out to the press.

The black preacher Henry Turner grabbed his copy of the Proclamation and ran up Pennsylvania Avenue to read it to a crowd of Negroes who were waiting on the corner with joyful impatience. New Year's had heretofore been "Heart-Break Day," set apart by custom for the changing of masters and the breaking up of families. Arriving out of breath, Reverend Turner handed the paper to another man, who read it aloud with earnest passion.

An old man named Thornton wept when he recalled a New Year's Day long ago. (The quotes that follow are taken verbatim from the *Washington Chronicle,* in the dialect journalists used in 1863.) "I cried all night. 'What de matter, Thornton?' Tomorrow my child is to be sold, neber more see till judgment—no more dat! No more dat! Can't sell your wife and children any more!"

Another said: "God has placed Mr. Lincoln in de President's chair, and I thanks Him that He would not let de rebels make peace until we black folks was free." Today "was hailed by the contra-bands as the dawn, not only of a new year, but of a new life." The black audience cheered, clapped, and sang a song of jubilee.

A crowd gathered in front of the White House. Blacks and whites called for the President. At last he came to the window and bowed. They cheered and blessed Lincoln, and someone cried out that if he would only "come out of that palace, they would hug him to death."

Whitman was not among them, consumed as he was with his work in the hospitals. He wrote in his notebook: "the phlegmatic coolness, all through Washington, under the new emancipation document, from the executive, is noticeable. I hear little allusion made to it in the public places of the city, where people most do congregate."

The jubilation in front of the White House on New Year's Day was rather isolated. After all, this was a Southern town, and most of its citizens did not welcome the liberation of slaves. The President had made some people happy (most of them faraway in the North) and many more furious. For a while many soldiers felt betrayed. A typical comment came from a Hoosier: "I think the Union is about played out. I use to think that we were fighting for the Union and Constitution but we are not. We are fighting to free those colored gentlemen. If I had my way about things I would shoot ever nigger I come across." Within weeks even a Boston antislavery group, accompanied by a Massachusetts senator, would call upon the President to complain that his Proclamation was a failure.

But Lincoln had calculated his risk. He guessed that the Emancipation Proclamation would inspire more volunteers for the Union cause than deserters. And he was right.

4

FEBRUARY 1863

General Tom Thumb, three feet tall, and his thirty-two-inch bride, Lavinia Warren, craned their necks while reaching up to shake the President's hand. The bride's head came to the level of his trouser pockets. She wore white satin and a diamond necklace, and was by all accounts strikingly beautiful. The "General" wore a black suit, patent leather boots, a faultless necktie, a large breast-pin of brilliants, a gold watch with an elaborate chain, and snow-white kid gloves. Despite P. T. Barnum's pleading, no photographs were permitted. Jokes were superfluous, though Lincoln could not resist chuckling: "God likes to do funny things; here you have the long and short of it."

The honeymooning couple were perfect White House guests for Valentine's Day in this bleak season. The entertainer Charles S. Stratton, age twenty-five, a.k.a. Tom Thumb, was known for cavorting half-naked onstage as Cupid, with a bow and a quiver of arrows. On February 13 Mrs. Lincoln gave a party honoring the newlyweds, with fifty of Washington's finest, including cabinet members Salmon P. Chase, Edwin M. Stanton, Gideon Welles, Montgomery Blair, and John P. Usher, some senators and congressmen, Generals Benjamin Franklin Butler and Thomas H. Clay, and a few newsmen.

On Valentine's Day this story brightened the newspapers. Lincoln had remarked to Tom Thumb that "he had thrown him completely in the shade"—which suited the President perfectly. Bad weather had throttled the war. John Nicolay quipped, "The Army of the Potomac is for the present stuck in the mud, as it has been nearly the whole of its existence."

Perhaps no man in the Federal City was happier than Walt Whitman. On Sunday afternoon, February 15, after making his rounds at the hospital, he had the fifth floor of the Paymaster's Office all to himself for his writing. This was one of the highest vantage points in the city. "The lovely Potomac spreads, reflecting the evening clouds—the great white Capitol with its huge, pope's tiara–looking dome, lifts itself calmly on Capitol Hill, with windows gilded by the day's last yellow-reddish halo." The dome stood unfinished upon Lincoln's inauguration. He had insisted the work go forward as a symbol of the Union's endurance, even as the war depleted the Treasury.

Whitman watched the shadows deepen rapidly around the towers of the Smithsonian. From his east windows he could see the Patent Office building, now serving as a hospital. "Its severe and grand proportions show well, as they catch the last flood of light . . . the mists and darkness grow heavier and heavier over there on the Maryland side." Toward the north he surveyed the long white barracks of hospitals as far as the Soldiers' Home, where the Lincolns spent their summer nights. A steamship was trailing smoke just to the north of the Potomac Bridge, beyond the gray stone of the half-finished monument to George Washington.

Above the river, on the darkening hills, the fires of forts and camps glowed and flickered.

"On the Virginia side I see the transparent copper-colored clouds hang up there, gradually fading—sweep my eyes in admiration around the unsurpassed broad-stretched environ-scenery of river, hill, and wood, that marks this one of the most beautiful natural locations on the continent."

He had a cheerful disposition that dispelled gloom. The newspaper lying on a desk reported, "The body of an infant, supposed to be only three or four days old, was found in the canal, at the foot of North Capitol Street." In a city with hundreds of brothels this was a common occurrence. Two months earlier, on the day Whitman arrived in Washington, a dead horse lay at the corner of Ninth and G Streets next to the Patent Office. A week later the newspapers were still ridiculing the authorities for not removing the carcass. The citizens relied upon packs of dogs, free-ranging pigs, and flocks of crows to dispose of garbage and carrion.

One week after Whitman described the city's beauty at twilight, Noah Brooks reported in the *Sacramento Union*, "At this writing the city of Washington is probably the dirtiest and most ill-kept borough in the United States." The streets were "seas or canals of liquid mud" with "conglomerations of garbage, refuse and trash, the odors whereof rival those of the city of Cologne which Coleridge declared to be 'seventy separate and distinct stinks.'" It was particularly noisome where Whitman worked, near the White House, where the Tiber Creek branch fed a polluted backwater. Brooks mentions the Mall, "the Island, upon which the Smithsonian Institution and other buildings [including Armory Square Hospital, where Whitman nursed soldiers] stand," and writes that it "is bounded on two sides (N. & E.) by a stagnant canal of ooze, open to the sun's hot rays, the receptacle of all the imperfect system of drainage," with human waste, dead cats, dead livestock, dead babies. At a sloping intersection, Brooks observed "a torrent of thick, yellow mud flowing in unruffled smoothness over the concealed crossing" and bearing on its surface the waste that had been swept or bailed out of houses, stables, shops, and saloons. He described the spavined horses condemned to toil in that noxious sludge until "turned out to wander in the bone through the scenes they knew in the flesh." Nags dropped dead and were carried away by the carrion cart, which in cold weather took its time. "Everybody has heard of the great corruption of the city," Brooks concludes, "but I will venture to say that its moral corruption is far exceeded by the physical rottenness of its streets."

Brooks expressed the majority opinion, which an earlier visitor put succinctly: "In truth it is impossible to imagine a more comfortless situation for a town, or a town more foolishly and uncomfortably laid out." Another critic, Charles Dickens, scorned the city plan, citing the absurd distances of the stone-and-marble Post Office, the Patent Office, the Treasury, and the Capitol from one another, and the lack of brick streets. He called it the "City of Magnificent Intentions" and a "monument raised to a deceased project."

But Walt Whitman, from his high window, idealized the Federal City and admired the sunset, which in 1863, much as today, was magnificent, owing to the particular atmosphere and low cloud formations produced by the tidal estuary. Then, looking down, he saw a string of army wagons lumbering along Fifteenth Street and turning onto Pennsylvania Avenue, white canvas arching over each wagon, each pulled by a six-mule team, with the teamsters walking alongside their mules. He watched squads of the provost guard march by, and a party of cavalry galloping along.

"I see sick and wounded soldiers (but that's nothing now—I have seen so many thousands of them)—the light falls, falls, touches the cold white of the great public edifices—touches with a kind of death-glaze here and there the windows of Washington—first lingers on the gilt balls and crosses on the steeples—I see the street-lamps beginning to be touched up, like bright sparks in the distance." A church bell tolled nearby, melodiously, mournfully, and Walt Whitman closed his notebook.

The Paymaster's Office was where Whitman worked between 9:30 A.M. and 2:00 P.M., to earn the few dollars he needed to pay for his lodging in the O'Connors' rented quarters at 394 L Street, his meals and ale, and such incidentals as writing paper. His notebooks were cheap papers folded in half and pinned together or stitched neatly by Nellie O'Connor. Whitman also made "some money by scribbling for the papers" in his bright third-story front room, next to the rooms of the O'Connors and their little girl. But most of his afternoons and evenings he spent in the hospitals—at Armory Square on the Mall, a twenty-minute walk from home; at Campbell Hospital, equidistant, at the north end of Seventh Street bordering woods and fields; and sometimes at the Patent Office wards in the city center. Depending upon the fighting there could be as many as forty thousand wounded men, Rebels and Federals warded together, in the fifty hospitals that had sprung up to accommodate them.

What began as a kindly visit to two Brooklyn boys in Campbell Hospital on January 2 became an obsession. "O my dear sister," he wrote the next day to Martha Whitman, "how your heart would ache to go through the rows of wounded young men, as I did—

and stopt to speak a comforting word to them." A hundred men lay in the long, neatly whitewashed hospital shed. One was groaning in pain. Whitman tried to comfort the boy and then, upon inquiring, found that no doctor had examined him.

"So I sent for the doctor, and he made an examination of him—the doctor behaved very well . . . said that the young man would recover—he had been brought pretty low with diarrhoea, and now had bronchitis, but not so serious as to be dangerous. I talked to him some time—he had not a cent of money—not a friend or acquaintance—I wrote a letter from him to his sister . . . I gave him a little change I had—he said he would like to buy a drink of milk, when the woman came through with the milk. Trifling as this was, he was overcome and began to cry."

Walt Whitman did not go to Washington to become an official soldier's nurse, or delegate of the Christian Commission of the YMCAs (to which he was appointed later that January), or a "Soldier's Missionary," as he somewhat ironically signed himself on the inside cover of his notebook. At first he had a more distinguished, if not higher, ambition.

Whitman eagerly explored the newly designed halls of Congress. When the Thirty-seventh Congress was in session the Capitol shone at night like a lantern. In the cold winter its warmth and gaslight acted as a magnet to the idle and the curious, to soldiers, journalists, lobbyists, and visitors from all over the world.

Approaching from the north, he admired the allegorical frieze set in the pediment overhead: a female figure of America in the blaze of the rising sun; on her right, a soldier, a tradesman, a student, a mechanic, and a sheaf of wheat. Upon the tympanum of the central pediment sits the "Genius of America" crowned with a star and bearing a shield. She faces a symbolic figure of Hope, whose attention she directs to a figure of Justice who holds the scrolled Constitution in her right hand, the scales in her left.

The magnificent dome of the Capitol, its marble statuary, and its corridors frescoed by Constantino Brumidi filled the poet with hope—despite his healthy cynicism concerning the nation's lawmakers. "All architecture is what you do to it when you look upon it," he had written in *Leaves of Grass*.

"You pass through a splendid corridor, I should say as beautiful a piece of interior finishing as there is in the world—the white ceiling, arched, and simply ornamented, the delicate colors of the tessellated pavement, blue, white, brownish, yellow . . ."

The poet stood in a window niche, scribbling in his notebook. "Then as you turn to go toward the gallery—the superb and massive marble balustrades and staircase with the columns of mottled brown & white, and the steps of pure white, the hodge-podge of pictures in the great panel (a masquerade or nightmare dream, of an overland emigrant train crossing the Rocky Mountains)—the blue bay of San Francisco frescoed underneath—the whole grandeur and beautiful proportions and color and enduring material of this staircase . . ."

Whitman was fascinated by the drama of the Hall of Representatives, with the members in session under the elaborate ceiling of iron and glass, "lighted from gas which is itself not visible, except as its powerful jets shine through the panels of astral glass overhead—pouring a broad flood of light down on the members—over the broad surrounding horse shoe of members desks . . . the members are idling in their seats—the galleries are full—the clock points to eight . . ."

He became a student of the legislature, a familiar figure in the halls of Congress, which in those days were accessible to everyone. Soon he would claim: "I have watched their debates, wran-gles, propositions, personal presences, physiognomies, in their magnificent sky-lighted halls—gone night and day . . ."

He was amused by how insignificant the politicians looked. "These then are the men who do as they do, in the midst of the greatest historic chaos and gigantic tussle of the greatest of ages.—Look at the little manikins, shrewd, gabby, dressed in black, hopping about, making motions, amendments.—It is very curious."

The congressmen seemed to Whitman unequal to their task. "What events are about them, and all of us? Whither are we drift-ing? Who knows? It seems as if these electric and terrible days were enough to put life in a paving stone,—as if there must needs form, on the representative men that have to do with them, faces of grandeur, actions of awe, vestments of majesty."

There must be an office here for him.

Shortly after arriving in Washington on December 29, 1862, Whit-man had written Ralph Waldo Emerson a curious and enigmatic letter:

I fetch up here in harsh and superb plight—wretchedly poor, excellent well, (my only torment, family matters)—realizing at last that it is necessary for me to fall for the time in the wise old way, to push my fortune, to be brazen, and get employ-ment, and have an income—determined to do it . . . I write to you, ask you as follows:

I design to apply personally direct at headquarters, for some place. I would apply on literary grounds, not political.

I wish you would write for me something like the enclosed

form of letter, that I can present, opening *my interview with the great man*.

Whitman's "enclosed form of letter" has not survived—a pity, since it might shed some light upon the obscurities and innuendoes of his petition. Who was "the great man"? Whitman knew that in February 1862 Emerson had been introduced to Abraham Lincoln by Senator Sumner of Massachusetts. Dapper Charles Sumner was a frequent guest of the Lincolns, and along with Secretary of State Seward and Secretary of the Treasury Chase he was one of the most influential men in Washington. Perhaps only Secretary of War Stanton stood in as powerful a relation to the President.

Emerson was enormously generous toward Whitman. Upon receiving *Leaves of Grass,* the Sage of Concord wrote Whitman a private letter, saying: "I am not blind to the worth of the wonderful gift of 'Leaves of Grass.' I find it the most extraordinary piece of wit & wisdom that America has yet contributed." Emerson forgave Whitman for all his eccentricities, his megalomania and vulgarity, his occasional condescension; he even forgave the poet for using, without permission, that private letter of praise in public advertisements, though its use infuriated the philosopher, who was slow to anger. He forgave Whitman everything because he understood his genius.

Now Whitman asked Emerson to write three letters on his behalf, to send one directly to Senator Sumner, and to enclose the others in envelopes addressed to Seward and Chase and post them to the poet to use at his own discretion. Whitman must have picked Sumner, Seward, and Chase because of their proximity to Lincoln—they were otherwise an unpromising combination. Sumner and Seward were mortal enemies, Chase and Seward disliked each other intensely, and Chase (Whitman had heard) considered *Leaves of Grass* "a nasty book." Yet Whitman was convinced that Emerson's letters to these three politicians would gain him a job.

"It is pretty certain that, armed in that way, I shall conquer my object," he wrote to Emerson.

Only Whitman, and perhaps Emerson, ever knew exactly what that "object" was. Once again Emerson proved his devotion by granting Whitman's peculiar request, roughly along the lines Whitman had set forth. Innocent of practical politics and office seeking, and in a state of manic excitement after his military adventure in Virginia, Whitman must have seemed to his wise friend to be possessed by delusions of grandeur. The poet likely imagined himself in the role he had assumed in *Leaves of Grass*, the bard of democracy, advisor to statesmen.

> *To hold men together by paper and seal, or by compulsion, is no*
> *   account,*
> *That only holds men together which is living principles, as the hold of*
> *   the limbs of the body, or the fibres of plants.*
>
> *Of all races and eras, These States, with veins full of poetical stuff,*
> *   most need poets, and are to have the greatest, and use them the*
> *   greatest,*
> *Their Presidents shall not be their common referee so much as their*
> *   poets shall.*

His country needed him, his government needed him; and surely the higher his office among what Senator Fessenden called this "shambling, half-and-half set of incapables," the more Whitman might contribute. He might, given the right audience, help to put an end to this bloodbath. It seemed not wholly unfeasible, in the close world of Washington politics, that the poet might get the President's attention.

Emerson was familiar with Whitman's hypomania, his boundless ego, and his occasional delusions, which were never harmful to anyone but himself. He discarded Whitman's "form of letter" (no copy of which has survived to indicate the office-seeker's true intention) and then wrote him letters that, while observing the spirit of that intention, did not so far satisfy Whitman that he ever thanked Emerson for his trouble. Emerson wrote frankly to Chase and Seward:

> Permit me to say that he [Whitman] is known to me as a man of strong original genius, combining, with marked eccentricities, great powers & valuable traits of character: a self-relying, large-hearted man, much beloved by his friends; entirely patriotic & benevolent in his theory, tastes, & practice. If his writings are in certain points open to criticism, they yet show extraordinary power, & are more deeply American, democratic, & in the interest of political liberty, than those of any other poet . . . A man of his talents & dispositions will quickly make himself useful, and, if the Government has work that he can do, I think it may easily find, that it has called to its side more valuable aid than it bargained for.

He enclosed the two letters in an envelope with a covering note to Whitman advising: "If you wish to live in that least attractive (to me) of cities, I must think you can easily do so. Perhaps better in the journalism than in the Departments." He posted the packet on January 12, and Whitman received it on the seventeenth. Emerson had done what Whitman asked, recommending him on literary rather than political grounds, knowing, as the naïve poet did not, that even he, Emerson, the most revered writer of his age, could never secure a government position on the basis of his literary achievement alone.

The letters Emerson wrote for Whitman—at least the two to Chase and Seward he had read—were not exactly what Whitman desired. So for a long time he did not use either of them. Rather, he depended upon the letter of recommendation he had not seen, to Emerson's friend Senator Sumner, to conquer his object.

Sumner was the one man in the Capitol whose face and figure, whose "vestments," in fact, approximated the grandeur Whitman was seeking. Charles Sumner worked in the North Wing, where Whitman was a stranger. Folks went to the halls and galleries of the House for diversion, for society, or to escape the cold and freezing rain of January, in rooms far from the chambers of the Senate. These rooms were private, hushed, particularly now that the Senate's numbers were reduced by the Secession. One went to the Senate, if at all, on serious business, as Whitman was doing on a day in late January when he summoned the courage to call upon the illustrious Senator from Massachusetts. Of the dignitaries to whom Emerson had written on Whitman's behalf, Sumner was the most likely to welcome him.

The fifty-two-year-old bachelor looked like the hero of a romance, with his wide-set eyes of deep blue, his square, dimpled chin, and his mane of wavy chestnut-colored hair streaked with silver. Chase's daughter Janet Hoyt described his "strangely winning smile, half bright, half full of sadness." He had an air about him that showed he was a man of the world. Paradoxically he could be childlike, pouting: his idealism blinded him to the practical motives of rivals, and even friends, such as Henry Adams. When Sumner finally recovered from the brutal caning he had received in 1856 from South Carolina Congressman Preston Brooks, he came to regard himself as a holy martyr to the cause of abolition. And indeed Brooks's bludgeoning of the antislavery Yankee at his desk—after Sumner had sharply censured the proslavery senators—shocked America and presaged the War of the Rebellion.

The strength of Sumner's jaw and broad brow did not diminish the sensitivity of the voluptuous, downturned lips. Sumner was a man of fierce resolutions and scarcely concealed vulnerabilities, an affectionate friend with little sense of humor about himself, a disappointed idealist. Six feet three inches tall and weighing 220 pounds, he was one of the few people in Washington who could stand eye to eye with Lincoln. This he did frequently, in agreement or discord, in friendship and loyal opposition. Sumner was distraught over Lincoln's delay in emancipating the slaves, and in letting them join the army. As an intimate friend of Mary Todd Lincoln, he enjoyed the freedom of the White House; as chairman of the Committee on Foreign Affairs, Sumner maintained easier access to the President than did any other senator.

Sumner's clothing, like his manners, reflected his familiarity with the European capitals, and especially London. In contrast to the black frock coats worn by other public men, Sumner sported light tweeds made to order in London, and English gaiters. Noah Brooks recalled that "his appearance in his seat in the Senate chamber was studiously dignified" and that "he once told me that he never allowed himself, even in the privacy of his own chamber, to fall into a position which he would not take in his chair in the Senate." He practiced his speeches before a pier-glass mirror in his sumptuous apartment at Thirteenth and F Streets.

His appearance was splendid, his vanity transparent. Sumner took pride in his long and shapely hands, especially their whiteness; in the Senate he would lean back in his chair, his head slightly inclined over his broad chest, and study his hands as they rested upon his crossed knees. He wore gloves to protect them, sometimes throughout entire sessions. Henry Adams said that Sumner's mind by 1863 "had reached the calm of water which receives and reflects images without absorbing them; it contains nothing but itself." It was Adams's gentlest way of calling Sumner a narcissist.

To his man-of-the-world air, during this particular month, was added a dreamy languor, as Sumner was taking belladonna for angina and a stomach ailment. He was so weak he did not leave his rooms except to go to the Capitol, where, he said, he was "obliged to lie down" on a divan against the gilded rear wall of the Senate. Supine, the Senator found new gestures to express his dignity, resting on an elbow while completing a period, waving his hand feebly, royally, to answer a roll call.

It was probably there, on that divan, that the Senator opened the letter from Ralph Waldo Emerson concerning Walt Whitman. Certainly he was lounging there when a page boy told him that the poet himself was waiting outside, in the Senate Reception Room.

Whitman sat under the stained-glass skylight for hours. Anybody could page a U.S. senator. And it was the custom for the senator to respond—but only at his leisure. So Walt Whitman waited. He studied the tessellated floor beneath his boots—the braids, lozenges, and mandalas of marble as colorful and ornate as a Persian carpet—and looked up at the Brumidi frescoes. And the show delighted him for a long time until he reflected: "These days, the state our country is in, and especially filled as I am from top to toe, of late with scenes and thoughts of *the hospitals* (America seems to me now, though only in her youth, but brought *already here* feeble, bandaged, and bloody *in hospital*) . . . all the poppy-show goddesses and all the pretty blue & gold in which the interior Capitol is got up, seem to me out of place beyond any thing I could tell . . ." He had more than enough time to study the frescoes of the vaulted cavern, a domed box, twenty-two feet square and twenty-two feet high. Everything was gilded: the four arches inlaid with cinquefoils, the arched doors and the arabesque metal-work of the wall panels, the eagles over the girandoles, and the acanthus and tobacco leaves of the chandelier hanging from a fresco of cherubs at the bull's-eye of the dome.

Seven dark-paneled wooden settees with claw-and-ball arms and feet were arranged against the walls. A small library table of the same style stood at the open end of the room where the page boys picked up messages to carry in to the senators.

This is where petitioners came to file suit: lobbyists, journalists, army widows demanding pensions, mothers begging that their sons—accused of desertion or sleeping on guard duty—be saved from hanging. And there were many office seekers. He watched people come and go, men and women dressed in black and a few women in colored dresses, capes, and shawls, who sat and rose gracefully, arranging their crinolines. Now and then a senator would appear, behind his page, and everyone would look up, hop-ing it was his or her senator. The long-awaited eminence would stand for a few minutes listening or talking quietly with his con-stituent. A shake of the hand, a bow, and the senator was gone, the petition denied, forwarded, granted, or—most commonly—tabled until a more "propitious" time. There was sighing and indignation, some smiling and strained laughter, and occasionally tears. More than anything there was the waiting, so the room was heavy with anxiety, dread, and boredom, which sooner or later took its toll on hope.

If the "poppy-show goddesses and all the pretty blue & gold" seemed out of place to Whitman, he too may have felt out of place under the curious glances of the well-dressed citizens around him. Since returning from his battlefield adventures in Falmouth, he had managed to get his linen scrubbed. But he had not yet assembled a new wardrobe. The photograph Mathew Brady took of him then shows the poet wearing a brown single-breasted jacket of heavy wool with a small collar that buttoned high. Whitman's black bow tie is knotted low, carelessly overlapping the lapels, defying its duty to close the white shirt collar; as always, his throat below the beard is bare. His trousers were a coarse woolen weave. For this occasion the poet would dress as well as he could, but he probably saw no need to look any different than he had for his last publicity photograph. He wore his wide-brimmed hat of soft felt in all weathers. ("I cock my hat as I please indoors or out.") So now one might well ask whether Walt Whitman did, or did not, remove his slouch hat when Senator Charles Sumner finally appeared before him in the Senate Reception Room.

Sumner towered above everyone, approaching with a distinctive bearing more sinuous than erect. He wore a brown tweed frock coat, a gray waistcoat, and lavender-colored trousers. His black tie was knotted in a perfect bow, beneath his square chin. He did not need to be told who Walt Whitman was, but with that smile that was "half bright, half full of sadness" walked up to the poet as he rose from the settee, and shook his hand.

Whitman looked into Sumner's eyes, the pupils dilated with belladonna. The next thing he would have noticed, after taking in the Senator's extraordinary distinction of person and attire, was the pallor of those hands. Washingtonians had come to speak of other pale things, such as snow and milk, as being "white as Sumner's hands."

The Senator, for his part, took in the roughly dressed, hirsute poet. The phrase "marked eccentricities" from Emerson's letter must have leapt to mind. Here was a case that required the utmost care, diplomacy, and discretion. Charles Sumner was the most ostentatiously literary man in Congress. He knew five languages and used them all in his orations. His best friends were Henry Wadsworth Longfellow and historian Henry Adams. Sumner and Whitman had many friends and acquaintances in common—not the least of whom was Emerson. They both knew the mercurial Horace Greeley. They knew Whitman's admirer William Dean Howells and Howells's charming friend John Hay. These names and many others would provide a conversational bridge between the poet and the statesman.

If Whitman clumsily mentioned the mysterious Count Adam Gurowski, an ardent Whitman fan who was a frequent guest at the O'Connor-Whitman dinner table, Sumner would change the subject. He had known Gurowski since 1851, when they vacationed in Newport, and had welcomed the exiled Pole to Washington. Then the Senator got him a job as a translator in the State Department so, it was rumored, Gurowski could spy on Secretary Seward, Sumner's enemy. But lately the hotheaded Pole had turned upon his benefactor, criticizing Sumner in his published diaries, calling him an intriguer and a coward. In the same book Gurowski called Whitman "the incarnation of a genuine American original genius." So these men could never agree about the one-eyed Count, or his scandalous memoir.

About Ralph Waldo Emerson, their friend, there could be no disagreement. He was wise and noble and kind, the greatest American writer, present company excluded. (Sumner's *Recent Speeches and Addresses* had been published in 1856.) Emerson had paid Whitman compliments in a letter, and the amiable Senator would not hesitate to repeat them. Whitman was flattered, but not more so than he was proud. He talked of his work in the hospitals, of the bravery of the young soldiers who lay wounded and dying in the wards. He told Sumner how much they appreciated his little gifts of fruit, tobacco, and postage stamps. Impressed, Sumner promised he would send someone to the Post Office next door and get Whitman some franked envelopes for the soldiers.

But this was not the reason Whitman had come to Washington or why he had sat cooling his heels for hours in the frescoed Reception Room. There was the matter of an office, a government position that would make the most of "a man of his talents and dispositions." This was a very troublesome thing, and as accustomed as Sumner was to approaching the subject, he addressed it now wearily, and slowly.

"Everything here," said Sumner, "moves as part of a great machine . . ." It was impossible for him to do what Whitman wanted; it was of some importance to appear as if he had tried. "You must consign yourself to the fate of the rest . . ."

Accepting the "fate of the rest" never came easy for Walt Whitman. But that year he would learn this and other important lessons as he pursued his government office. The Senator promised Whitman he would do what he could, but the process had to begin with the support of the poet's home-state legislators. Sumner said he would speak to Senator King of New York presently, and prepare King for a visit from Walt Whitman in, say, two weeks, when there might be better prospects for him. Sumner was getting tired. He stood up, and shook Whitman's hand, acknowledging the poet's thanks; bid him good day; and returned to the Senate Chamber to lie down.

So this was the way things worked in the Federal City. Whitman would attend to his soldiers in the hospitals until it came time to go back to the bedizened vault of the Senate Reception Room. There he would wait for a page to lead Senator Preston King from the high, gilded hall of the legislators.

If Sumner had planned to send the poet on a wild-goose chase he could not have chosen a more useless bird than Preston King. Fat Preston King was moribund and, at the moment, nearly powerless. His figure was an emblem of gluttony and greed. The lame-duck Senator was fond of food and the lobbyists who picked up the checks, a connoisseur of good wine and the seven-course dinners at the Willard: leg of mutton, fricandeau of veal, pheasants, woodcocks, sweetbreads with peas, cherry pie, blancmange. Within a month the fifty-seven-year-old legislator would give up his seat in the Senate. After a troubled tenure as collector of the Port of New York—a position that had corrupted better men—in 1865 he would end his life by tying a bag of bullets around his neck and leaping from a ferryboat in New York Harbor.

Whitman knew nothing of King's problems. On February 11, 1863, at one o'clock in the afternoon, Senator Preston King came lumbering into the Reception Room, harried, squinting, his narrow porcine eyes looking for this Walt Whitman who had stirred him from his cushioned seat in the Senate chamber.

The poet stood up and addressed him, man to man. Mr. Sumner had spoken to Whitman about Senator King. Had not Mr. Sumner also mentioned to Senator King Whitman's desire for an office in one of the departments?

"He did not know me," Whitman confided to his diary.

King eyed with amusement Whitman's shabby jacket, loose bow tie, broad-brimmed felt hat, and unclipped beard, and said: "Why, how can I do this thing, or any thing for you—how do I

know but you are a secessionist—you look for all the world like an
old Southern planter—a regular Carolina or Virginia planter."
The remark had a kind of theatricality calculated to evoke laughter
in onlookers too polite to have giggled at the poet's appearance
before being given permission by the distinguished lawmaker.

Whitman stood his ground. "I treated him with just as much
hauteur as he did me with bluntness." In other words, the poet kept
his hat on. At first King could not recall that Sumner had spoken to
him about Whitman, but as Whitman persisted, holding him with
his eye, King "at last had a vague recollection of something."

Whitman later wrote to his brother Jeff: "Charles Sumner had
not prepared the way for me, as I supposed, or rather, not so
strongly as I supposed." So the next day, February 12, Whitman
was back in his spot on the settee, studying the innumerable orna-
ments of the gilded vault, waiting for Senator Sumner to answer
his page and to explain the curious behavior of Preston King.
Charles Sumner then "talked and acted as though he had life in
him, and would exert himself to any reasonable extent for me to
get something." By now Whitman may have gotten the drift that
the "something" he might get was not really what he hoped for.
Sumner would speak to Preston King once more; Whitman was to
return tomorrow and page the New York Senator a second time.

On the morning of Friday the thirteenth, Preston King, his
bulk fairly bursting from his black frock coat, approached Whitman in the familiar setting, with robust good humor, and bearing
"a sort of general letter, endorsing me from New York," Whitman
wrote; "one letter is addressed to Secretary Chase, and another to
Gen. Meigs [quartermaster general]." Now he had two letters for
Salmon Chase, who hated his poetry.

"I like fat old Preston King, very much—he is fat as a
hogshead, with great hanging chops . . ." Whitman appreciated

that "King was blunt, decisive and manly . . . My impression of King was good, I think Sumner is a sort of gelding—no good." The poet's instincts about Sumner were narrow but keen: although there is no evidence that the Senator was homosexual, his marriage in 1866 to the beautiful Alice Hooper dissolved quickly because, it was widely rumored, the bridegroom was impotent. Alice herself was the ultimate source of the rumor. The fact that Charles Sumner was a superb statesman and Preston King little more than a shrewd politician was beyond the poet's comprehension.

"It is very amusing to hunt for an office—so the thing seems to me just now—even if one don't get it," Whitman wrote to his brother good-naturedly, with evident humor about himself. He told Jeff: "I have not presented my letters to either Seward or Chase—I thought I would get my forces all in a body, and make one concentrated dash, if possible with the personal introduction of some big bug . . ." Jeff Whitman provided a letter from his friend Moses Lane commending Walt to E. D. Webster, a minor clerk in Seward's office. Walt welcomed this with the enigmatic comment, "I do not so much look for an appointment from Mr. Seward as his backing me from the State of New York." So what if the poet got his "forces all in a body"—Senator Sumner; Senator King; Secretary of State Seward, who hated Sumner and Chase— where did he mean to go to make his "one concentrated dash"?

On Friday, February 20, 1863, Whitman tried Sumner for the last time. He inquired: "If I don't succeed for the present—don't get anything till the 4th of March [the close of the Thirty-seventh Congress], may I count on your then giving me a boost?"

And Senator Sumner said: "Yes, I will—if I can."

That is the last recorded communication between the poet and his most powerful advocate. And it would be Walt Whitman's last stab at job seeking for a long while. He had learned an important lesson about the Federal City: that the political game in Washington was both larger and smaller than he had believed. His daily walks might be the closest he would come to the White House.

But if Whitman had no luck, Lincoln's situation was even worse. That same Friday, a week after the White House gala for Tom Thumb, the clouds were full of snow. It was the anniversary of Willie Lincoln's death, and the President and his wife were in mourning. Lincoln has been called "the loneliest man in Washington," and his loneliness during this season had much to do with Mary Todd Lincoln's inconsolable grief over the death of her child Willie. Mary's mental illness, which progressed rapidly in her early forties, after Lincoln was elected President, has eclipsed the radiance she had in her youth as a wife and mother. Abraham, whom she always called "Father," was the love of her life. She had been witty, energetic, and far prettier and better educated than any woman Lincoln had ever hoped to marry. They had been passionately in love (he had fought a duel to defend her honor), and her passion, physical as well as spiritual, was bound up in her belief in his destiny. She thought he would be President long before anyone else did. This sense of his destiny expressed itself in a variety of ways: her concern about his clothing and manners, her fretting about his diet and health, as well as her fierce defense against his enemies, real and imagined. He would not have missed her so much these days if she had not been such a comforting presence in his life before her descent into madness.

Although etiquette required only six months of first-degree mourning, for a year after Willie's death Mary wore black dresses and flounces. She chose a black crape bonnet with a long veil, so rigid that when she went out she could not turn her head, as if grief had so transfixed her that she could not see to either side of it. According to one witness, when she went to church, the New York Avenue Presbyterian, in her immense dark veil, "one could scarcely tell she was there."

Indeed, Mary Lincoln was not all there. She had retreated into the twilight of the spirit world for solace, attending séances in Georgetown with and without her husband. She invited several eminent mediums home. According to many accounts, there were no fewer than three and as many as eight séances held in the Red Room of the White House, in which the spirits conveyed word from Willie as well as opinions on affairs of state for the President's benefit.

Mary told her friend Charles Sumner, "a very slight veil separates us from the loved and lost and to me there is comfort in the thought that though unseen by us they are very near." Mary and the Senator shared many confidences. Sumner stood proudly among Mary's male favorites, as one about whom there was never a whiff of scandal. Unlike other men who held her hand in the charged darkness of séance parlors, the Senator would not take advantage of Mary's emotional vulnerabilities.

Sumner, however, may have abused his privileges in the White House in other ways. He had come between Abraham and Mary by converting her to his point of view that it was time to emancipate the slaves. Lincoln had freed only the slaves in the rebel states, fearing that general emancipation would alienate the Border States, which were essential to winning the war. Preservation of the Union remained more important to the President than abolition. The decree of January 1 even exempted many parishes of Louisiana (including New Orleans), much of Virginia, and all of West Virginia. Lincoln wanted a gradual emancipation that the states would initiate. His stance defied Sumner's abolitionism and the radicalism dominating the Republican Party, which was forcing Lincoln into political isolation. Not even his marriage was free of the dispute, now that Sumner had converted Mary. She drew closer to her Negro seamstress, Elizabeth Keckley, a woman in her thirties who had known the cruelties of slavery firsthand. Keckley also had turned to mediums for comfort when her only son was killed in the war. Now the President slept in one bedroom with his little boy, Tad, while Mary, in a new bed of mahogany and rosewood carvings, slept in another room, with her ghosts.

"Willie lives," she told her half-sister Emilie Helm. "He comes to me every night and stands at the foot of the bed with the same sweet adorable smile he always has had. He does not always come alone. Little Eddie is sometimes with him."

Knowing the precarious state of his wife's nerves, Lincoln did not burden her with his troubles. A Boston antislavery group, accompanied by Massachusetts Senator Henry Wilson, had called upon Lincoln on January 25. They complained that the Emancipation Proclamation was a failure, partly because the generals in the field did not promote it. The President told the delegation: "My own impression . . . is that the masses of the country generally are only dissatisfied at our lack of military successes. Defeat and failure in the field make everything seem wrong."

At the root of Lincoln's political problems was his army's failure in a war that had dragged on for almost two years. Republicans in the lame-duck Congress that met that winter blamed Lincoln for their defeat in the recent elections. Conservatives from the Border States cursed the Emancipation Proclamation, while Northern Radicals charged their defeat to Lincoln's delay in ending slavery. But everyone seemed to agree then upon "the utter incompetence of the President," and inevitably the criticism focused upon Lincoln's shortcomings as commander-in-chief.

Exasperated with McClellan's blundering through the Battle of Antietam, and his slowness in pursuing Robert E. Lee, Lincoln had replaced him as head of the Army of the Potomac with Ambrose E. Burnside. Burnside's ineptitude led to the massacre of Federal troops upon the terraces of Fredericksburg in December, a blow from which the North was still reeling. Then the efforts of Grant and Sherman to take Vicksburg resulted in at least one failure— the Battle of Chickasaw Bluffs—reminiscent of Fredericksburg. The *Cincinnati Commercial* called Grant "a jackass in the original package," and declared: "He is a poor drunken imbecile."

Desperate, and facing public pressure to reinstate McClellan, on January 26, 1863, Lincoln appointed General Burnside's most vocal critic, "Fighting Joe" Hooker, to replace him as commander. Noah Brooks said General Hooker was the handsomest soldier he had ever seen—tall, well built, his fair skin glowing with health, his blue eyes sparkling with wit, his copper-colored hair tossed back upon his shapely head. "He was a gay cavalier, alert and confident . . . and cheery as a boy." He was also known as a hard drinker, who had called the President and his administration "imbecile and played out." He told one reporter that nothing would go right "until we have a dictator, and the sooner the better," to which Lincoln responded: "Only those generals who gain successes, can set up dictators. What I ask of you is military success, and I will risk the dictatorship." The appointment of the brash Hooker, whose open contempt for Lincoln's government made him a popular choice in the North, provided some relief from criticism for the President during the late winter.

Nonetheless, in the words of historian David Herbert Donald, "Republicans of all factions were ready to court-martial the President at the first safe opportunity." Richard Henry Dana Jr., the

Boston lawyer and abolitionist, was visiting Washington at the
time and noted: "the most striking thing is the absence of personal
loyalty to the President. It does not exist." "King Lincoln," as the
Copperheads (Northerners sympathetic to the South) called him,
had censored the press, suppressed free speech, and jailed political
dissidents.

Lincoln fell into a depression. "His hand trembled . . . and he
looked worn and haggard." Another White House visitor, Admiral John Dahlgren, wrote, "I observe that the President never tells
a joke now."

The Federal City was visited by the ghosts of soldiers, and the
White House was haunted by the Lincolns' dead children. Perhaps
the President himself was troubled by a voice that existed out of
time: the conscience of America calling him to account. In a dark
mood some nights he would read poetry; John Hay remembered
Lincoln reading aloud to him from Shakespeare until the young
secretary's eyes drooped. Lincoln loved *Macbeth,* which contains
this famous passage:

> *I have liv'd long enough: my way of life*
> *Is fall'n into the sear, the yellow leaf;*
> *And that which should accompany old age,*
> *As honor, love, obedience, troops of friends,*
> *I must not look to have; but in their stead,*
> *Curses, not loud but deep, mouth-honour, breath,*
> *Which the poor heart would fain deny, and dare not.*

It is the nature of poetry to endure in the mind, especially one
as retentive as Lincoln's. He once told his friend Joshua Speed:
"My mind is like a piece of steel—very hard to scratch anything

on it, and almost impossible after you get it there to rub it out."
The American conscience had never spoken more insistently and
memorably than in *Leaves of Grass*.

> *Have you considered the organic compact of the first day of the first*
>   *year of independence of The States?*
> *Have you possessed yourself of the Federal Constitution?*
> *Do you acknowledge liberty with audible and absolute*
>   *acknowledgment, and set slavery at naught for life and death?*

> *Meanwhile, corpses lie in new-made graves—bloody corpses of*
>   *young men;*
> *The rope of the gibbet hangs heavily, the bullets of princes are*
>   *flying, the creatures of power laugh aloud . . .*

What would Walt Whitman think of this presidency?

5

THE SOLDIER'S MISSIONARY

*A*bandoning the search for an office in Lincoln's administration, Whitman turned his energies to the work that lay all around him, demanding his attention and peculiar gifts—work that brought immediate gratification. He devoted his free time and thoughts to the wounded soldiers. Thirty-five hospitals had sprung up in Washington, some with more than a thousand patients.

The poet was a night owl. He didn't rise until after 8:00 A.M., when he dressed and then fetched a pitcher of water from the pump on the corner. He sang all the while, ballads and marches. After enjoying a hearty breakfast with William and Nellie O'Connor at 8:30, he arrived at his desk in the Paymaster's Office at 9:30. He was usually done with his copying early in the afternoon. In 1863 he spent almost all his afternoons and evenings in the hospital wards, taking a rest between 4:00 and 6:00 to nap, bathe, and share an early dinner with the O'Connors.

"The O'Connor home was my home," said Whitman. "They were beyond all others—William, Nelly—my understanders, my lovers: they more than any others . . . A man's family is the people who love him—the people who comprehend him." His relatives certainly did not comprehend him. The careworn, meager Nellie was in love with Whitman, as her letters to him later attest. He was a comfort to Nellie in her troubled marriage. Her handsome, philandering husband was devoted to Whitman, but William O'Connor was moody, and the men wrangled bitterly over politics. While Whitman's thoughts about slavery matched Lincoln's, O'Connor was a radical abolitionist who had made his opinions public in his novel *Harrington*. They quarreled. At least once the police rapped at the door to inquire "What all the yelling was about." (With suspicious characters like Count Gurowski visiting, the police had more than one reason to watch this house.) Yet William O'Connor was awed by Whitman's commitment to the soldiers.

In a dispatch to the *New York Times* in late winter, Whitman recorded his impressions:

> Upon a few of these hospitals I have been almost daily calling on a mission, on my own account, for the sustenance and consolation of some of the most needy cases of sick and dying men . . . One has much to learn to do good in these places. Great tact is required. These are not like other hospitals. By far the greatest proportion . . . of the patients are American young men, intelligent, of independent spirit, tender feelings, used to a hardy and healthy life; largely the farmers are represented by their sons—largely the mechanics and workingmen of the cities. Then they are soldiers. All these points must be borne in mind.

The newer hospitals were built "pavilion style"—clusters of wooden barracks surrounded by tents for cooking, laundry, and storage. The buildings were "long, one-story edifices, sometimes ranged along in a row with their heads to the street, and numbered," or sometimes lettered, Wards 1, 2, 3; Wards A, B, C; etc. The middle shed, marked with a flagstaff, was the office of the surgeons. Each ward contained sixty or more cots. There was a ward master in each shed, and a nurse for every ten or twelve men.

That winter Whitman frequented a pavilion-style compound called Campbell Hospital out on the Washington flats, at the terminus of a horse-railway track on Seventh Street. On a chilly afternoon he entered Ward 6. He counted more than eighty patients, half of them wounded, more than half sick. The plain board shed was whitewashed inside. Slender-framed iron bedsteads were ranged against the walls under the exposed roof-beams. Whitman walked down the central aisle, a row of soldiers on either side of him, their feet toward him, their heads to the wall. Fires burned in large iron stoves. There were no partitions, so he could hear "groans, or other sounds of unendurable suffering, from two or three of the iron cots, but in the main there is quiet—almost a painful absence of demonstration; but the pallid face, the dull'd eye, and the moisture on the lip, are demonstration enough."

Whitman wore a wine-colored suit with large pockets, his baggy pants tucked into his black morocco boots. With his rosy cheeks, white beard, and the leather haversack slung over his shoulder, it was no wonder the boys called him Santa Claus. According to Nellie O'Connor, one Yuletide Whitman was coming from the hospital when a suspicious policeman ordered him to "remove that false face!" Walt showed him the face was really his own, but then asked the policeman, "Do we not all wear 'false faces'?" He was delighted to have been mistaken for St. Nick.

The sack, no bigger than a cavalry "coach bag," with a single clasp, was bulging with goodies: a jar of strawberry jam, oranges and apples, pickles, books, newspapers, and plugs of tobacco. The patients' greatest desire seems to have been for writing paper, envelopes, stamps, pens and pencils, so the bag always held a good stock of those, too. Much of Whitman's time was taken up writing letters for men without the strength, education, or hands to write their own.

He had bought a new wide-brimmed hat with a black and gold lacing that fastened under his chin with a clasp of gilded acorns. If he would not remove his headwear for Senator Sumner, now that proud hat was "for the first time, taken involuntarily off from an effect upon us of humility that all the Presidents, Princes, Congresses, Generals of the world could never begin to produce."

Whitman set down his sack beside the corporal in bed 25, Henry Boardman of the Twenty-seventh Connecticut, Company B. Boardman's family lived at Northford, near New Haven. Whitman pulled up a chair next to the twenty-year-old soldier and tenderly covered his hand with his own. "A noble-behaving young fellow—I get quite attached to him—proud spirited—would not accept any money—extremely weak, vomiting everything he took down—bad diarrhea also." For a while he would accept nothing from the poet but a pipe and tobacco.

Whitman wanted to know what else he could do for him.

"I have a hankering for a good home-made rice pudding . . . think I could live a week on one," the soldier said. Whitman jotted this in his notebook: a request to Nellie O'Connor to cook the rice pudding which was, in fact, the only nourishment that kept Boardman from starving.

In bed 59 lay Janus Mafield of the Virginia Volunteers, eighteen years old. "Illiterate, but cute—can neither read nor write. Has been very sick and low, but now recovering. Have visited him regularly for two weeks, given him money, fruit, candy & c." The last often serves as Whitman's shorthand for affection; "& c" was the thing Mafield needed most. "Always the sick and dying soldiers forthwith begin to cling to me in a way that makes a fellow feel funny enough." It was an intimacy that Whitman craved. He wrote: "These thousands, and tens and twenties of thousands of American young men, badly wounded, all sorts of wounds, operated on, pallid with diarrhea, languishing, dying with fever, pneumonia . . . open a new world somehow to me, giving closer insights, new things, exploring deeper mines than any yet, showing our humanity."

Sometimes he would put himself "in fancy in the cot, with typhoid, or under the knife." He was making good on the prophetic verses he had published seven years earlier:

Not a cholera patient lies at the last gasp, but I also lie at the last
*   gasp,*
My face is ash-colored, my sinews gnarl . . .

I am the man . . . I suffered . . . I was there.

In that same ward lay two servicemen from Brooklyn. "I had known both the two as young lads at home, so they seem near to me. One of them, J.L., lies there with an amputated arm, the stump healing pretty well." Whitman had seen him on the battlefield in December, "all bloody, just after the arm was taken off. He was very phlegmatic about it, munching away at a cracker in the remaining hand."

In bed 23 was one who "had set his heart on a pair of suspenders." Walt gave the soldier thirty cents instead, promising to bring the suspenders the next time.

Slowly, heedfully, the soldier's missionary made his way among the cots, "observed every case in the Ward, without, I think, missing one; gave perhaps from twenty to thirty persons, each one some little gift, such as oranges, apples, sweet crackers, figs . . ."

Whitman's hospital notebook records the men's wounds and illnesses, and what they asked of him. Everything in Washington was expensive, so he solicited funds from friends in New York and Boston. "I have distributed quite a large sum of money, contributed for that purpose by noble persons in Brooklyn, New York (chiefly through Moses Lane, Chief Engineer, Water Works there). I provide myself with a quantity of bright new ten-cent and five-cent bills, and give small sums of, 15 or 20 cts or 25, 30 and occasionally 50 cts.—Ah, if the friends who have sent me this money could see what pleasure they have diffused, and little comforts they have brought . . ."

Chester H. Lilly (bed 6) 145th Penn down with Erysypelas and jaundice also wounded / wants some preserve or Jelly . . . shirt and drawers for J.H. Culver Ward G. bed 24 . . . Albert J. Maurier co B 55th Ohio amputated left leg—toothbrush . . . Erastus Haskell ward E Typhoid . . . young man in Ward H or I sitting in chair waiting to have his arm taken off—I saw him on the operating table, frothing at mouth . . . *dead* . . . J.W. Smith co. G 25th Ohio comp[lications] from right thigh also some fever / some fruit (strawberries or sweet peaches) . . .

Whitman's dispatches to the New York press, as candid as they are, do not capture the grisly scenes in the wards as vividly as do his blood-spattered notebooks, raw directories of the wounded and their pathetic yearnings.

Wm C Thomas, we are there as—the dresser bed sores great hole in which you can stick—round edges rotted away / flies— / two men hold him / the smell is awful / great sores— the flies act as if they were mad / he has one horrible wound three bad ones / a fracture— / & several shocking bed sores—

John Berry Co E. 25 N.J.—gave him 20 cts . . . an apple & c. rheumatism—consumptive no parents—can read but not write . . .

Corp Justus F. Boyd bed 22 co D 6th Mich cavalry been in five months, four sick, affection of the kidneys and pleurisy— wants some paper and envelopes and something to read gave him 12 sheets paper, & 12 envelopes & three of them franked by Mr. Sumner . . .

The least Sumner could do for Whitman was to provide postage for his patients.

Approaching the bedside, Whitman would adapt to each case: some wanted to be humored; some were addled; many just wanted the gentle fellow to sit near them and hold them by the hand. Some would want him to read aloud from a book or letters, while others asked him to write to a parent, sister, or lover. Some, wounded in wrist or shoulder, liked to have Whitman feed them. Others asked for a cooling drink. He would go around a ward from cot to cot with a jar of raspberry preserves in one hand and a spoon in the other, offering the sweet stuff to all takers.

Above all it was the gift of his kind presence that the soldiers valued. He told his mother, "the reason I am able to do some good in the hospitals, among the poor languishing & wounded boys, is that I am so large and well—indeed like a great wild buffalo, with much hair."

What had frightened the Senators charmed the boys. Soldiers from the west and far north especially took to such a man "that has not the bleached shiny & shaved cut of the cities and the east." In his little book *Memoranda During the War* he recalled, "it was in the simple matter of Personal Presence, and emanating ordinary cheer and magnetism, that I succeeded and help'd more than by medical nursing, or delicacies, or gifts of money, or anything else." He prepared for his visits by fortifying himself with a nap, a bath, "clean clothes, a good meal, and as cheerful an appearance as possible."

Whitman was troubled by how young the soldiers were, a lot of them under seventeen. He told Nellie O'Connor that many had run away from home to escape the severity of their fathers. He opined that while mothers were loving and sympathetic, he considered "the institution of the father a failure."

"My profoundest help to these sick and dying men is probably the soothing invigoration I steadily bear in mind, to infuse in them through affection, cheering love, & the like, between them and me. It has saved more than one life. There is a strange influence here." He called it his "Magnetism."

The doctors and ward masters had never seen anything quite like it; soon they gave Whitman complete freedom of the wards, to come and go as he pleased.

At first Whitman divided his time among Campbell Hospital, Armory Square, Judiciary Square, and the Patent Office wards. From October 1861 until March 1863, the Patent Office, a Doric marvel on the corner of Seventh and F Streets, had given up an entire wing—three large apartments of the model-room—for the care of soldiers. Whitman was fascinated by these "immense apartments filled with high and ponderous glass cases, crowded with models in miniature of every kind of utensil, machine or invention . . ." Some of the trophies on display there were engines of war.

Between the lighted cases, and in a long double row of cots up and down the middle of the hall, the badly wounded, sick, and dying men were crowded. In a gallery running above this corridor there was another row of beds. "The glass cases, the beds, the forms lying there, the gallery above, and the marble paving under foot—the suffering, and the fortitude to bear it in various degrees . . ." together made an ironic display of war's barbarity amid Lincoln's precious "Discoveries and Inventions."

Whitman visited there many times, especially at night "to soothe and relieve particular cases." The worst surviving casualties from Antietam and Fredericksburg, men dying from botched or infected amputations, catastrophic wounds, fevers, pneumonia, and diarrhea, were all kept in one large ward here, overseen by the surgeon and sculptor Horatio Stone. One winter evening, as Whitman stood near the cot of a dying soldier, this doctor told the poet that "of all who had died in that crowded ward the past six months, he had still to find the *first man* or *boy* who had met the approach of death with a single tremor, or unmanly fear."

After the Patent Office cleared out the wards in March 1863, Whitman spent most of his time on the Mall, at Armory Square Hospital. He devoted himself to this hospital because, as he wrote his mother, "it contains by far the worst cases, most repulsive wounds, has the most suffering & most need of consolation."

The eleven long pavilions of Armory Square were built side by side along the noxious canal at the foot of Seventh Street. The flagstaff building with its curved tin roof and cupola housed a reception room, offices for the chief surgeons, and a post office, dispensary, linen room, and officer's quarters. Behind this building stood the mess hall and main kitchen, and the laundry shed. Five ward pavilions were positioned north and south of the flagstaff. Each wood-framed ward was 150 by 25 feet, and rose 13 feet from the wide floorboards to the ridgepole of the peaked roof. At one end lay the water closet, the ward master's room, and the bath room. A ward held fifty or more beds.

"I am very familiar with this hospital," Whitman noted, "have spent many days & nights in it—have slept in it often—have seen many die here."

Early spring of 1863 provided a spell of relative calm after the disastrous battles of the previous fall and winter, and an ebb tide of the wounded in the hospitals. Doctors and nurses, like the public, hoped and believed that the worst bloodshed was behind them, as General Hooker prepared the Army of the Potomac to surround General Lee in Chancellorsville. Hooker improved morale. The President was cautiously optimistic, as was Whitman. "My plans are perfect," Hooker declared. "May God have mercy on General Lee, for *I* will have none."

Whitman witnessed such awful suffering at Armory Square in March 1863, it did not occur to him that things could get much worse. And he saw how he was making a difference. Some men were dying. But thanks to him many more were leaving the wards to return home, or to their ranks. During this month his letters show that he was exhilarated, elated by the work that had begun while he was waiting for his government job. "I cannot give up my hospitals yet. I never before had my feelings so thoroughly and (so far) permanently absorbed to the very roots, as by these swarms of dear, wounded, sick, dying boys—I get very much attached to some of them, and many of them have come to depend on seeing me, and having me sit by them a few minutes, as if for their lives."

He was happier than he had been for years, in love with life and his "boys." "Much of the weather here is from heaven," he wrote to his friend Fred Gray.

That promising spring, during the lull in the war, Whitman was able to answer the question that haunted Abraham Lincoln during his darkest hours: Was the Chief Executive doing his best for the country?

"I think well of the President," Whitman wrote to Gray on March 19. "He has a face like a hoosier Michael Angelo, so awful ugly it becomes beautiful, with its strange mouth, its deep cut criss-cross lines, and its doughnut complexion." The intimacy of the description, especially of the skin, suggests it was drawn not from photographs but from recent observation; taking habitual walks by the White House he had probably glimpsed Lincoln. Soon the poet would be seeing the President so often he took it for granted. "My notion is, too, that underneath his outside smutched mannerisms, and stories from third-class county bar-rooms, (it is his humor,) Mr. Lincoln keeps a fountain of first-class telling wisdom. I do not dwell on the supposed failures of his government; he has shown . . . supernatural tact in keeping the ship afloat at all [how this would have pleased Lincoln!], with head steady, not only not going down, and now certain not to [this is both a vote of confidence and a poet's prophecy], but with proud and resolute spirit, and flag flying in sight of the world, menacing and high as ever."

In this letter, for the first time, he used the nautical metaphor that would shape his most famous poem: "I say never yet captain, never ruler, had such a perplexing, dangerous task as his, the past two years. I more and more rely upon his idiomatic western genius, careless of court dress or court decorums."

Few men would have romanticized the embattled President as the poet then did. For most of the country Lincoln was practically a pariah. This effusion marks the beginning of hero worship that would culminate after the war in Whitman's great elegies for Lincoln. Whitman was falling in love with the President, just as he had fallen in love with his soldiers, leaves of grass on the storm-torn battlefield of America.

Nellie O'Connor kept bringing up the subject of marriage, in the abstract, and in Whitman's particular case, and he always told her that marriage was "the true and ideal relation between the sexes." Then he would explain that he doubted it would have been well for him "to have formed that closest of ties," because he was too fond of his freedom.

"True if I had been caught young," he told her, "I might have done certain things, or formed certain habits." He also confided to Nellie that he "did not envy men their wives, but he did envy them their children." Years later she recalled a day the two were walking along the street, and a little girl—a total stranger—smiled at Whitman and said, "I know you." Upon which he returned her smile and responded, "I wish I knew you."

As long as he was enamored of his "boys" as a group, he did not need to fear acting immorally. But his passionate diaries and letters show that it was inevitable that his affection would become particularized and erotic. Whitman's sensitivity and ardor made him a natural soldier's missionary; the same temperament made him vulnerable to his patients.

In December he had met in Falmouth a nineteen-year-old Confederate captain who had just had his leg amputated. Whitman did what he could to cheer him up ("poor boy, he has suffered a great deal, and still suffers—has eyes bright as a hawk, but face pale") and soon found that his ardor for the soldier was reciprocated. The Captain followed Whitman to Washington, where he was admitted to Emory Hospital. Visiting him there in January Whitman confessed, "our affection is quite an affair, quite romantic—sometimes when I lean over to say I am going, he puts his arm around my neck, draws my face down, & c. quite a scene for the New York Bowery [a popular Manhattan theater]."

Whitman understood the danger in this particularization of his "love of comrades." Ironically he cautions other nurses against it in a *New York Times* dispatch: "He who goes among the soldiers with gifts, etc. must beware how he proceeds . . . there is continual discrimination necessary . . . Some hospital visitors, especially the women, pick out the handsomest-looking soldiers, or have a few for their pets. Of course, some will attract you more than others . . . but be careful not to ignore any patient." It was advice meant for himself. No woman visiting Armory Square could have been more susceptible to male beauty or the mingling of Eros and Thanatos than Whitman, who captured in his notebook "The shining beauty of the young men's hair dampened with clots of blood."

Poor fellows, too young they are, lying there with their pale faces and that mute look in their eyes. O how one gets to love them, often particular cases, so suffering, so manly and affectionate!

Lots of them have grown to expect as I leave at night that we should kiss each other . . . I have to go around; poor boys—there is little petting in a soldier's life in the field, but . . . I know what is in their hearts—always waiting—though they may be unconscious of it themselves.

Whether he wanted to or not, in the intoxication of that first year in the hospitals he lost his perspective—he began to interpret certain soldiers' craving for attention as romantic love. This is painfully evident in a series of letters he wrote that spring to Sergeant Thomas P. Sawyer after his discharge from Armory Square.

Sawyer had occupied the same Ward K as Lewis "Lewy" Brown, another of Whitman's favorites. Brown was eighteen when he enlisted in Purnell's Legion. A year later, on August 19, 1862, a Confederate bullet shattered his left leg. A prisoner of war, Lewy lay for days among other wounded Union soldiers before an exchange permitted his transfer to Washington. Sergeant Sawyer received a less serious wound while serving in the Eleventh Massachusetts Infantry at the Second Battle of Bull Run. The twenty-one-year-old soap maker from Cambridgeport—like his comrade Lewy from Elkton, Maryland—was semiliterate. Thomas Sawyer, thanks in part to Whitman's affectionate ministrations, would be strong enough in about six months to return to active duty; Lewy Brown, after more than a year of agony, would lose his leg.

By the time Thomas Sawyer was ready to leave Washington in March, the poet was hopelessly in love with him. He bought Sawyer a fine blue shirt, new socks, and underdrawers, and then waited for the young man to come to him in his third-story room on L Street to gather them before departing for the front. The poet did not wrap the gifts in paper and string to take to Sawyer at the hospital or depot; he got him to agree to come to his room, where Whitman sat on his bed in the fading light of day from the south window, waiting. He waited at first with his heart pounding in exquisite anticipation. Then as evening turned to night and the bells tolled for vespers he waited in gloom, fearing the fellow had forgotten his promise, had a change of heart. He thought of Sawyer trying on the new clothes in this room and his heart ached.

"I am sorry you did not come up to my room to get the shirt and other things," he would write to his love. "I should have often thought now Tom may be wearing around his body something from *me* . . ."

He waited for weeks to hear from the soldier, to get some explanation, or at least an account of Sawyer's new adventures with the Army of the Potomac. In the meantime he took comfort in his attachment to Sawyer's best friend in Ward K, Lewy Brown. At last, on April 21, Whitman wrote a love letter in which his passion for the two comrades is nearly indistinguishable.

"Tom, I was at Armory last evening, saw Lewy Brown, sat with him a good while . . . Lew is so good, so affectionate—when I came away, he reached up his face, I put my arm around him, and we gave each other a long kiss, half a minute long."

Then Whitman grows wistful, plaintive, as he describes his life since Sawyer left town. "I go around some, nights, when the spirit moves me, sometimes to the gay places, just to see the sights. Tom, I wish you was here. Somehow I don't find the comrade that suits me to a dot—and I won't have any other, not for good."

Was his description of Lewy's long kiss an attempt to make Sawyer jealous? For all of Whitman's high-minded and sincere dedication to the health of his boys in the abstract, the poet was only human, a lonely forty-four-year-old bachelor. Consciously or not, he was searching through the wards of needy soldiers for a man who might be his comrade "for good."

"Dear comrade, you must not forget me, for I never shall you. My love you have in life or death forever." When the war is over, he fantasizes, the men will live together in idyllic bliss. "We should come together again in some place where we could make our living, and be true comrades and never be separated while life lasts—and take Lew Brown too, and never separate from him. Or if things are not so to be—if you get these lines, my dear, darling comrade, and any thing should go wrong . . . my soul could never be entirely happy, even in the world to come, without you, dear comrade."

Such romantic poetry stands in contrast to the harsh world of facts and human contingencies. It is not unlike Whitman's naïve expectation of a political office based "on literary grounds," his idolizing a President widely regarded as incompetent, or his faith on March 19, 1863, that the ship of state was certain to stay afloat. Whitman was no realist. A realist would have seen that the war was a stalemate. His strengths as a poet were consonant with his weaknesses as a man. Inspired, he could rise to the heights of prophecy, but he could also descend into foolish self-deception. He never considered that as grateful as the boys were for his kindness, he was part of a nightmare most of them wanted to forget.

Probably embarrassed, Thomas Sawyer did not respond for nearly a year to Whitman's letter, or to the ones that followed, by turns pleading, scolding, desperate for some reciprocal expression of love. When his answer came, it was terse. Thankful as he might be, he would never see the poet again.

Whitman's emotions were powerful and unstable. Hopeful, exhilarated by his success in the hospitals, and in love with Sawyer, he was as happy in mid-March as he could be. But Sawyer's departure, and his disappointing silence, coincided with the darkening clouds of war. Writing to him on April 21, Whitman reported: "there is great excitement now about the Army of the Potomac, no passes allowed, mails held over . . . they seem to be shoving troops off from here all the time . . . So I suppose something is up." General Hooker was about to make his move. Two weeks earlier the Union had suffered its worst naval loss of the war, at Charleston, and Whitman admitted: "the war news is not lovely is it? We feel disappointed about Charleston—I felt as blue about it as anybody."

The hospitals were beginning to take a toll on Whitman despite his boasting about perfect health. He wrote to his mother on April 15, "if you or Mat [his sister-in-law] was here a couple of days, you would cry your eyes out. I have to restrain myself and keep my composure—I succeed pretty well." He had begun to complain of severe humming in his ears and occasional deafness, "stupor-like at times," that made him unfit for work. He thought this came from a head cold. But it was probably high blood pressure, which also accounted for his rosy cheeks; it presaged the strokes that would paralyze him after the war. Nevertheless, he was in good spirits.

Then the news came from Chancellorsville.

On May 1, 1863, hardly a Union man in the Federal City doubted that General Hooker had Robert E. Lee exactly where he wanted him, and the Rebellion would soon be over. The Rebels were outnumbered 130,000 to 60,000. The Army of the Potomac was in excellent condition, Hooker's strategy seemed foolproof, and the General himself exuded confidence. It was believed he could not fail.

The city was in a state of denial, lulled by a "Congratulatory Order" Hooker issued on April 30 stating, "the enemy must either ingloriously fly or come out from behind his defenses and give us battle on our own ground, where certain destruction awaits him." The drama had seemingly unwound, and the citizens sought diversion in sporting events and stage plays. Hundreds left on trains bound for Charlestown, Maryland, to see a *real* fight, between Joe Coburn of New York and Mike McCoole, regarded as the Champion of the West, who would battle bareknuckle to the finish on May 5 for the championship of America. According to the *Morning Chronicle*, "The largest collection of the sporting fraternity ever collected on this continent assembled to witness the fight," some five thousand fans. Coburn, the lighter of the two, "had everything his own way" against the stronger McCoole, who was heavy and slow. Coburn was declared the winner after sixty-nine rounds, by which time McCoole's "face was beaten to a jelly, and his head swelled to twice its usual size. He was taken from the ground completely disabled."

While this news reached Washington promptly, the casualties from Chancellorsville were signaled only by the boatloads of wounded and dying men arriving at the Sixth Street wharves.

On May 5 the *Washington Star* was still quoting the Congratulatory Order, the last word from the General, commenting, "Our readers can rely upon it that the great battle of the war is now being fought by the Union troops under Hooker with a determined and persistent bravery that augurs conclusive results and a victory that shall sound the death knell of the rebellion."

Lincoln loved the theater, Shakespeare especially. So he might have liked to see *Othello* at the Washington Theatre, had it not been for the torrential rains the nights of May 4 and 5. John Wilkes Booth had leased the playhouse on the corner of Eleventh and C Streets; with Alice Gray in the role of Desdemona, and Booth as the homicidal Moor, the young actor/manager was enjoying enormous success. The *Chronicle* reviewer began by saying such a role should be attempted only by a great actor, and ended by declaring that Booth "lacked nothing, either physically or intellectually, to satisfy the lover of Shakespeare in his interpretation . . . We have rarely seen so good a performance, and, we might add, never a better one."

But for the President, who attended more than a hundred plays in Washington, this was no time for costume drama. He had what Gideon Welles called "a sort of intuitive sagacity" and did not altogether trust the blustering General Hooker. From May 1, when he began his attack, until May 5, when the battle was over, the General wired no reports. News correspondents on the scene filed contradictory stories. No one in Washington had hard intelligence concerning the outcome.

Desperate for dispatches, the Commander-in-Chief haunted the telegraph office in the War Department. Lincoln wryly observed that "the most depressing thing about Hooker . . . is that he is overconfident." Lincoln had been informed of Hooker's battle plan: to pull 80,000 Union troops from their camps across the river from Fredericksburg and march them in a wide arc, to attack the enemy from the rear (west). Meanwhile 40,000 men under Major General John Sedgwick would hold the Confederate soldiers in their entrenchments near the town.

This was a fine plan. But it did not take into account Lee's genius or Stonewall Jackson's audacity. Hooker sent all of his cavalry on the left flanking movement, leaving his right flank "in the air." Frightened by the sudden appearance of a line of Confederates blocking his way at Chancellorsville, Hooker dawdled; amazingly, he ordered his generals to pull back into defensive positions. This gave Jackson time enough to move 26,000 troops around the Union's unprotected right flank. On the evening of May 2, the Union Eleventh Corps on the right was shattered by Jackson's attack, and only heroic charges by some Pennsylvania cavalrymen in the middle of the Southern advance, and the coming of night, prevented the complete rout of the Army of the Potomac.

By courageously splitting his smaller army, Lee had managed to overpower Hooker in every part of the field. Chancellorsville is widely considered among the greatest tactical achievements in military history, Lee's masterpiece. Yet if Hooker had not retreated, he could have scattered Jackson's extended line or overwhelmed Lee's 15,000 men with his greater numbers.

The night of May 3, Lincoln kept a vigil at the telegraph office until 11:00, in "a feverish anxiety to get facts." Nothing was coming through but rumors (mostly from Richmond), yet Lincoln had awful forebodings. On May 4, Hooker was still not responding to his Commander-in-Chief's telegrams. At 3:10 P.M. Lincoln wired Hooker: "We have news here that the enemy has reoccupied heights above Fredericksburg. Is that so?"

On May 5, at a morning cabinet meeting, the distraught President read the General's telegraphic response—it *was* so. Was there no hope that Hooker might recover and renew the battle? That same day Walt Whitman observed: "the condition of things here in the Hospitals is getting pretty bad—the wounded from the battles around Fredericksburg are coming up in large numbers. It is very sad to see them."

According to Noah Brooks—who was at the White House on May 6—while there was still no proof, the President "was certain in his own mind that 'Hooker had been licked.' " At 2:00 P.M. Lincoln asked if Brooks would wait with Dr. Anson Henry, a friend from Springfield who was staying at the White House, in the guest room across from the oval library. Lincoln was going over to the telegraph office and wanted Brooks and Henry to wait where he could find them in case there was important news.

An hour later Lincoln walked into the bedroom where the journalist and the doctor were talking. He held a telegram in his hand. He shut the door behind him. Brooks said he would "never forget that picture of despair . . . His face, usually sallow, was ashen in hue." The wall behind him was papered in a pattern of "French gray," and Brooks thought, "the complexion of the anguished President's visage was almost exactly like that of the wall."

Lincoln handed Brooks the telegram. In a trembling voice Lincoln said, "Read it—news from the Army."

Hooker had withdrawn his beaten army across the Rappahannock the night before. When the bodies were counted it would be known that the Army of the Potomac had lost 17,278 men to Lee's 12,821, having outnumbered the rebels more than two to one on the field.

"Never, as long as I knew him," said Brooks, "did he seem to be so broken, so dispirited, and so ghostlike. Clasping his hands behind his back, he walked up and down the room, saying, 'My God! My God! What will the country say! What will the country say!' "

Lincoln seemed unable to find any other words to express his heartache, and soon rushed out of the room. His doctor, who had known Lincoln most of his life, burst into tears. Secretary Stanton, among others, was afraid that the President might commit suicide.

Looking out the north window under the portico, Brooks and Henry saw a carriage approach the porte cochere bearing General-in-Chief Henry Halleck. They watched the tall, dark form of the President climb into the vehicle, which then rattled away through the mud, bound for the wharf where the yacht was waiting to take the Commander-in-Chief to Falmouth. He was headed for Virginia to see, firsthand, what had become of the Army of the Potomac.

Before news of the defeat, the dead and wounded began arriving in Washington, in the driving rain of early May. Major General Hiram George Berry, Third Army Corps, while trying to recover ground lost by the Union Eleventh Corps of Maine, was struck by a minié ball, which pierced his lungs and heart. He had been a prominent citizen of Maine. On May 5 the *Chronicle* reported: "Gen. Berry's remains were embalmed by Drs. Brown and Alexander and placed in a handsome coffin." That afternoon Lincoln sent his son Tad around to the funeral home with "a beautiful bouquet of rare and fragrant flowers, and a wreath of evergreens" to place upon the coffin. "Lists of the killed and wounded will be found elsewhere in our columns," the *Chronicle* added.

The night before, 250 sick and wounded soldiers arrived from Aquia Creek, Virginia. They were the first of the casualties that would fill the hospitals where Whitman was working. On May 11 he wrote to Moses Lane that he had never seen "more heart-rending cases, than those now coming up in one long bloody string from Chancellorsville and Fredericksburg battles, six or seven hundred every day. We have already over 3000 arrived here in hospital from Hooker's late battles."

Whitman stood at the landing on Sixth Street in the darkness of early evening as two boats tied up at the pier. A few torches cast light on the scene as "the poor, pale, helpless soldiers had been debark'd." A violent shower made the torches smoke and sputter. Soldiers lay on the wharf and in the mud all around, on blankets and old quilts, probably grateful for the rain. "Bloody rags bound round heads, arms, and legs." There were few attendants, only some overworked ambulance drivers. "The wounded are getting to be common," Whitman observed, "and people grow callous." Men patiently waited their turn. The worst cases were carried off in stretchers. At last the ambulances began to arrive in caravans; one by one the horse-drawn wagons would back up to take their painful loads. The eerie silence in which the men suffered astonished Whitman. "A few groans that cannot be suppress'd and occasionally a scream of pain as they lift a man into the ambulance."

"The bad cases are yet to come," one of the medics told Whitman.

"If that is so I pity them, for these are bad enough," the poet reflected. The wounded were arriving at the rate of a thousand a day.

Lincoln, headed in the opposite direction on the presidential steamer, the *Carrie Martin,* was perforce more concerned with the men in the ranks. Arriving at headquarters in Falmouth, the President interviewed the surviving corps commanders individually. He was relieved to find that the army was still intact. But Hooker's generals were furious about his ineptitude in the field.

Hooker himself remained maddeningly "cool, clear and satisfied," convinced he had been on the verge of victory when a cannonball hit his headquarters and a falling beam knocked him on the head, throwing him into confusion. If the ball had been aimed a little lower, Lincoln mused, and had erased Hooker, then the Union might have won the day. He had learned nothing from his mistakes. And while the President continued to support him publicly ("I wouldn't throw away a gun because it didn't fire the first time"), he knew that he would soon have to replace this general.

The man who would eventually relieve Hooker, the irascible, hatchet-faced George Gordon Meade, wrote to his wife about his conversation with the President at headquarters in Falmouth. "The President remarked that the result was in his judgment most unfortunate; that he did not blame any one . . . Nevertheless he thought its effect, both at home and abroad, would be more serious and injurious than any previous act of the war." Public expectations had never been higher. Now, as the Boston *Journal* wrote, "the victory that was to be is not."

The rest of the month proved to be one of the gloomier passages of Lincoln's presidency. Admiral Samuel Francis Du Pont's ironclads had failed in Charleston harbor; Hooker had failed at Chancellorsville; General William Starke Rosecrans was stalled in Eastern Tennessee; and while General Grant was winning battles in Mississippi, he had yet to advance upon Vicksburg. As Lincoln declined to blame any of his generals, the public censured the Commander-in-Chief for the bloodshed, for this seemingly endless war. More and more politicians and journalists, Republicans as well as Democrats, called Lincoln's administration incompetent. Military failures prompted demands for peace negotiations. And the President was roundly condemned for curtailing civil liberties: his support of Burnside's suspension of habeas corpus in arresting ex-Congressman Clement Vallandigham for treasonable speeches; his suppression of "seditious" newspapers in Indiana.

Although Robert E. Lee had lost Stonewall Jackson, his "strong right arm," at Chancellorsville, he knew he had taken a significant step toward victory. Emboldened by his army's power and morale, contemptuous of the Union generals, Lee began a carefully screened movement northward.

And during May and June, General Hooker did nothing to stop him. On May 14 Lincoln wrote to Hooker from the White House: "I have some painful intimations that some of your corps and Division Commanders are not giving you their entire confidence. This would be ruinous, if true . . ." This was a roundabout way of describing Lincoln's plight as well as Hooker's. Critics of Lincoln's performance as commander-in-chief were driven by radical politics: they wanted Hooker, Halleck, Grant, and Rosecrans replaced by generals who were also abolitionists. Lincoln simply wanted generals who would fight.

"Will the President realize," wrote General John Frémont to Charles Sumner—in a letter concerning the enlistment of colored troops—"that if this summer's campaigns are not successful the Confederacy is well nigh established?"

The President understood this all too well.

6

THE LOOKING GLASS

*T*he war was nearing its climax that summer. And Lincoln found himself in a domain beyond the looking glass, a place and time when it became difficult to know truth from illusion, or friends from enemies, even in his own home. The nation had been thrown into chaos, and somehow the entire complex structure must change, adapt, if it was ever to regain stability.

> *Will the whole come back then?*
> *Can each see signs of the best by a look in the looking-glass? is there*
>   *nothing greater or more?*
> *Does all sit there with you, and here with me?*
>
> —WHITMAN, "A SONG FOR OCCUPATIONS"

The eyes of the world were upon the President, but many of the people he counted on for approval or succor had withdrawn. His faithful secretary John Hay, whom he regarded with almost paternal affection, had left for Georgia's Sea Islands and Florida to survey fortifications, and would not return until July. Hay and John Nicolay, Lincoln's other secretary, shared a bedroom across from the President's office. They were the first people to see him in the morning as he shuffled down the hall in his carpet slippers between six and seven to begin his desk work. And they were often the last ones to see him at night as the three worked late together. Tad, who adored his father, would play in the office and lie around until he fell asleep. Ten years old, the boy was a slow learner, and he spoke with a lisp. His difficulties, and Lincoln's grief over Willie, made Tad all the more dear to him. Around ten o'clock Lincoln would carry the child off to bed.

A journalist described John Hay as "exceedingly handsome—a slight, graceful, boyish figure," with kind, lustrous brown eyes and rosy cheeks. He was charming, brilliant, and tactful. There was no one else in the household like Hay, to whom Lincoln confided so many personal matters as well as secrets of State. John Nicolay, gaunt, hawk-faced, with thinning hair and a scraggly goatee, guarded the gate between the long rectangular waiting room and the President's office while Hay dealt with the cascade of mail, answering most of Lincoln's letters. When he had put aside the mail, Hay welcomed visitors. With his kind voice and winning smile, he knew the art of "temporing unreasonable aspirations," as one newsman put it, and "giving to disappointed ambitions the soft answer which turneth away wrath." To a woman weeping he might offer his handkerchief; for a gentleman, on a hot day, he might fetch a glass of water. It was this young aide who made the White House appear a generous, humane stronghold, a sanctuary for yearning or distressed visitors during wartime. Now he was gone, and gruff John Nicolay remained.

Both Hay and Nicolay detested Mary Todd Lincoln. Hay nicknamed her "Hellcat" for her temper. Whatever her youthful virtues had been, by the time she became First Lady she was vain, jealous, profligate, and given to heroic tantrums. Admittedly, she had inherited a White House in disrepair, yet "Mrs. President Lincoln had overspent the $20,000 four-year allowance [for redecorating] in less than a year," writes Jean Baker, the preeminent biographer of Mary Lincoln. The commissioner of White House purchases—whose appointment Mary engineered—was William S. Wood. According to Baker, the President soon received an anonymous letter of warning (to which the biographer gives credence) that his wife and Wood were having an affair.

The debts Mary Lincoln ultimately incurred in redecorating the White House and purchasing lavish dresses created a public-relations nightmare. "As her debts increased, she may have initiated the exchange of her influence on Lincoln for a bill paid or new material for a dress," Baker reports. Then, in 1862, she was accused of espionage when she allegedly leaked an advance copy of the President's State of the Union message to one of her admirers, named Henry Wikoff, a secret correspondent for the *New York Herald*.

From time to time, during the first year of the war, Mary visited Campbell or Douglas Hospital, and she was pleased to see this recorded in the newspapers. She gave a thousand dollars to purchase fruit for soldiers threatened with scurvy, and she forwarded to the hospitals gifts of liquor that came to the White House. Upon Elizabeth Keckley's urging she raised relief monies for the "contrabands," the homeless freed blacks who were camping on the parade grounds in back of the White House and crowding the city. But as Mary's health failed in 1862, Keckley took over these charities herself.

By 1863, when Mary Lincoln was not tormenting her husband, she was neglecting him; and as intimate as they had been five years earlier, now he must have missed her sorely. "The President's wife wanders around among watering places unprotected by any member of her family or by the company of any respectable gentleman and lady or worthy consort of her husband," one journalist observed. Three times a year or more she left town to go shopping in New York, Boston, or Philadelphia. During the last half of 1863, she was absent most of the time. Although she had been an attentive mother to the older boys, "now Tad evoked memories of Willie." According to Baker, Mary left Tad to her husband, and the child clung to him day and night.

After Willie's death Mary became even more erratic, withdrawing into the world of spiritualism, escaping into the circle of flatterers she called her "salon," which included gentlemen and rogues on whose behalf she approached her husband for jobs. "Favor seekers recognized in her an experienced influence peddler and made known their claims," Baker writes. To keep Nettie Colburn, her favorite spirit medium, in Washington, she secured her a position in the Interior Department.

Her mind was unbalanced, and Lincoln pitied her. According to Elizabeth Keckley, during one of Mary's fits of hysteria Lincoln led her to a window with a view of the lunatic asylum and gently explained: "Mother . . . try and control your grief or it will drive you mad and we may have to send you there." He always called her "Mother," and he treated her with unfailing tenderness. To Mary he had been "truly my all—Always-lover-husband-father and all, all to me." They continued to love each other. But by the spring of 1863 Mary Lincoln was no more of a helpmate to her husband than he was to her—consumed as he was by the duties of his office.

After March 28, 1863, the Lincolns ended their Saturday afternoon receptions. On April 6 Mary and Tad accompanied Lincoln

as he reviewed Hooker's army in Virginia. Excepting a séance in
the Red Room on April 23 (which Lincoln walked out on before
the spooks appeared) and a couple of visits to the theater, the tele-
scopic record of the Lincolns' life during that spring shows that
the couple spent little time together by day. At night they slept
apart. On June 4 the President and his wife attended a "recitation
from Shakespeare at a private residence near Chain Bridge,"
according to General Samuel P. Heintzelman's *Journal*. Then
Mary grew restless and prepared to leave Washington.

From the tone of his letters to Mary that month, and the fact
that he saved none of hers, it appears that Lincoln was relieved to
see her go. In their black barouche, with the rubber on the wheels
worn thin, the President rode with his wife and boy to the Baltimore & Ohio Railroad station just north of the Capitol. He kissed
them goodbye and put them on a three o'clock train to Philadelphia. He had no idea when she would return.

Mary booked rooms at the Continental Hotel in Philadelphia,
and no historian has ever discovered whom she saw or what she
did there that June. In the one note of hers that has survived from
those weeks, she politely refused to see some friends who asked to
call upon her.

Lincoln wrote to his wife on June 16: "It is a matter of choice
with yourself whether you come home. There is no reason why
you should not, that did not exist when you went away." The letter
suggests the residue of a recent quarrel, and not much affection on
either side.

Without his wife and little boy, and without John Hay's cheerful presence, Lincoln spent his days consumed with military decisions and the tedious defense of his suspending the writ of habeas
corpus. He slept fitfully, tormented by nightmares. Once he
dreamed that Tad killed himself with a cap pistol. Several times he

dreamed of his own murder, but he would not allow more security guards. The President had no idea how many deadly conspirators watched him. But one of his friends was obsessed with it.

———

Marshal Ward Hill Lamon could be found late at night in the smoky gentlemen's saloon of the Willard Hotel across from the White House, drinking a glass of old rye whiskey. This giant walrus of a man wore a dark swallowtail coat over a yellow double-breasted vest buttoned tightly over his paunch, a white neckcloth, and a ruffled silk shirt. He also wore, as suited the occasion, two revolvers, a bowie knife, and brass knuckles.

Lincoln and Lamon had been friends since the 1850s, when they were law partners on the Eighth Circuit in Illinois. After the election, Lamon came along to protect the President-elect on his journey to the capital. Allan Pinkerton, a detective working for the railroad, uncovered a plot to murder Lincoln in pro-Confederate Baltimore. When this was confirmed by the Secretary of State and General Winfield Scott, Mary Lincoln begged Lamon not to leave her husband's side. Armed with two pistols, two derringers, and two knives, Lamon accompanied Lincoln as he surreptitiously entered Washington at dawn.

Lincoln made Lamon marshal for the city of Washington and chief of protocol at White House events. At public receptions Lamon introduced visitors to the President—from this vantage point he could spot any suspicious characters as they came through the door.

Lamon's style was equal parts riverboat gambler, troubadour, and Wild Bill Hickok lawman of the Wild West. Thirty-five years of age, the bull-necked self-appointed "bodyguard" of the President played Falstaff to Lincoln's Prince Hal. Lincoln admired

Lamon's baritone, his wit, and his brute strength, which he had seen in action. "Hereafter," the President warned him, "when you have occasion to strike a man, don't hit him with your fist; strike him with a club or crowbar or something that won't kill him." The marshal was larger than life in several ways, including his concern about the President's safety. Lincoln told him: "I think, for a man of accredited courage, you are the most panicky person I ever knew; you can see more dangers to me than all the other friends I have. You are all the time exercized about someone taking my life . . ."

Lamon was nearly as tall as the President. His sagging jowels and great girth bespoke gargantuan appetites, and his long, black, pomaded hair and beard were groomed to affect a studious nonchalance. He was renowned for the quantity of pure rye whiskey he could put away while still managing to repeat the romantic tongue-twister "She stood at the gate welcoming him in." He was also known for his rich singing voice. "Sing me a little song," Lincoln would beg, and Lamon would pick up his banjo and strike up one of the President's favorites, such as "Camptown Races" or "The Blue-Tail Fly."

But tonight Lamon was in no mood for singing. He was in the mood for drinking. When his eyes were not on the President, the marshal was troubled, and the more he worried the more he drank. It was Lamon's job to do the worrying. Spies and assassins lurked all around—in the bushes, in high windows, in theaters, in the Willard saloon—and Lincoln would never know the number of plots his guardian "Hill" had discovered and undone.

Lincoln, who was philosophically opposed to bodyguards and hated military surveillance, made the watchman's duty very difficult. His carelessness in coming and going at all hours, unescorted, to the telegraph office, or riding horseback on a lonely road three miles to the Soldiers' Home, where he spent summer nights, was the despair of his friends and staff. Such behavior passed beyond courage; it seemed foolhardy, tempting fate.

General-in-Chief Scott ordered Colonel Charles Stone to keep an eye on the President, with an effort not to attract attention. They did not consult Lincoln about this, knowing his "almost morbid dislike of guards and escorts," and Scott felt it was inadvisable "that it should appear that the President of the United States was, for his personal safety, obliged to surround himself with armed guards." The first time Lincoln noticed armed troopers on horseback at the gates of the White House, he protested. "It would never do for a President to have guards with drawn sabers at his door, as if he fancied he were, or were trying to be, an emperor." He sent them away. "Why put up the bars when the fence is down all around? If they kill me, the next man will be just as bad for them; and in a country like this, where our habits are simple, and must be, assassination is always possible, and will come if they are determined upon it." What some considered the President's bravery, his nonchalance about his safety, others called rashness.

One day Congressman Cornelius Cole walked into Lincoln's office, unchecked, unannounced. When he lectured the President about the danger of such accessibility, Lincoln was unmoved. At last he said, "When I first came here, I made up my mind I would not be dying all the while." He was thinking perhaps of the line from Shakespeare's *Julius Caesar,* "The valiant never taste of death but once." Or he might have been recalling the calm verses of Walt Whitman,

> Slow-moving and black lines creep over the whole earth—they never cease—they are the burial lines.
> He that was President was buried, and he that is now President shall surely be buried.

Lincoln took time to explain to Cole: "I have observed that one man's life is as dear to him as another's and he could not expect to take my life without losing his own. Besides, if anyone wanted to, he could shoot me from some window as I ride by daily to the Soldiers' Home."

This was exactly the possibility that drove the marshal to drink, now that it was late June and Abraham Lincoln was sleeping, or tossing or turning, or lying in his own blood for all Lamon knew, in the summer residence on a hill to the north overlooking the city. Sometimes nobody could *find* him. The summer before, while Lincoln was riding on horseback alone on the toll road to the Soldiers' Home, at eleven at night, a would-be assassin shot a hole through the President's stovepipe hat. Lincoln made a funny story out of it, which Lamon did not think was a bit funny. Because the Lincolns could not be persuaded to give up the cool, salubrious air of the Soldiers' Home in the summer, they were forced to accept a cavalry escort between the White House and the fourteen-room Victorian "cottage" overlooking Washington. But when his wife and Tad were away, Lincoln would not bother with the barouche and the horseguards; he often rode out by himself on "Old Abe," his favorite horse.

Only one man in the city made Lincoln uneasy, and that man was Walt Whitman's old friend from Pfaff's rathskeller, the Polish Count Adam Gurowski. More than once the President had told Lamon: "So far as my personal safety is concerned, Gurowski is the only man who has given me a serious thought of a personal nature. From the known disposition of this man, he is dangerous wherever he may be. I have sometimes thought he might try to take my life. It would be just like him to do such a thing."

As the Count appeared to Lincoln at receptions or on the street, the burly fellow, with his large round head, his bulging brow, stubbly beard, and blue-tinted spectacles, cut a sinister figure. He wore the dark glasses to protect his good eye—he had ruined the other by falling on his jackknife as a child—and to spare others the sight of the mutilation. Gurowski, fifty-eight, balding, wore a long black cape and a bell-shaped hat, like a spy in a cartoon. He did not so much walk the streets around the White House as march, with an aristocratic air, like a foreign army of one.

Gurowski's operatic appearance and his baroque politics were like nothing Lincoln had ever seen in Illinois or Indiana. The urbane Charles Sumner had known the Count for many years, although they had recently had a falling out. In Cambridge, Henry Wadsworth Longfellow, James Russell Lowell, and Edward Everett had welcomed the Count's cosmopolitan point of view, his offbeat perspective on American culture, and his understanding of European history. As a Polish revolutionary, he had played an active role in that history. Now a Boston publisher was bringing out his diaries, in which he described wartime Washington, offering his opinions on everything from military matters to cabinet appointments. Whitman considered him a man of "great keenness," and a "splendid intellect."

In his diaries Gurowski attacked Sumner, Seward, and Lincoln himself. (For instance, the entry for November 5, 1862, reads: "Lincoln-Seward politically slaughtered the Republican Party, and with it the country's honor. The future looks dark and terrible. Dishonor on all sides.") Then he wrote the President rambling letters of advice whose tone was hysterical and imperious. Having fled the political chaos of Eastern Europe, the Pole was doomed to witness an unparalleled tragedy in his adoptive country. In print, and on street corners to passersby, Gurowski denounced the President as "a beast," Seward as "a clever charlatan." He could not conceal his contempt for the President even in his presence. At best he was condescending, showing disgust at Lincoln's jokes and tales. Sometimes Lincoln felt a palpable threat in the Count's cyclopean stare.

There were more serious concerns. Gurowski carried a pistol, and he had been seen brandishing it out of the folds of his cape upon little provocation. Under surveillance by the constabulary since the first inauguration, Gurowski had a record that included the following charges: When words failed him in an argument with reporter Adams Hill in the *Tribune* office, he drew his gun on Hill, threatening to blow out his brains. Gurowski put away the weapon, but thereafter was barred from the office. One autumn he was riding a horse-drawn streetcar and he ordered the driver to make an unscheduled stop. When the streetcar passed the corner where the Pole had wished to alight, Gurowski pulled out his revolver and commanded the driver to stop the vehicle. Somebody yelled for the police. They arrested Gurowski and led him before the magistrate, who fined him twenty dollars.

Perhaps the most bizarre scene, which Whitman evidently witnessed, occurred one summer. The poet and his radical friend were watching some firemen dousing a burning building with hand-pumps and hoses. Something about their dawdling, or ineptitude, irritated the Count. Out came the pistol, which he waved at the firefighters as an incentive to pursue their duty with more vigor. A patrolman arrested him, and this time he was locked in the station house for a while before facing the judge who fined him. Years later, when questioned about the event, Whitman said, "That fire incident . . . looks worse than it was," a curious comment, suggesting either that the crew needed lashing, or that his friend meant no harm in pointing a gun at them, as if the firearm had been no more than a conductor's baton.

So Lincoln had positive evidence of the Count's violence to

add to the troubling tone of his writings. On June 5 Gurowski wrote: "I often meet Mr. Lincoln in the streets. Poor man! He looks exhausted, care-worn, spiritless, *extinct*. I pity him! Mr. Lincoln's looks are those of a man whose nights are sleepless, and whose days are comfortless. That is the price for a greatness to which he is not equal. Yet Mr. Lincoln, they say, wishes to be reelected!"

The night of his first election Lincoln had lounged in his bedroom, opposite a bureau with a swinging mirror above it. "And looking in that glass," he recalled, "I saw myself reflected nearly at full length; but my face, I noticed, had *two* separate and distinct images . . . one of the faces was a little paler—say five shades—than the other." It gave him a pang, he told Noah Brooks, and when he told Mary about the ghost in the mirror it frightened her: she said this was a sign that he would be elected to a second term but would not live to finish it. Now, Lincoln mused, if he were to be reelected, it might be over the dead body of Adam Gurowski.

Gurowski subsisted as a houseguest of Fanny Eames, whose husband Charles was counsel for the Department of the Navy. Fanny presided over one of the most brilliant salons in the capital, "a sort of focal point in Washington society, where one meets . . . the brains of society—politicians, diplomats, authors and artists," wrote John Nicolay, who with John Hay liked to visit the house on the northwest corner of Fourteenth and H, between eight and eleven on Sunday evenings. Hay wrote in his diary, "saw Count Gurowski come into the parlor & go growling out because I was there." Charles Sumner, a frequent visitor, had the same effect then on Gurowski. But the Count and Fanny Eames were devoted to each other. She was patient with his rages and nursed him in his illnesses.

This gadfly was under more and more constant surveillance as the war dragged on and as his criticism of the administration grew more vehement. Hill Lamon appointed his younger brother Robert to aid him as deputy marshal. Between them, and their detectives, the city police, the adjutant general, and two companies of cavalry and infantry lately assigned to protect the President, they made sure that neither Gurowski nor any of his bohemian associates escaped notice. The Lamon brothers would not have overlooked the ménage at Fourteenth and L Streets where Gurowski sometimes went to dine with the radical abolitionist William O'Connor and his friend Walt Whitman, the infamous author of *Leaves of Grass*, whose politics no one quite understood.

Readers of the *Washington Star* on June 22 knew that the President was taking up his residence that very day at the Soldiers' Home. Anyone—whether he be a patriot, a newsman, or an aspiring assassin—with the slightest interest in seeing the Chief Executive, on horseback or riding in his barouche, might observe Lincoln traveling along an unvarying route to and from the White House.

The carriage, with new rubber on its wheels, drawn by two horses, picked up the President from the north portico. As they drove through the gate and out the semicircular drive, the Light Guard of cavalry from Ohio fell in behind them. The carriage rattled and the horseguards' sabers clattered. They passed the two-story house of the State Department at the corner of New York Avenue, across from the Paymaster's Office where Whitman worked. They turned north on Fourteenth Street, under the Eameses' windows, and drove for five blocks past L Street, where Whitman lived with the O'Connors, just south of the circle where the party would pick up Vermont Avenue, which took them north to the toll road and out of town.

The brawny, shaggy-looking fellow in the light gray summer coat with huge pockets, haversack slung over his shoulder, leaning on an umbrella, obviously had more than a casual interest in looking upon his President. Lincoln's schedule was not wholly predictable, although he generally left the mansion before suppertime and returned in the morning after breakfast. Yet this distinctively accoutred graybeard always managed to appear, somewhere in the neighborhood of Fourteenth and L Streets, near the curb, in full view of the President. He would wave and bow in the most courteous, friendly manner. His luminous gray eyes, which resembled Lincoln's, shone with a delight that verged upon adoration. The viewer did not look like other men. He was peculiarly intense.

Sergeant Smith Stimmel of the horseguards, like all of the Ohio detail, had been instructed to be vigilant, to look from the tops of buildings on either side of the street to the windows shaded with striped awnings. He was to take note of any men or women who appeared regularly in the President's line of sight. Such idlers might be up to no good. Zealotry of any sort was threatening: the man who worships from afar on a Monday may want to murder his idol on a Friday.

If Lincoln, Sergeant Stimmel, and Stimmel's fellow horseguards took no notice of this particular "fanatic" when the company rode out along Fourteenth Street on Monday, June 22, 1863, they certainly had sized him up by Monday evening, June 29.

The next day Whitman wrote to his mother: "Mr. Lincoln passes here (14th St) every evening on his way out—I saw him last evening about ½ past 6, he was in his barouche . . . I had a good view of the President last evening—he looks more careworn than usual—his face with deep-cut lines, seams, & his *complexion gray*, though very dark skin, a curious looking man, very sad."

The poet said to a lady standing near him, "Who can see that man without losing all wish to be sharp upon him personally? Who can say he has not a good soul?"

She did not wish to argue, but was nevertheless "vindictive on the course of the administration," complaining that it lacked nerve.

Whitman observed that the carriage was shabby and the horses looked like what his Broadway drivers called "old plugs."

"The President dresses in plain black clothes, cylinder hat." The day before, Whitman had seen him stop alone at Stanton's house on K Street, without the cavalry escort, and Lincoln "sat in his carriage while Stanton came out & had a fifteen minute interview with him . . . —& then wheeled around, & slowly trotted around the corner and up Fourteenth st." By this time the horseguards were in hot pursuit.

"I really think it would be safer for him just now to stop at the White House," Whitman judged, meaning he should stay in the safety of the mansion and not risk the commute to the Soldiers' Home. This was exactly Marshal Lamon's opinion during that awful, hot summer, when the stench from the mud, carcasses, and sewage in the canal grew pestilential, and Walt Whitman and Abraham Lincoln saw more and more of each other.

Whitman became a President-watcher, loitering at the corner of L Street, or sauntering down Fourteenth Street at twilight, toward the block of newspaper offices across from the Willard, on his way to Armory Square. His hopes and efforts often met with success. And one could not be a President-watcher in those days without being watched in turn by the President and his guard. Who is that jolly-looking old duffer with the baggy pants stuffed into his boots, the shaggy one with the haversack and the bulging pockets? There he is again, right about where we left him yesterday. The poet, Walt Whitman, Gurowski's friend, studying the President.

So the horseguards whispered to one another—word passed through the ranks—ever vigilant. Whitman's personal magnetism is well documented; it won him such friends as the astute naturalist John Burroughs, who had seen nothing like the poet in all of nature. Burroughs described him at this time, "his large benevolent look . . . of infinite good nature and contentment, and the curious blending of youth and age in his expression; also the transparent skin which allows the summery, motherly nature to shine through, and rich mellow voice, indicative of deep human sympathies and affinities . . ." It was the benevolent look that had so much healing power in the hospitals. But there was something else in Whitman's gaze that the naturalist could not quite describe, a look "as in that of the mother of many children." The beauty and expressiveness of Whitman's eyes seemed to Burroughs uncanny. "It is as if the Earth looked at me—dumb, yearning, relentless, immodest, inhuman. If the impersonal elements and forces were concentrated in an eye, that would be it . . . not piercing, but absorbing and devouring—the pupil expanded, the lid slightly drooping, and eye set and fixed." Like a mirror of the cosmos.

Now as the lonely President passed, mopping his brow with a handkerchief, worrying over Lee's army and whether or not they were moving into Pennsylvania, and when, exactly, he would remove General Hooker from command and replace him with General Meade; as the sad President passed with the weight of the nation on his shoulders, the fate of several hundred thousand men, their fearful wives and mothers, and the grief of a hundred thousand more who dressed in mourning, Walt Whitman fixed him with that "benevolent look . . . of infinite good nature," that look of a mother or Mother Earth, a gaze that merged "deep human sympathy" with an "impersonal and elemental force."

At some point, that week or the next, the President looked back at Whitman, met his gaze and acknowledged it, with a nod of his head or a slight wave of his hand. That eye-to-eye contact began to form a bond, as order formed out of chaos. Lincoln would not, of course, have stopped the barouche if it had been an archangel who blessed him in passing; yet neither Lincoln nor any of the Light Guard ever displayed concern about Whitman's persistent attention, no matter how near he came to hail the President. The poet had become a welcome and comforting fixture on the road to Lincoln's lonely summer retreat.

This gentle communion became central to Whitman's routine that summer. After his nap and bath in the late afternoon, the poet took his supper. Then he dressed in his cleanest clothing, packed up his haversack, and went to see the President. Whitman recalled how he would "pass a word with" Lincoln sometimes, as he rode by. The Commander-in-Chief probably needed the love and comfort the poet delivered in his slow gaze, needed this as much as any feverish soldier in Armory Square Hospital. And the sight of Lincoln's transparent goodness inspired Whitman. The soldier's missionary would bear that memory with him as a rapture or charm into the infernal regions of the sick wards.

Lincoln's infamous melancholia lifted during those last days of June, on the eve of the Battle of Gettysburg. His leadership grew bold, as he replaced the timid Hooker with General Meade, and parried the Ohio Democratic Convention's challenges concerning his exiling the Copperhead Vallandigham. As Lee's Army of Virginia swept through Maryland, panic was selling newspapers from Washington to Boston. HARRISBURG IN IMMINENT DANGER, blared one headline, and PITTSBURGH TO BE INVADED, SACKED AND BURNED, said another, but Lincoln remained in high spirits.

John Hay, back in Washington, arranged the newspapers on Lincoln's desk. What did those editors know? Although the President was not sure exactly where the Rebels were, somehow he felt optimistic that Lee's invasion of the North would present the most favorable opportunity yet to surround and crush the Confederate army.

Lincoln had grown frighteningly gaunt. "I am growing as thin as a shad," he quipped, "yea worse—as thin as a shadder." Hay was pleased to find that the President had recovered his sense of humor. When they learned that one Captain James Cutts Jr. had been caught peering through a keyhole and over a transom at a woman undressing, Lincoln commented, "He should be elevated to the peerage for it, with the title of Count Peeper."

During ponderous hours in the cipher room in the War Department telegraph office, Lincoln sat in his shirtsleeves with his feet propped up on Major Thomas Eckert's writing table next to the iron safe, telling stories. He loved the tale of the congressman who had been watching the Battle of Bull Run from a hill as if the war were some sporting event, how the congressman outran the pack, his legs a blur as he led the race back to the capital when the Union soldiers retreated.

"I never knew but one fellow could run like that," said Abraham Lincoln.

He was a young man out of Illinois who had been sparking a girl much against the wishes of her father. In fact, the old man took such a dislike to him that he threatened to shoot him if he ever caught him on the premises again. One evening the young man learned that the girl's father had gone to the city, and he ventured out to the house. He was sitting in the parlor with his arm around the girl's waist and then he suddenly spied the old man coming around the corner of the house with a shotgun. Leaping through the window into the garden, he started down the path at the top of his speed like greased lightning. Just then a jackrabbit jumped up in the path in front of him. In about two leaps the boy overtook the rabbit. Giving it a kick that sent it high in the air, he yelled, *Git out of the road, gosh dern you, and let somebody run that knows how!*

News of Lee's position was slow in coming to the men in the cipher room. Lincoln ran his fingers through his hair. He advised the dour Montgomery Meigs (the same quartermaster general who ignored Senator King's letter recommending Walt Whitman for a job) to read the humorous writings of Orpheus C. Kerr. This was the pen name (punning on the crush of *office-seekers* in Washington) of Robert Henry Newell, a columnist for the New York *Mercury*. "Any one who has not read them must be a heathen," Lincoln said to no one in particular, gazing about the small, square room. At a desk on the adjacent wall to the President's right sat the cipher operator waiting in vain for information, staring at the open fireplace opposite. In the center of the room at a rectangular table sat Meigs, impassive. Welles or Stanton would drift in one of the doors across from where Lincoln was holding forth, take a seat for a while, and finding there was no news, would wander off again.

"The most interesting natural curiosity here, next to Secretary Welles' beard," wrote Orpheus C. Kerr from Washington, "is the office of the Secretary of the Interior. Covered with spider-webs, and clothed in the dust of ages, sit the Secretary and his clerks, like so many respectable mummies in a neglected pyramid."

Then there was the Kerr story about the two Quakers in the railway coach. One says to the other: "I think Jefferson Davis will succeed." And "Why does thee think so?" asks the second.

"Because Jefferson is a praying man," he replies. "And so is Abraham a praying man," says the second Quaker. "Yes," says the first, "but the Lord will think Abraham is joking."

The reservoir of Lincoln's good humor would be nearly drained in the days to come. Mary returned from Philadelphia. At ten o'clock on the morning of July 2, she was riding from the cottage into town. Near the Mount Pleasant Hospital the carriage driver's seat became detached from its springs, throwing the man to the ground. A saboteur had loosened the bolts. While the horses were in full gallop, Mary leapt from the runaway barouche, sustaining a blow to the back of her head, which bled profusely. Surgeons from the nearby hospital promptly treated her, then took her to the White House.

Lincoln wired his son Robert not to worry, that the injury was not serious. But the wound became infected, and she lay for weeks in a state of confusion, from which, some believe, she never wholly recovered. The attack intended for Lincoln had wounded his wife.

That same morning the silence in the telegraph office was broken by the staccato of General Meade's wire dispatches from Gettysburg. The armies had met there, by fateful coincidence, the day before, and now toiled in the largest battle ever fought in America. Eighty-eight thousand Federals and seventy-five thousand Rebels marched against one another armed with cannon, pistols, rifles, swords, and bayonets. Meade had told his officers: "Corps and other commanders are authorized to order the instant death of any soldier who fails in his duty at this hour."

"The balls were whizzing so thick," said a Texan, "that it looked like a man could hold out a hat and catch it full." Soldiers five feet apart fired rifles into each other's faces, hacked away with saber strokes. Men went down on their hands and knees spinning like tops in the cyclone of gunfire, swallowing blood—soldiers legless, armless, headless.

A private from Massachusetts recalled the sound of the battle: "The hoarse and indistinguishable orders of commanding officers, the screaming and bursting of shells, cannister and shrapnel as they tore through the struggling masses of humanity, the death screams of wounded animals, the groans of their human companions, wounded and dying and trampled underfoot by hurrying batteries, riderless horses and the moving lines of battle . . . —a perfect hell on earth, never, perhaps to be equaled, certainly not to be surpassed, nor *ever* to be forgotten in a man's lifetime."

Many books have been written about this ferocious battle, with its dramatic reversals of fortune. On the third day the valiant Rebels—charging precipitously—were overwhelmed by Meade's greater force. Confederate Brigadier General Josiah Gorgas wrote in his diary: "Yesterday we rode on the pinnacle of success; to-day absolute ruin seems to be our portion. The Confederacy totters to its destruction." By nightfall on July 3 there were more than seven thousand dead on both sides, and fifty thousand casualties.

Robert E. Lee said, "It was all my fault," and retreated. He had lost a third of his army.

Far away, on July 4, the Confederate garrison at Vicksburg surrendered to General Ulysses S. Grant at 10:00 A.M. The same hour, Lincoln issued a triumphant press release: "News from the Army of the Potomac, up to 10. P.M. of the 3rd is such as to cover that Army with the highest honor."

The President knew that the tide had turned. But his euphoria was short-lived. It never occurred to him that Meade would not press his advantage and annihilate Lee's army as it fled. Meade had greater numbers and reinforcements at the ready. A downpour flooded the Potomac, making it impossible to ford; for days the

Army of Virginia lay trapped between the Federals and the swollen river, yet Meade did nothing, while the flood drained. For reasons understood only by the commanders in the field—whose advice Meade sought—the Union army rested while the Rebels escaped.

Lincoln could not contain his disappointment or his wrath. He told his son Robert: "If I had gone up there I could have whipped them myself." He wrote to Meade of "the magnitude of the misfortune involved in Lee's escape . . . He was within your easy grasp, and to have closed upon him would, in connection with our other late successes, have ended the war. As it is, the war will be prolonged indefinitely . . . Your golden opportunity is gone, and I am distressed immeasurably because of it."

In the bedroom down the hall, his wife lay delirious from the infected wound in her head.

Whitman wrote to his mother: "One's heart grows sick of war, after all, when you see what it really is—every once in a while I feel so horrified & disgusted—it seems to me like a great slaughterhouse & the men mutually butchering each other . . ." Perhaps this was the sentiment that paralyzed Meade's generals. "Then I feel how impossible it appears, again, to retire from this contest, until we have carried our points." He felt it "cruel to be tossed from pillar to post" in these conflicting emotions.

"It is curious—when I am present at the most appalling things, deaths, operations, sickening wounds (perhaps full of maggots), I do not fail, although my sympathies are very much excited, but keep singularly cool—but often, hours afterward, perhaps when I am home, or out walking alone, I feel sick & actually tremble when I recall the thing & have it in my mind again before me."

One evening Whitman went with the O'Connors to visit the Unitarian minister William Ellery Channing. Channing found the usually calm poet in a state of extreme agitation, pacing restlessly and wringing his hands.

"I say stop this war, this horrible massacre of men!" Whitman exclaimed.

"You are sick," the minister said. "The daily contact with these poor maimed and suffering men has made you sick; don't you see that the war cannot be stopped now? Some issue must be made and met."

Whitman was not alone in his disillusionment. In the Midwest, white mobs attacked conscript officers in protest against Lincoln's "war for Negro freedom." In mid-July came the incendiary draft riots in Manhattan. A crowd of workingmen, mostly Irish-Americans, set fire to the draft office. Then they went on a rampage, looting saloons and seizing rifles from an armory on the way to the Negro ghetto where they burned Negroes and hung them from lampposts, killing hundreds. They torched an orphanage. It took the police force, militia, naval forces, a company from West Point, and a detachment of soldiers from Gettysburg to restore order.

In Washington the general feeling was that New York should be cannonaded and the rioters all hung in a body. The President was ill over it, could not even bring himself to convene his cabinet on the sixteenth. "None of us were in the right frame of mind for deliberation," said the Secretary of the Navy, Gideon Welles, "—he [Lincoln] was not." Whitman, weary of the war, feared the draft, feared that his brother Jeff might end up in uniform, and did not lack sympathy with the rioters. "I remain silent, partly amused, partly scornful, or occasionally put a dry remark, which only adds fuel to the flame—I do not feel it in my heart to abuse the poor people, or call for rope or bullets for them, but that is all the talk here, even in the hospitals."

The poet was ailing in several ways. He was lonely and homesick. William and Nellie O'Connor had moved out of the house on L Street that summer, and Whitman was spending entire days and nights at Armory Square in flight from solitude. He had cut his hand while assisting a surgeon in July and the hand had become infected. The wound was slow to heal and he wore a bandage on it until early August. He went to bed feeling weak and dizzy, and woke in the morning drenched with sweat.

"I see so much of butcher sights, so much sickness and suffering," he wrote his mother, "I must get away a while I believe for self-preservation."

The weather that summer was insufferable, the temperature rising to 104 degrees. The newspapers daily reported men, women, and horses dropping in the streets from sunstroke. Whitman carried an umbrella and a fan in the daytime—"quite a Japanee," he remarked.

Only late at night did the poet take any pleasure in retracing the dusty length of Pennsylvania Avenue from the Capitol to the White House. At the beginning of August the moon was full; the moonlight on the white pilasters and balustrades bestowed upon Lincoln's dwelling-place a rare splendor, to Whitman a true glory. He described "the tender and soft moonlight, flooding the pale marble, and making peculiar faint languishing shades, not shadows . . . the brilliant and extra-plentiful clusters of gas, on and around the façade, columns and portico, & c.—everything so white, so marbly pure and dazzling, yet soft.—the White House of future poems, and of dreams and dramas, there in the soft and copious moon——the pure and gorgeous front, in the trees, under the night-lights, under the lustrous flooding moon, full of reality, full of illusion."

He neared the clover and fleur-de-lys ironwork of the open northeast gates of the portico. A sentry armed with a carbine sat on a stone post in front of a great gate-pier. The gas lanterns atop the gate-piers shone upon that soldier and his fellow sentries pacing there in their blue coats, "stopping you not at all," Whitman observed, "but eyeing you with sharp eyes, whichever way you move."

"I see the President almost every day," Whitman wrote on Wednesday, August 12, "as I happen to live where he passes to and from his lodgings out of town."

That morning found Whitman on his watch, at Vermont Avenue near L Street, as he heard the cavalry rattling in from the north and saw the horseguards with their naked sabers held upright over their shoulders. Lincoln himself was on horseback this morning, on a large easygoing gray horse, "dress'd in plain black, somewhat rusty and dusty; wears a black stiff hat, and looks about as ordinary in attire, & c, as the commonest man." At his left rode a lieutenant, with yellow shoulder-straps; and following behind rode the Ohio detail, two by two, horseguards in yellow-striped jackets, at a slow trot, their sabers and bridles clanking.

"I see very plainly Abraham Lincoln's dark brown face, with the deep cut lines, the eyes . . . always to me with a deep latent sadness in the expression."

It seemed that no one's sorrow escaped the President's notice. The sight of the ragged, starving "contrabands" tugged at his heart. On Monday he had met with Frederick Douglass, the lecturer, author, and suffragist, a freed slave. On Tuesday a one-legged colored man had stopped Lincoln on the street, begging for help. It was 94 degrees in the shade. Lincoln hurriedly wrote a check out of his personal account at Riggs & Co.: "*Pay to* colored man, with one leg *or bearer* Five . . . *Dollars* $5/oo. A. Lincoln." That was a day consumed with cabinet meetings and tedious arguments with New York Governor Horatio Seymour over the draft. This morning, Wednesday, he would be settling a dispute between General Grant and the disgraced Major General John McClernand, whom Grant had dismissed from his command. The same day he must find time to write Stanton on behalf of a Mrs. Baird. The widow had three sons in uniform, one of them under arrest for desertion, who should have been pardoned under a recent dispensation. Lincoln wanted the Secretary of War to return the boy to duty. "I think too, he should have his pay for duty actually performed. Loss of pay falls hard upon poor families."

Such thoughts passed through his mind that morning as he rode down Vermont Avenue toward the White House. And there once again the smiling graybeard with the beautiful gray eyes stood by the curb, his face beaming goodwill and encouragement, waiting to bestow his benediction.

"We have got so that we always exchange bows, and very cordial ones," wrote Walt Whitman.

7

HALLOWEEN

*A*utumn of 1863 was a cruel season for the Whitman family. Walt's brother Andrew, stricken with consumption, lay on his deathbed; their mother had severe rheumatism in her arms and legs so she could hardly take care of her retarded son Edward, or her older son Jesse, whose mental illness had taken a violent turn. Walt himself was exhausted, although he would not admit it. He had tested his courage in the hospitals, and the things he had seen and done there were undermining his health. He talked to his friend John Hay, Lincoln's secretary, about going home to vote in the November election, and to see what he might do for his family.

In late October, Hay approached his New York acquaintance Albert Marshman Palmer to see if he could help Whitman. Palmer, with his lantern jaw, wide-set piercing eyes, and jutting chin, had inherited from his father, the Baptist preacher and poet Albert Gallatin Palmer, a rare combination of severity and vulnerability. A. M. Palmer, as he was called, had graduated from law school in 1860 but never practiced law. Well connected, Palmer pursued a mazy, unprincipled career in the New York government before his confessed peculations forced him into a second profession, as a theater manager.

Palmer, like Hay, was twenty-five years of age. They had many things in common, including charm, precocity, and influence, both serving as private secretaries to powerful men. Palmer's boss Hiram Barney, collector of the Port of New York, was the highest-paid public official in the country, making even more money than the President. Secretary of the Treasury Chase wanted to replace Lincoln as chief executive, and the customhouse was a key to political influence in New York, Secretary Seward's state. Control over that customhouse with its hundreds of jobs became a point of furious contention between the ambitious Chase and the loyal Seward.

Salmon Chase had won the first round, in getting his Ohio friend Barney the post. But Barney faltered in the job. Now Seward's crony, Republican boss Thurlow Weed, had taken Barney's secretary under his wing, and Palmer was adroitly gaining control of the customhouse patronage. People had begun to call him "the collector de facto."

Over drinks, the young men chatted in the Willard, where Palmer was staying during the last week in October. Hay had a favor to ask . . . the poet Walt Whitman wanted to go home to Brooklyn. Palmer may have feared the favor on the tip of Hay's tongue involved the customhouse. For all of the secretary's influence, he would not be able to get an office there for the notorious author of *Leaves of Grass*.

Palmer was relieved to find it was a simpler matter: the poet was almost penniless, having spent all his money on treats for his soldiers. Election Day was coming. If Palmer could procure a round-trip train ticket to New York City for Whitman, Hay would get him a furlough to go home and vote.

A simple matter. When you are "the collector de facto" of the Port of New York, train tickets are to be had for the asking.

So, three days before Allhallows, John Hay "went down to Willards . . . & got from Palmer who is here a free ticket to New York and back for Walt . . . who is going to New York to electioneer and vote for the Union ticket," Hay wrote in his diary on October 29. He told Whitman he would have the train tickets and the furlough ready for him if he would drop by the White House on Halloween, Saturday the thirty-first, a slow day in the President's office.

Walt Whitman had gotten his hair cut and his beard trimmed. ("All my acquaintances are in anger & despair & go about wringing their hands.") In a letter to his mother he joked that among his friends the recent battles in Charleston and Tennessee were "insignificant themes in comparison" to his hairstyle and his dignified new frock coat of black broadcloth. He also had bought a shirt of white linen. Perhaps it was to reassure a prospective landlady— on October 16 he moved to 456 Sixth Street, five blocks north of Armory Square. The landlady was old and feeble, and was taking care of her four-year-old granddaughter; she would have preferred her boarders to look like gentlemen. And certainly Whitman's year in Washington had taught him that, outside of the sick wards, there were social circles that were inaccessible to a man who looked like a Southern planter or a buffalo hunter.

On the northeast corner of Seventh and D Streets, just across the street from Whitman's new dwelling, stood Shepherd & Riley's Bookstore, where the poet bought paper, pencils, and books. A long awning surrounded the corner where the journals were racked and stacked outside. And up above the bookstore was Alexander Gardner's Gallery, four windows across the front and two in the peaked loft between the twin chimneys, to light the subjects of his photographs. Gardner, a former associate of Mathew Brady, advertised the finest apparatus and "every arrangement has been adopted which could in any way facilitate the production of 'Beautiful Pictures.' " Also, his ads explained, "the light has been constructed so as to obviate all heavy and unnatural shadows under the eyebrows and chin." And Gardner was cheaper than Brady.

Dressed in his new coat, Walt Whitman went to have his picture taken in Gardner's Gallery. The artist posed him against a square pier, leaning with his elbow upon the capstone, his hand smoothing his elegant goatee. His white mustaches are slightly upturned as if he has been twirling them. The look in his gray eyes is serious but gentle. His throat is covered by a black neckcloth and—as if he were quite proud of his haircut—his hat is nowhere to be seen.

For the first time in his life Walt Whitman looked fit to be introduced to the President. This meeting never had seemed more likely to the poet than on Halloween, 1863, when his friend and admirer John Hay invited him to the White House on official business. Having greeted the President many times, Whitman could not doubt that the Chief Executive would recognize his face if he saw him again up close. Whitman had published some pieces in the *New York Times* that autumn celebrating the Federal City; perhaps Hay had shown these to the President.

"I fully believe in Lincoln," the poet wrote to his sister on October 15. "Few know the rocks & quicksands he has to steer through."

Whitman's direct route to the White House ran past the marble

portico of the Patent Office and due west on F Street, past newpa-
per row, and by the Paymaster's Office. The weather was unseasonably cold. To supply the fortifications around the city with fuel,
great swaths of forest had been felled and 150 wagons engaged to
haul the cordwood to the camps.

On Ninth Street a six-hundred-pound wheel of New Jersey
cheese aged slowly in the window of Barnes & Company, grocers,
a wonder to the neighborhood. On Tenth Street a poster
announced that John Wilkes Booth would appear on Monday at
Ford's Theatre as the villainous Richard III.

Anything seemed possible. Halloween was gaining popularity
in wartime—America was obsessed with the macabre, haunted by
a crowd of the newly dead. A day without news of bloody battles
seemed dull. Brady and Gardner were doing a brisk side business
in selling grisly photographs of corpses on the battlefields. This
morning's *Chronicle* included a long and poetic essay on Halloween: "The wisest and gravest of men for this one October night
forget their wisdom and calmness, and loyally believe in fairy-
land, the midnight revelry of witches . . . All we have done in an
evil way will be remembered and punished; and all good deeds will
receive the reward that the kind dispensers [fairies] of happiness
and hope have in their power to bestow."

Although fairies no longer ride through the air on cream-
colored horses; and the demons and minions of the Evil One no
longer scatter their curses and famines and disease, "the human
heart is still the same, with its hopes and loves and fears." The
anonymous columnist concludes: "Our hills may not have the
romance of the Highlands, nor has the Potomac the poetry of the
Bonnie Doon. But on hills and river let the fairies meet tonight,
and we wish them joy in their revels under the waning moon."

One can only imagine the excitement Whitman felt on this day, after so many walks near "the White House of future poems, and of dreams and dramas." For the first time he passed the sentries at the gate and advanced through the Ionic columns up the steps to the broad platform in front of the entrance. He entered the enormous vestibule, where Edward McManus, the doorkeeper, directed him to a flight of stairs on the left. Through an archway at the top of the stairs he found John Hay, at his work with the President's mail in the anteroom.

They greeted each other warmly, the distinguished author grateful for the favors Hay had done him, the handsome, boyish secretary with the soft brown eyes proud to be of service to the great poet. Yes, the President was in. They could hear his gentle voice and see his dark-clad, gaunt figure through the doorway. This was an unusually quiet day here. The President wrote a couple of requests to the Attorney General for pardons, authorized a few passes, and informed some congressmen-elect of the form of credentials required of them. Now Lincoln was taking the leisure to meet with a friend.

Hay gave Whitman an envelope with the train tickets and the furlough as the poet watched and listened to the President a few steps away. Whitman "saw Mr. Lincoln standing, talking with a gentleman, apparently a dear friend," he wrote that day. "—his face & manner have an expression & were inexpressibly sweet— one hand on his friends shoulder the other holding his hand."

Noting the poet's rapt attention, Hay would not hurry him. Nor did the secretary dare to interrupt Lincoln during this intimate interview to inform him that here was Walt Whitman, the author of *Leaves of Grass*. Whitman would not have ventured to ask it. If the President noticed Whitman there, dressed now in formal black, with his hair clipped and beard trimmed, like a lobbyist, maybe Lincoln would not have recognized him. No, it must suffice for the poet to identify with the dear friend whose hand the President held, his other hand on the visitor's shoulder, while he gazed upon him with a look "inexpressibly sweet."

And of course there would be plenty of time in the future to meet the President. Whitman thanked Hay, bid him farewell, and left the mansion in a mood of wistful euphoria.

On All Souls' Day he wrote in his diary: "I love the President personally."

> *Over the carnage rose prophetic a voice,*
> *Be not dishearten'd—affection shall solve the problems of Freedom*
>   *yet;*
> *Those who love each other shall become invincible—they shall yet*
>   *make Columbia victorious.*

part three

DRUM-TAPS

8

THE GREAT CHASE

$\mathscr{D}$uring the month when Whitman was on holiday in New York, the President infuriated his wife by attending the social event of the season without her. The wedding of Salmon Chase's daughter Kate to Senator William Sprague of Rhode Island was a chief topic of conversation in Washington high society and the obsession of journalists, from the dignified *Washington Intelligencer* to the influential *New York Times*.

Mary Lincoln had hated Kate Chase long before her engagement. Twenty-two-year-old Catherine Jane Chase had the social poise and natural beauty that made her a great asset to her ambitious father, in a town where Mary's provincial habits and demeanor were a constant source of amusement. And now Kate was marrying one of the wealthiest men in America.

The hostility began upon Lincoln's inauguration, and it was triggered by Mary's fierce partisan defense of her husband against all rivals. Salmon Chase wanted to be president as much as any man has ever desired that much-coveted office. He could never quite accept the fact that homely Abraham Lincoln, with his lack of executive experience, his poor schooling, low breeding, and rudimentary drawing-room manners, had won the prize, while he, Salmon Chase, had been passed over. He had gone to Dartmouth. He had served as a U.S. senator and then as governor of Ohio. His uncle was a bishop. With his bold, square features, handsome from any angle, and the dignified dome of his bald head, he *looked* like a President. He feared God and served the Church and the cause of abolition. Indeed, it had been his "radical" approach to freeing the slaves that had cost him his party's nomination.

Because the Secretary of the Treasury had been a widower for some time, Kate managed their three-story brick town house at Sixth and E Streets, acting as hostess at Chase's frequent formal dinners and receptions. Father and daughter entertained graciously: breakfasts for congressmen and visiting lobbyists; sumptuous dinners honoring foreign ministers, bankers, generals, and senators, who enjoyed Chase's plentiful stock of wine, liquor, and cigars. Not the least of the attractions there was "pretty Kate," as John Hay called her.

Salmon Chase was six feet two inches tall, and broad-shouldered; his hyper-erect posture made him look even larger than he was. Lincoln once said of the proud Secretary, "Chase is about one and a half times bigger than any other man I ever knew." Bald and clean-shaven, he also seemed frosty, remote; this was due in part to his nearsightedness. A contemporary quipped: "Mr. Chase is nearsighted and does not see men." Kate did. And by all accounts she was the most brilliant woman in the city, strikingly beautiful, statuesque, and exceedingly clever. Her hair was chestnut-colored, with red-gold highlights, and her dark, wide-set eyes, with long lashes, sparkled with wit.

The upper crust of Washington society had been invited to a

lavish celebration, a wedding of power and beauty. Although Kate could hardly be improved by adornments, Sprague—heir to a textile fortune and former governor of Rhode Island—gave her a tiara of matched pearls and diamonds worth fifty thousand dollars as a wedding gift. On the evening of November 12, 1863, the bride in her white velvet gown, her veil encircled by the tiara, descended the stairs to meet her father in their living room. Sprague, a few inches shorter than Kate, waited there with the Bishop of Rhode Island, in his miter, cope, and cassock. The room was crowded. The President, cabinet members and their wives, senior military officers, family members, and a select group of legislators were thrilled to witness the marriage. The President's wife was not among them.

We cannot know for certain that Mary Lincoln was personally jealous of Kate Chase Sprague. But she surely saw the extravaganza of this wedding party for what it was: a carefully choreographed political event. Mary wanted no part of it. As father and daughter approached the groom and the Bishop, the marine band played a march written for the bride by the popular composer Frederick Kroell (it is now called "The Kate Chase Wedding March"). The room wanted only bronze eagles and bunting to complete the picture.

There is no greater evidence of Lincoln's high-mindedness and political shrewdness than the way he handled his obstinate Secretary of the Treasury. Throughout his tenure the moody, humorless Chase caused the President nearly as much trouble as the rest of his cabinet combined. Lincoln needed Chase far more than Chase needed a place in the cabinet—particularly the Treasury. Chase would not have minded being Secretary of State, and so he resented Seward. At the outset he knew next to nothing about monetary policy or finance, and only arduous study enabled him to master the complex duties of his office. Lincoln needed this progressive Ohio Republican for balance in his administration; newly reelected to the Senate, Chase was an abolitionist and a Midwesterner, and he could be relied upon not to placate the Rebels. Chase would have preferred remaining a senator, and he made this clear to Lincoln, who would not take no for an answer. The Secretary served virtually under protest. Knowing that Chase would not stop running for president even during a war, Lincoln had wanted him on board, in the cabinet, where it would be harder for him to stir up strife to serve his own agenda—support for the presidential nomination in 1864.

Now 1864 was fast approaching, and the progressive wing of the Republican Party, including Horace Greeley, wanted Chase in the White House. A single term was customary, and no president since Jackson had served more than four years. Almost everyone agreed that Kate Sprague would make a splendid first lady. The idea appalled Mary Lincoln, who was so deeply in debt that only the prospect of four more years of a presidential salary might bail her out. For his part, Lincoln felt that if he was not offered a second term during wartime it would amount to a verdict of failure on his first four years. Publicly he remained noncommittal, but he believed he was the best man to bring the war to conclusion and direct the Reconstruction.

Lincoln was amused by what he called Chase's "voracious desire for office . . . from which I am not free myself," and said the Secretary was like "a horsefly on the neck of a plowhorse." But Chase was more than a nuisance. He spread stories of Lincoln's military blunders and his naïveté about finance. He enlarged the myth that Lincoln was a pawn of Secretary of State Seward and big-money interests in New York. Chase challenged the President's policies at every turn, while filling Treasury posts with sycophants who would electioneer on his behalf. When controversy arose over General Rosecrans's crucial failure at Chickamauga, John Hay told Lincoln: "Chase will try to make capital out of this Rosecrans business."

The President chuckled and said: "I suppose he will, like the blue-bottle fly, lay his eggs in every rotten spot he can find."

Hay noted in his diary that Lincoln "seems much amused at Chase's mad hunt after the Presidency. He says it may win. He hopes the country will never do worse."

Soberly, Hay advised his boss that "he should not by making [endorsing] all of Chase's appointments make himself *particeps criminis* [accomplice to the crime]." Hay cited Chase's appointment of Homer Plantz as district attorney of Florida. "Plantz went down with but two ideas," said Hay, "to steal money for himself and votes for Chase." The President acted like it was just "a devilish good joke. He prefers letting Chase have his own way in these sneaking tricks than getting into a snarl with him by refusing what he asks," Hay wrote. Lincoln chose his battles carefully.

At the end of November, on a quiet Saturday morning, John Hay sat drinking whiskey with his friend Wayne McVeagh in the bedroom across from the President's office. McVeagh, chairman of the Pennsylvania Republican Central Committee and a staunch Lincoln supporter, was worried that Lincoln might not carry Pennsylvania, and he was alarmed over the support Chase was getting in New York.

"Chase is at work night and day, laying pipe," said McVeagh. Chase had attracted Kansas Senator Samuel Pomeroy, who had much to gain from the Treasury's backing in building the Kansas-Pacific Railroad, in which Pomeroy owned stock. Pomeroy assembled a Chase-for-president cabal that included Ohio Senator John Sherman, Major General (soon-to-be-Congressman) James

Garfield, and a radical senator from Missouri called B. Gratz Brown. The committee also included the gang of Chase's Treasury agents in New Orleans; it was generously funded by the brilliant financier Jay Cooke (who marketed the enormous Civil War loans of the Union) and Chase's new son-in-law, William Sprague.

Chase needed a new campaign biography. Casting about for a writer who would do him justice, the candidate hooked a thirty-seven-year-old poet and author of boys' books named John Townsend Trowbridge. Trowbridge's most famous book, *Neighbor Jackwood* ("a true New England novel"), had gone to the stage with moderate success in 1857. With Cooke's deep pockets and powerful editorial contacts, Chase was able to make the writer an irresistible offer. In late November, the Secretary invited Trowbridge to come to Washington and be his guest in the town house at Sixth and E Streets.

Despite the sadness Whitman had seen and felt in his family home, he returned to Washington on December 2 refreshed from a month of opera-going and dining out with his friends in Manhattan. After three weeks of recreation he had written to a soldier at Armory Square Hospital: "I have had enough of going around New York—enough of amusements, suppers, drinking & what is called *pleasure* . . . I cannot bear the thought of being separated from you—I know I am a great fool about such things . . . at the gayest supper party, of men, where all was fun & noise and laughing & drinking, of a dozen young men, & I among them, I would see your face before me . . . & my amusement or drink would be all turned to nothing."

His New York friends were witty, handsome, and well edu-

cated; some were rich and others were published authors; all were
good men, he believed. Yet now he perceived something was lacking in their company: "there has never passed so much between
them & me as we have," he wrote to his soldier, including all the
wounded men and their nurses, "there is something that takes
down all artificial accomplishments, & that is a manly and loving
soul."

Although the constant strain of caring for Eddie and Jesse had
taken its toll on Louisa Whitman, Walt found his sixty-eight-year-
old mother "active and cheerful." Andrew was dying of consumption, struggling for breath. "My brother is bound for another
world," Walt wrote to Charles Eldridge, "he is here the greater
part of the time." Andrew did not want to die in the squalor of his
own lodgings, and his drunken wife Nancy, furiously jealous,
stormed into Louisa's home to make scenes. Nancy would lead the
invalid away, and the next day Andrew would hobble back again to
be nursed by his sister-in-law Martha, Jeff's wife, and his mother.
Martha's children were Hattie, two years old, and the newborn
Jessie Louisa.

Whitman marveled over his mother's strength and courage
"under her surroundings of domestic pressure—one case of sickness & its accompanying irritability—two of grown helpless-
ness—& the two little children, very much with her . . ." While
Walt's presence was always a comfort, there was not much he
could do for his dying brother or for Louisa either, besides helping
with the babies a few hours a day. The minute he could get out of
that house he was gone, crossing on the Fulton Ferry to join his
friends in Manhattan. He had learned something about triage and
survival, and he meant for this month in New York to strengthen
him for the work that lay ahead.

He was bound to leave Brooklyn—by the terms of his fur-

lough—on December 2, although he could see that Andrew's life
hung by a thread. Back in the Federal City on December 3, Walt
received the telegram informing him of his brother's death. He
could not return for the funeral, but sent his regrets that he had not
stayed in Brooklyn a little longer.

He narrowly escaped a spectacle that would have canceled
whatever good his leave of absence had done him. Andrew began
to suffocate the morning Walt left Brooklyn. By that evening the
dying man's torment was so pitiful that his wife drank herself into
a stupor and passed out beside him. According to Louisa, "In the
morning she [Nancy] brought such a smell that Jeffy got sick."
Poor Andrew inhaled that stench with his final breath. Meanwhile
the lunatic Jesse was so unhinged by the trauma he threatened to
strike the wailing child Hattie, and to clobber her mother, Jeff's
wife. Jeff wrote to Walt, "to have this infernal pup—a perfect
hell-drag to his mother—treat Martha so—to threaten to brain
her—call her all the vile things he could think of—is a little more
than I will stand . . . Had I been home I would have shot him dead
on the spot. I wish to God he was ready to put along side of
Andrew." Jeff and Walt began their planning to have Jesse committed.

Years later Whitman told a biographer: "I was always between
two loves at that time—I wanted to be in New York; I had to be in
Washington. I was never in the one place but I was restless for the
other." He meant that his vocation in Washington ("It was a religion with me") had become his guiding star, his master, superced-
ing his devotion to his family. But he never admitted that he left
Brooklyn in part for the same reason his brother George enlisted in
the Thirteenth Regiment: the crowded family home on Portland
Avenue was bedlam, a sinkhole more threatening to the healthy
brothers than the War of the Rebellion.

He was relieved to return to his third-floor garret on Sixth Street, "a very good winter room, as it is right under the roof & looks south, has low windows, is plenty big enough, I have gas"— gaslight, but no heating fuel. For cooking and heating he used a little sheet-iron stove, which he fed parsimoniously with sticks of wood. "I am quite by myself, there is no passage up here except to my room, & right off against my side of the house is a great old yard with grass & some trees back, & the sun shines in all day . . ." There was a good big bed, a pine table, and several chairs stacked with newspapers. He made a cupboard out of an oblong pine box by setting it on end against the wall.

His interval in Brooklyn—where the muses had first discovered him—had reminded Whitman: "I *must* be continually bringing out poems—now is the hey day. I shall range along the high plateau of my life and capacity for a few years now, & then swiftly descend." This was prophetic. He had returned to Washington with forty-odd poems, most of them written before 1863, that he now planned to publish under the title *Drum-Taps*. The sheaf of poetry lay in a steamer trunk at the foot of his bed. Since he arrived in Washington he had written a good deal of fine journalism but few verses. "I must bring out *Drum-Taps*," he told Charles Eldridge, his former publisher.

Unknown to Whitman, just across the street an old friend of his, John Trowbridge, was plotting with Salmon Chase to defeat Lincoln in the next presidential election. Three years earlier, while Whitman was reading the proof sheets for the third edition of *Leaves of Grass* in Charles Eldridge's stereotype foundry in Boston, John Townsend Trowbridge had first met the poet. Trowbridge remembered, "The tremendous original power of this new bard, and the freshness, as of nature itself, which breathed through the best of his songs . . . inspired me with intense curiosity as to

the man himself." Upon first seeing him that spring day, Trowbridge was struck by the contrast between the grandiose, renegade
speaker of *Leaves of Grass* and the gentle, soft-spoken, and plainly
dressed fellow bent over his proofs in the dingy office. Later,
Trowbridge could recall from that meeting only a single line of
conversation. When he asked Whitman how the poems impressed
him at this rereading, all set up in type, the poet replied, "I am
astonished to find myself capable of feeling so much." This is a
striking reminder of Whitman's emotional vector—how far he
journeyed from his apathy in the early 1860s to his passionate
awakening in wartime Washington.

The two writers shared a sense of humor, a delight in wordplay, and admiration of Emerson. Whitman told Trowbridge that
when he had worked as a carpenter he carried a volume of Emerson in his lunch pail, and read about the "Over-Soul" and "Spiritual Laws" while seated on a pile of boards, taking his noon meal.
Emerson had helped Whitman find himself. To Trowbridge the
poet confided, "I was simmering, simmering, simmering; Emerson
brought me to a boil." By the time Whitman left Boston, Trowbridge felt that "a large, new friendship had shed a glow on my
life."

Late in 1863, finding himself in the Federal City in Chase's
employ, John Trowbridge asked his fellow Bostonian William
O'Connor, "Where's Walt?"

"What a chance," O'Connor replied. "Walt is here in Washington, living close by you, within a stone's throw of the Secretary's door." O'Connor asked Townsend to come around on
Sunday for dinner, and he would have Whitman there, too.

Trowbridge was a handsome, slender gentleman of thirty-six,
with a goatee, a Roman nose, and wide-set, slightly down-turned,
watery eyes. Barbarous treatment by an oculist, who scored the

sclera of both his eyes with a lancet when the boy was twelve, had left his eyes permanently weak and rheumy—a challenge to his literary ambitions. More than anything he had wanted to be a poet; he had published verse in the *Atlantic,* but his poetry would never get as much attention as his "juvenile fiction," and so his affection for Whitman was complex, tinged with envy.

He found Whitman much the same as before, "except that he was more trimly attired, wearing a loosely fitting but quite elegant suit of black." That day, December 6, was probably the day of Andrew's funeral. Trowbridge recalled that Walt "was in the best of spirits; and I remember with what a superb and joyous pace he swung along the street, between O'Connor and me, as we walked home with him, after ten o'clock."

Whitman led his friends to the ramshackle wooden house and up the dimly lit stairs, unlocked his door and swung it wide, scratched a match for the gaslight, and welcomed them to his room. A gust of winter wind swept in an open window. He did not light a fire. Whitman cleared the chairs of newspapers, and the three sat in their overcoats—Walt and John on the chairs, William on the bed—passionately conversing, making ghosts with their breath. They talked about books, about Shakespeare and Francis Bacon, and whether Bacon had or had not written the works of Shakespeare. They talked of *Leaves of Grass.* "In my enjoyment of such high discourse," Trowbridge recalled, "I forgot the cheerless garret, the stove in which there was no fire, the window that remained open (Walt was a fresh-air fiend), and my own freezing feet."

Trowbridge does not record any talk of politics, which would have been awkward. Whitman recently had told his mother: "Mr. Lincoln has done as good as a human man could do . . . I realize here in Washington that it has been a big thing to have just kept the

United States from being thrown down & having its throat cut—
& now I have no doubt it will throw down secession & cut its
throat . . ." Whitman had believed this before Gettysburg. Trowbridge—if not wholly cynical or mercenary—had come to Washington with a different opinion about Lincoln. With his pen,
Trowbridge would try to help Salmon Chase unseat Whitman's
"redeemer President."

No clashing of politics rippled the stream of the men's literary
conversation, which was so absorbing that Trowbridge forgot the
lateness of the hour. "I also forgot that I was a guest at the great
house across the quadrangle, and that I was unprovided with a
latch key," he later wrote. Long after midnight he said goodbye to
Whitman and O'Connor, and hurried to Secretary Chase's door.
Trowbridge was locked out. His embarrassment was eased by the
thought that during wartime the Secretary was accustomed to
receiving dispatches at all hours. The guest rang boldly, the
vestibule gas lamp increased its glow, and a servant let him in.

———

"In the fine, large mansion, sumptuously furnished, cared for by
the sleek and silent colored servants, and thronged by distinguished guests, dwelt the great statesman; in the old tenement
opposite, in a bare and desolate back room, up three flights of
stairs, quite alone, lived the poet," Trowbridge recalled, years
later. He would savor the irony that he had known them both,
"passing often from the stately residence of the one to the humble
lodging of the other . . . Great men both, each nobly proportioned
in body and stalwart in character, and each invincibly true to his
own ideals and purposes; near neighbors, and yet very antipodes in
their widely contrasted lives." Chase was by nature solitary, happi-
est in his study. His best friend in Washington was the erudite

Charles Sumner, equally somber, righteous, and aristocratic, if more gregarious. Chase was so wealthy that "the slenderest rill of [his riches] would have made life green for the other [Whitman], struggling along the arid ways of an honorable poverty."

Both men were ambitious, Chase believing it was his destiny and right to be the next president, Whitman determined to become the great American poet, the bard of freedom and democracy for the ages. While Trowbridge admired and respected the Secretary, for Whitman he felt so powerful an attraction he could only describe it as "something like a younger brother's love."

On the morning of December 8, Trowbridge was invited to breakfast with Whitman in his garret. The poet warned his friend not to come before ten o'clock.

At that hour John Trowbridge found Whitman partly dressed, cutting slices of bread from a loaf with a jackknife. A fire glowed in the little stove, on which a teakettle simmered. Trowbridge speared a bread slice with a sharpened stick and began toasting the bread through the open door of the stove, over the sparse coals. Whitman buttered the bread with his knife, then poured tea into cups at a corner of the table that had been cleared of newspapers and books for that purpose. "His sugar bowl was a brown paper bag. His butter plate was another piece of brown paper," in which he had carried away the lump of butter from the corner grocery.

While they breakfasted they conversed. When the last slice of toast had been eaten, the paper went into the stove to burn. With no dishes to wash, the writers could get on with the main item on their agenda, which was poetry. Whitman unlatched his trunk and brought out the manuscript of *Drum-Taps*, almost ready for publication.

For an hour Whitman read his poetry aloud, and then they discussed it. The poet had started his book early in the war as a cluster of reveille poems, a call to arms ("taps" was short for "tattoo," the sound of the war drum); it would be years before the irony of the title could be fully appreciated. Taps, of course, is the bugle melody played at military funerals, a dirge. Writing the reveille poems, Whitman had no idea what a calamity he was summoning, for his countrymen and for himself.

1

FIRST, O songs, for a prelude,
Lightly strike on the stretch'd tympanum, pride and joy in my city,
How she led the rest to arms—how she gave the cue,
How at once with lithe limbs, unwaiting a moment, she sprang:
(O superb! O Manhattan, my own, my peerless!
O strongest you in the hour of danger, in crisis! O truer than steel!)
How you sprang! how you threw off the costumes of peace with
  indifferent hand;
How your soft opera-music changed, and the drum and fife were
  heard in their stead;
How you led to the war, (that shall serve for our prelude, songs of
  soldiers,)
How Manhattan drum-taps led.

2

Forty years had I in my city seen soldiers parading;
Forty years as a pageant—till unawares the Lady of this teeming
  and turbulent city,
Sleepless, amid her ships, her houses, her incalculable wealth,
With her million children around her—suddenly,
At dead of night, at news from the south,
Incens'd, struck with clinch'd hand the pavement.

3

A shock electric—the night sustain'd it;
Till with ominous hum, our hive at day-break, pour'd out its
  myriads.

4

From the houses then and workshops, and through all the doorways,
Leapt they tumultuous, and lo! Manhattan arming.

5

To the drum-taps prompt,
The young men falling in and arming,
The mechanics arming, (the trowel, the jack-plane, the blacksmith's
  hammer, tost aside with precipitation,)
The lawyer leaving his office and arming—the judge leaving the
  court;
The driver deserting his wagon in the street, jumping down, throwing
  the reins abruptly down on the horses' backs,
The salesman leaving the store, the boss, book-keeper, porter, all
  leaving;
Squads gather everywhere by common consent and arm . . .
.   .   .

6

Mannahatta a-march!—and it's O to sing it well!
It's O for a manly life in the camp!

7

And the sturdy artillery!
The guns bright as gold—the work for giants—to serve well the
  guns:

Unlimber them! (no more as the past forty years, for salutes
    for courtesies merely;
Put in something now besides powder and wadding.)

8

And you, Lady of Ships! you Mannahatta!
Old matron of the city! this proud, friendly, turbulent city!
Often in peace and wealth you were pensive, or covertly frown'd
    amid all your children;
But now you smile with joy, exulting old Mannahatta!

Trowbridge recalled that Whitman "read them unaffectedly, with force and feeling, and in a voice of rich but not resonant tones." The poems dramatically descended from patriotic exuberance to disillusionment and horror.

1

A SIGHT in the day-break grey and dim,
As from my tent I emerge so early, sleepless,
As slow I walk in the cool fresh air, the path near by the hospital-tent,
Three forms I see on stretchers lying, brought out there, untended
    lying,
Over each the blanket spread, ample brownish woolen blanket,
Gray and heavy blanket, folding, covering all.

2

Curious, I halt, and silent stand;
Then with light fingers I from the face of the nearest, the first, just
    lift the blanket:
Who are you, elderly man so gaunt and grim, with well-grey'd hair,
    and flesh all sunken about the eyes?
Who are you my dear comrade?

3
Then to the second I step—And who are you, my child and darling?
Who are you, sweet boy, with cheeks yet blooming?

Then to the third—a face nor child, nor old, very calm, as of
beautiful yellow-white ivory:
Young man, I think I know you—I think this face of yours is the
face of the Christ himself;
Dead and divine, and brother of all, and here again he lies.

Whitman claimed that the experience of war had made him a great poet. "This is the very centre, circumference, of my whole career . . . but for this I never would have had *Leaves of Grass.*" Many readers disagree, and so did Trowbridge, for all his admiration of these "fine, effective, patriotic and pathetic chants." Of course he would not tell his friend then and there, but he "did not find in them anything comparable with the greatly moving passages in the earlier *Leaves.*" The tone was more literary, with lapses into conventional poetic diction.

1
Come up from the fields, father, here's a letter from our Pete;
And come to the front door, mother—here's a letter from thy dear son.

2
Lo, 'tis autumn,
Lo, where the trees, deeper green, yellower and redder,
Cool and sweeten Ohio's villages . . .

We may find fault with *Drum-Taps*—the diction of individual lines, their sentimentality, or the overall quality of the poems—yet there is no doubt that these poems, and the poems in *Sequel to Drum-Taps* (which Whitman completed soon after Lincoln's death), represent the apotheosis of Whitman's role as the bard of democracy in our American drama. He felt that every poem he had published before the war was a prophecy of the tragic conflict as well as the inevitable triumph of the Union. In the end the poet came to believe that *Drum-Taps* (with its sequel) was the narrative climax of the completed opera of *Leaves of Grass*. And now, whatever one's opinion of the relative merits of this or that cluster of poems, it is difficult to dispute him.

4

Bearing the bandages, water and sponge,
Straight and swift to my wounded I go,
Where they lie on the ground after the battle brought in;
Where their priceless blood reddens the grass, the ground;
Or to the rows of the hospital tent, or under the roof'd hospital;
To the long rows of cots, up and down, each side, I return;
To each and all, one after another, I draw near—not one do I miss;
An attendent follows, holding a tray—he carries a refuse pail,
Soon to be fill'd with clotted rags and blood, emptied, and fill'd
      again.

5

I onward go, I stop,
With hinged knees and steady hand, to dress wounds;
I am firm with each—the pangs are sharp, yet unavoidable;
One turns to me his appealing eyes—(poor boy! I never knew you,
Yet I think I could not refuse this moment to die for you, if that
      would save you.)

6

On, on I go—(open doors of time! open hospital doors!)
The crush'd head I dress (poor crazed hand tear not the bandage
*   away;)*
The neck of the cavalry-man, with bullet through and through, I
*   examine;*
Hard the breathing rattles, quite glazed already the eye, yet life
*   struggles hard;*
(Come, sweet death! be persuaded, O beautiful death!
In mercy come quickly.)

7

From the stump of the arm, the amputated hand,
I undo the clotted lint, remove the slough, wash off the matter and
*   blood;*
Back on his pillow the soldier bends, with curv'd neck, and side-
*   falling head;*
His eyes are closed, his face is pale, he dares not look on the bloody
*   stump,*
And has not yet looked on it.

8

I dress a wound in the side, deep, deep;
But a day or two more—for see the frame all wasted and sinking,
And the yellow-blue countenance see.

9

I dress the perforated shoulder, the foot with the bullet-wound,
Cleanse the one with a gnawing and putrid gangrene, so sickening, so
*   offensive,*

While the attendant stands behind aside me, holding the tray and
*   pail.*

10
I am faithful, I do not give out;
The fractur'd thigh, the knee, the wound in the abdomen,
These and more I dress with impassive hand——(yet deep in my breast
*   a fire, a burning flame.)*

                                        ——from "The Dresser"

Whitman may have written his greatest poems before the war.
But war was in the air in the 1850s, as Lincoln, Sumner, Chase,
Seward, John Brown, and Robert E. Lee all knew. With the poet's
gift for prophecy and transcending the quotidian, Whitman had
published the first edition of *Leaves of Grass* knowing it was part of
a larger vision. "Song of Myself" not only belonged to the future, it
had been called into being by poems that were yet to be written. No
poem in Whitman's book was self-generating or self-sustaining——
all were interlinked, directed toward an end that lay beyond the war,
a new bible that would comprehend the fiery crucible and the triumph of the democratic ideal. It was meant to heal the nation.

———

"I thought no man more than Whitman merited recognition and
assistance from the government," John Trowbridge recalled. He
asked his friend if he would accept a job in one of the departments.
Whitman said he thought it unlikely he would ever get an appointment. But then he mentioned in an offhand way that he still had a
letter that Emerson had written to Salmon Chase on his behalf.
Intrigued, Trowbridge asked if he could see it.

Later Trowbridge asked if he might hold on to the Emerson

letter until such a moment as seemed proper to show it to the Secretary of the Treasury, "and with such furthering words as I could summon in so good a cause." Whitman remained skeptical. A government worker had once told him that upon seeing *Leaves of Grass* on his center table, Chase had said, "How is it possible you can have this nasty book here?" The poet insisted that if Trowbridge's venture failed, he wanted the precious Emerson letter returned to him.

There is something suspicious about this passage of Trowbridge's affectionate "Reminiscences of Walt Whitman," published forty years later. The Tuesday they breakfasted together was the opening day of the Thirty-eighth Congress, when Lincoln delivered his annual message to the House and Senate. The President praised the Treasury's performance and the enacting of the national banking law, its crowning achievement. Chase was polishing the Report of the Secretary of the Treasury, which would fill the front pages of the newspapers, and he was the subject of lavish editorial praise. He could not have been more proud than he was on December 10, busier, or more convinced of his chance to win the Republican nomination for president.

That Thursday morning, after breakfast, John Trowbridge followed the Secretary into his book-lined private office in the mansion. After some pleasant conversation, Trowbridge said: "I'm about to overstep a rule I laid down for myself on entering this house."

"What rule?" Chase's handsome features were distorted by a single flaw: his right eyelid drooped involuntarily, giving him a sinister look.

"Never to repay your hospitality by asking you any official favor."

Salmon Chase replied that he was happy to do for his friends the sort of things he was constantly asked to do for strangers. So Trowbridge laid Whitman's case before him, especially praising the poet's patriotic work in the hospitals. Then he showed his host Emerson's letter. Chase's eyes widened as he read the page. He was an avid autograph collector.

Having listened politely to Trowbridge's plea on Whitman's behalf, Chase responded with characteristic gravity, his deep voice marred by a lisp. "I am placed in a very embarrassing position. It would give me great pleasure to grant this request, out of my regard for Mr. Emerson." Then he went on to say that *Leaves of Grass* had made the author notorious; Chase was given to understand that Whitman was a rowdy—that he had even described himself as "one of the roughs."

Trowbridge said, "He is as quiet a gentleman in his manner and conversation as any guest who enters your door."

Nevertheless, Secretary Chase concluded, "his writings have given him a bad repute, and I should not know what sort of place to give such a man." The candidate for the presidency was taking no chances; if he could not fill a position with a partisan, he surely wasn't going to fill it with a poet of ill fame. If Trowbridge did not know this, and know of Whitman's devotion to Lincoln, he had no business calling himself Whitman's friend, or Chase's biographer.

Trowbridge offered to spare all three of them further embarrassment by withdrawing the Emerson letter; but Chase glanced again greedily at the Sage of Concord's signature and concluded, "I have nothing of Emerson's in his handwriting, and I shall be glad to keep this."

What could Whitman's friend have done? After all, the letter had been addressed to Salmon Chase.

Walt Whitman was an obsessive collector, too, which may be one of the reasons why he never had parted with Emerson's introductions to Seward or Chase. So when Trowbridge showed up at Whitman's lodging on Friday morning, abashed, the poet was scarcely disappointed that Chase had rejected his suit, but he "showed his amused disgust" when his friend explained how the letter had been pocketed by the Secretary.

Knowing that the Treasury had been accused of corruption, Whitman quipped, "He is right in preserving his saints from contamination by a man like me!" Trowbridge defended Chase, saying his employer could not be blamed for taking a writer at his word when he described himself as "rowdyish," "disorderly," and worse. He quoted Whitman his own line, "I cock my hat as I please, indoors and out," and Whitman laughed. He said, "It's about what I expected."

So one must wonder exactly what John Trowbridge's agenda had been on December 8, when he took the Emerson letter across the street from the tenement to the mansion. What feelings of remorse the writer must have suppressed when, forty years later, he apologized. "I should probably have had no difficulty in securing the appointment if I had withheld Emerson's letter, and called my friend simply Mr. Whitman, without mentioning *Leaves of Grass*." This is absurd. The novelist had tangled himself in his own web, covering an old lie with a new one. Trowbridge knew perfectly well he could not get Walt Whitman a position in Chase's department, but he certainly had delighted his new employer with the present of the Emerson autograph—briefly. Unknown to Trowbridge, Chase's conscience troubled him, and he surrendered the famous letter to the Treasury files.

To give some idea of the amount of money that was changing hands to get Chase nominated: Jay Cooke paid $2,000, a fortune in

Civil War dollars, to a bookseller in Boston to act as agent for a single transaction—to place a chapter of Trowbridge's campaign biography of Chase in the April issue of the *Atlantic Monthly*. (The President's monthly salary in 1863 was $2,022.34.) It is not known how much Chase's backers were paying Trowbridge for his writing. By December 22 Chase had agreed to release $640,000 of Treasury funds for the use of the Kansas-Pacific Railroad, which became the main source of money to finance the Chase-for-president movement; then the railroad men joined Kansas Senator Pomeroy and newsman Whitelaw Reid on the committee.

Although Salmon Chase had no sense of humor, his effort to appear uninterested in the presidency while pursuing the office with fanatic ambition and acrobatic exertions seemed comical to Lincoln and Hay—until it became a genuine challenge. Only Chase had the stature and the progressive credentials to consolidate the radical wing of the Republican Party, and abolitionists like Charles Sumner and Horace Greeley had long been out of patience with Lincoln's moderate leadership. Chase was a real threat. On January 18, 1864, the Secretary wrote to a major supporter in Ohio: "At the instance of many who think that the public interest would be promoted by my election in the chief magistry, a committee, composed of prominent Senators and Representatives and citizens, has been organized here for taking measures to promote that object." Chase hastened to add that all his protests had failed to discourage the venture, and "under these circumstances, I desire the support of Ohio." He had made it public that he was available.

Mary Lincoln's feelings about Chase anticipated a chorus of Lincoln's friends who cried that the traitor ought to be drummed out of the cabinet. The President, fully aware that Salmon Chase was the most formidable opponent against him for the nomination, seemed unperturbed by his politicking, or by charges that Chase had been filling department posts with men who would get him elected. As long as the Secretary performed his duties competently—and he did—Lincoln said he had no intention of replacing him.

By late summer Lincoln had all but given up hope of a second term. But, by one of those perverse tricks of history that must have tormented Chase until the day he died, he was not the man to dash Lincoln's hopes. Chase appears to have been undone by his own immoderate ambition, which infected the men he trusted to promote him, in surprising ways.

Lincoln, with his uncanny political instincts, may have sensed that Chase or his men would overdo things. When he found himself bewildered about how to handle a problem, Lincoln's style was to sit back and wait it out. So he waited for Chase to blunder. In all fairness, it was not Chase who blundered—it was his "committee." The Chase-for-president committee might have been an inspiration for the Keystone Cops or the Gang That Couldn't Shoot Straight. As the dignified candidate looked on in horror, they sank his promising campaign in only six weeks, eight full months in advance of the election.

Chase's publicists began by sending out an anonymous pamphlet, "The Next Presidential Election," a diatribe against Lincoln and all those who were trying to secure his nomination for a second term. This "vascillation [*sic*] and indecisiveness of the President . . . the feebleness of his will" and his "want of intellectual grasp . . . has been the real cause why our well-appointed armies have not succeeded in the destruction of the rebellion." Ward Hill Lamon first saw this "most scurrilous and abusive pamphlet" on February 6. It drew a little support for Chase in the religious press and the more radical dailies. But the tone of the circular was so

vehement it attracted far more attention among Lincoln's supporters than Chase's. When it appeared in Ohio under the frank of
Senator Sherman, one correspondent wrote that the document was
so dastardly that "it will brand with infamy your character as a
statesman and your honor as a gentleman."

Certainly the Chase committee's circular was insolent and ill
timed; moreover, the authors had underestimated Lincoln's political organization and grassroots support in states they had targeted.
Oblivious, in mid-February the publicists circulated a second anti-
Lincoln pamphlet announcing that the reelection of Abraham Lincoln was "practically impossible" and would damage "the cause of
human liberty and the dignity and honor of the nation." This time
the manifesto was signed by Kansas Senator Samuel Pomeroy.
And he boldly announced that Salmon Chase possessed "more of
the qualities needed in a President during the next four years, than
are combined in any other available candidate."

The infamous "Pomeroy Circular," widely published, galva-
nized support for the incumbent President, and it embarrassed
Secretary Chase, who claimed that he had no knowledge of the
tract before it was printed, and that he was a reluctant candidate
who had been ill used by his admirers. A cabinet member, he now
appeared a traitor to the man who had appointed him.

Chase offered his resignation. Lincoln, after letting him floun-
der for a week, calmly responded that he did "not perceive occasion for a change" in the Treasury. He chose not to accept the
resignation, knowing what lay in store for his shamed adversary.

On February 24, the Ohio State Republican convention urged
Lincoln's nomination; three days later Lincoln's friend Congressman Francis P. Blair Jr. attacked Chase on the floor of the House,
blaming him for widespread corruption in the Treasury Department. And referring to the Pomeroy Circular, Blair expressed

surprise "that a man having the instincts of a gentleman should remain in the cabinet after the disclosure of such an intrigue . . . every hour he remains sinks him deeper in the contempt of every honorable mind."

Humiliated, Chase withdrew his candidacy on March 5, 1864. He explained that his home state, Ohio, preferred another candidate. Chase had ended his run for the presidency, although almost no one believed it.

9

WILDERNESS

January's bitter cold gave way in February to a southern wind and two weeks of mild weather that thawed the earth and began to dry the roads, promising an early spring.

Sometime during that winter of 1863–1864, according to William O'Connor's brief biography *The Good Gray Poet* (1865), Walt Whitman was taking a stroll along the rutted road in front of the White House. "Slow of movement," a friend had described him, "inclined to walk with a lounging gait which somebody has likened to an elephantine roll . . . head massive, complexion florid-tawny." His white hair and the wrinkles in his brow made him look older than his forty-five years.

As O'Connor tells it, a congressman, accompanied by his friend A. Van Rensellaer, had come to visit the President on business. When they found that Lincoln was not in his second-story office, they looked for him downstairs. The three met in the vestibule, and the President led them into the East Room, where they stood by the front windows. There the congressman had his four-minute interview with Lincoln and handed him a letter. Lincoln glanced at it, then raised his eyes to watch as a man passed by outside. The figure was familiar to him from his summer carriage rides to the Soldiers' Home—the old man with kind eyes who had stood by the curb on Vermont Avenue in the evenings, waving to him, nodding, exchanging courtesies. The man moved slowly, his hands thrust into the pockets of his overcoat, his broad-brimmed hat tipped back on his head.

Lincoln asked who the man walking by the White House was. Van Rensellaer told the President that the fellow was Walt Whitman, the poet who had written *Leaves of Grass* and other things, letters and articles for the New York press.

"Mr. Lincoln didn't say anything but took a long look till you were quite gone by," Van Rensellaer reported to Whitman in a letter on July 30, 1865.

"Then he says," Van Rensellaer wrote, "(I can't give you his way of saying it but it was quite emphatic and odd) 'Well,' he says, '*he* looks like a *man*.' He said it pretty loud but in a sort of absent way and with the emphasis on the words I have underscored. He didn't say any more but began to talk about the letter and in a minute or so we went off."

Because this is the only testimony apart from Whitman's that the President ever recognized him by sight, the letter has been scrutinized repeatedly. (After Whitman's death the document passed into the distinguished collection of Oscar Lion.) Reverend William E. Barton called the letter a fraud, arguing that Van Rensselaer did not exist. Trying to prove, in the late 1920s, that a man did *not* exist in 1865—when a letter with his signature on it has survived—is a tortuous exercise. Anyone interested may read Barton's elaborate complaint in his 1928 book on Whitman and Lincoln.

Let us imagine that Lincoln's observation of Whitman that winter happened as described. Even Barton, after all, admitted: "The incident as related in the letter of A. Van Rensellaer is not inherently improbable. It might even have occurred just as it is told."

Historiography assigns due weight to hard facts, prudently distinguishing degrees of authenticity that separate myths from true events. Van Rensellaer's story is not intrinsically significant history, even in a book about Lincoln and Whitman. And it has been vigorously disputed. Its importance lies in the value with which Whitman, his friends, and subsequent generations have endowed it. Whitman believed that the President had spoken those words. The affinity he felt for Lincoln was thereby sanctioned: Lincoln might have taken courage in the poet's quiet affection, his salubrious influence, even from afar.

During this season, the President had been bedridden with variola minor (a kind of smallpox), overwhelmed by military responsibilities and problems in planning for Reconstruction, and surrounded by schemers worse than Salmon Chase. Lincoln must have felt like a prisoner. One of his best friends, Illinois Congressman Owen Lovejoy, was dying. At fifty-three, Lovejoy was three years younger than the President. Visiting his friend's sickbed on February 6, Lincoln said: "This war is eating my life out. I have a strong impression I shall not live to see the end." Yet he was bound to be reelected. Ambition had lured him into the marble mansion, and now his sense of duty had trapped him there.

Gazing out the window at the freewheeling poet ambling past, tall, brawny, his hair and beard growing wild, the spirit of the open country breezing about his loose clothing, Lincoln might certainly have remarked with admiration and envy, "Well, *he* looks like a *man*," as much as to say, *There's nobody here in this mausoleum who*

looks much like a man these days, including myself. The President
would have been struck by the difference between the guileless,
homespun poet of *Leaves of Grass,* avatar of truth and liberty, and
the slick courtiers who assailed him daily in the White House.

Fact or myth, the story endures. It has earned an important
place in the Lincoln-Whitman dossier because the poet so passionately loved and believed it.

———

Spring brought the fragrance of lilacs and blossoming magnolias,
the purple Judas trees, sassafras, and the spreading branches of
white-blossomed dogwood. The war would heat up with the
weather.

Weary of his routine in Washington, Whitman confided in an
officer friend, "I had a great desire to be present at a first class battle." Having studied the war's effect on his soldiers, he wanted to
witness the gunfire and saber strokes that caused their wounds.
More than once he had expressed his wish to join the army and
fight side by side with his comrades. That spring he would write,
"it has no terrors for me, if I had to be hit in battle, as far as I
myself am concerned—it would be a noble and manly death, & in
the best cause."

Accompanying his boss Major Hapgood on a paymaster's mission to Culpeper, Virginia, in February, Whitman came close
enough to the front lines to help out in division hospitals. He found
no wounded men there, only "some poor creatures crawling about
pretty weak with diarrhea . . . they keep them till they get very bad
indeed, & then send them to Washington." He saw no battles or
bloodshed, and wrote to his mother: "have had a very good time,
over woods, hills, & gullys, indeed a real soldier's march . . . I
never cease to crave more & more knowledge of actual soldiers'

life and to be among them as much as possible." A few days of it
satisfied Whitman, who understood that his duty lay in the Washington hospitals. "I am very clear that the real need of one's services is there after all—there the worst cases concentrate, &
probably will, while the war lasts."

There was not much fighting until April, so it was mostly "sick
cases" that arrived at the hospitals. Diarrhea was the worst
scourge, killing more soldiers than gunfire. In addition, Whitman
wrote, "There is a great deal of rheumatism & also throat diseases,
& they are affected by the weather." One soldier, who seemed to
Whitman quite young, groaned as the stretcher bearers carried
him through the hospital gates. When they set down the stretcher
to examine him they found he had died. "The worst of it is too that
he is entirely unknown . . . it is enough to rack one's heart, such
things—very likely his folks will never know in the world what
has become of him—poor, poor child, for he appeared as though
he could be but 18."

Whitman's letters home are full of dread, "to think that we are
to have here soon what I have seen so many times, the awful loads
& trains & boat loads of poor bloody & pale & wounded young
men again . . . I see all the little signs, getting ready in the hospitals
& c." Anticipating Grant's offensive in May, the commanders in
the South were clearing out the division hospitals, sending the
dregs of the sick and wounded to Washington. At the end of
March Whitman wrote: "I feel lately as though I must have some
intermission . . . my feelings are kept in a painful condition a great
part of the time—things get worse and worse, as to the amount &
sufferings of the sick . . ." And the doctors and nurses were getting "more callous and indifferent."

During those tense months of waiting for the next offensive,
the poet developed a strong attachment to an Ohio boy named

Oscar Cunningham. He had arrived at Armory Square with a bad gunshot wound high in his right thigh. Whitman said that when he first saw Oscar he thought the fellow ought to be a sculptor's model, "for an emblematical figure of the west." He was a handsome giant with a large head and golden hair, "thick and longish & a manly noble manner and talk." The doctors were trying to save his limb. But as of April 12, the poet noted it was in "horrible condition, all livid & swollen out of shape." Erysipelas had inflamed his leg and foot. While the doctors remained hopeful about this case, Whitman was disheartened.

Another man who occupied the poet's thoughts was one of many wasting away from dysentery. The soldier's dwindling from the full figure of manhood—from flesh, blood, muscle, and sinew to skin and bone—became an allegory of Whitman's own waning strength and courage during that terrible season.

At night the patient to whom Whitman only refers by the pathetic sobriquet "the diarrhea man" desired Whitman to ask God's blessing on him before leaving. "I am no scholar & you are," he whispered to the poet.

"Poor dying man, I told him from the bottom of my heart God would bless him, & bring him up yet—I soothed him as well as I could, it was affecting, I can tell you."

Much of Whitman's correspondence from this period concerns the whereabouts and welfare of his brother George, still a captain in the Fifty-first New York Regiment, under Burnside's command. George was not able to write nearly enough letters to please his mother and assure her of his safety. In the Federal City, between the military hospitals and the halls of Congress, Whitman had rich sources of intelligence concerning troop movements, and sometimes second- or third-hand news of George himself. The poet's circle of friends in Washington had grown to include John

Burroughs, working in the Treasury; Ohio Congressman James Garfield; and New York Congressmen Martin Kalbfleisch and Anson Herrick. If Lincoln got reelected, there was still a possibility Whitman might have a job in the administration.

But for the time being he was giving his full attention to the hospital work, grateful for every day that passed without his brother coming through the door of Ward K on a stretcher. So one can imagine Whitman's excitement after the rainy night of April 24, as he woke to the sun breaking through the clouds and rumors that Burnside's army was marching in from Annapolis. There was nothing about troop movements in the newspapers.

Burnside's entire Ninth Corps, thirty thousand strong, was on its way to join Grant's army in Virginia. The parade marched down Fourteenth Street in mud past the Willard Hotel, where the President waited with General Burnside to review the troops. Lincoln stood with his head uncovered on that cool, clear day, behind the curved balustrade above the southeastern portico, smiling at the soldiers, from the first flag-bearer and drummer to the last footsore private; the tall Commander-in-Chief kept smiling and waving most of the day. John Burroughs joined Walt Whitman for three hours, as he stood across the street just to Lincoln's left, alternately watching the President and looking north, scanning the faces of oncoming soldiers, looking for his brother.

Now and then a mud-spattered soldier would recognize Whitman, leap out of line and hug his old friend, then run to rejoin his outfit.

After three hours Walt picked George out of the ranks. "I joined him just before they came to where the President & General Burnside were standing with others on a balcony." In the excitement of seeing his brother for the first time in a year, Captain Whitman forgot to salute the President, forgot indeed to search for Lincoln's face in the group looking down on the parade and the crowd. Walt fell in to march at his brother's side, greeting him warmly before pointing out President Lincoln behind them on the portico. George "was a little annoyed at forgetting it—I called his attention to it, but we had passed a little too far on." And Captain Whitman, observing strict military decorum, "wouldn't turn round even ever so little."

The Corps was headed south for Long Bridge, the wide ranks stepping quickly, and the poet marched with his brother "for some distance & had quite a talk—he is very well, he is very much tanned and looks hardy, I told him all the latest news from home— George stands it very well, & looks & behaves the same good & noble fellow he always was & always will be." According to John Hay: "This is the finest looking & best appointed force I have ever seen . . . a little gorgeous and showy . . ." Both Hay and Whitman admired the five regiments of new black troops, Hay observing that they "looked well & marched better than others: As in fact they always do," and the poet expressing the anomaly of the President saluting Negroes, "with his hat off to them just the same as the rest as they passed by."

Whitman's letter to his mother the next day captures the glory of the five-hour parade, and also his underlying sadness. "Mother, it was a curious sight to see these ranks after ranks of our own dearest blood of men, mostly young, march by, worn & sunburnt & sweaty . . . it is a great sight to see such a big Army . . . they are all so gay too, poor fellows." Whitman did not know exactly where the army was headed, "only that there is without doubt to be a terrible campaign here in Virginia this summer . . . I do not feel to fret or whimper, but in my heart and soul about our country, the army, the forthcoming campaign with all its vicissitudes & the wounded & slain—I daresay, Mother, I feel the reality more than some because I am in the midst of its saddest results so much."

Walt's brother and the rest of Burnside's army were marching into the nightmare Battle of the Wilderness, less than ten days away.

———

On April 27 Whitman sat at the bedside of a soldier of the Sixth of Maine who had just had his leg amputated. The boy was calmed now, by morphine and the poet's presence, and Whitman was taking a quiet moment to write a letter to James Kirkwood, a patron. "The sick are coming in pretty freely here, poor wrecks and phantoms—a sign of action, as they are breaking up the field hospitals. One's heart bleeds for them . . . if you have any friends able to send me aid . . . show them this letter . . ."

The sight of Lincoln's kind face on Monday had inspired him. "I see the President often. I think better of him than many do. He has conscience & homely shrewdness—conceals an enormous tenacity under his mild, gawky western manner." Tenacity was what Whitman wanted, the strength to endure the crisis in Washington. "The difficulties of his situation have been unprecedented in the history of statesmanship. That he has conserved the government so far is a miracle in itself."

That Lincoln kept himself sane was another kind of miracle. With only the vaguest sense of Grant's battle plans, the President awaited a catastrophe. "Grant has gone into the Wilderness, crawled in, drawn up the ladder, and pulled in the hole after him," the President told the curious. Some who saw him that week said he was so despondent they could hardly look at him without weeping. Yet John Hay recalled that one night when the secretaries were working after midnight the President came into the office laughing uproariously. He was wearing his nightshirt and clutching a volume of Thomas Hood's humorous writings. He couldn't contain his mirth, but had to read aloud to Nicolay and Hay the tale about "An Unfortunate Bee-ing." Lincoln was oblivious that with the nightshirt "hanging about his long legs & setting out behind like the tail feathers of an enormous ostrich he was infinitely funnier than anything in the book he was laughing at."

Hay was struck, as Whitman would have been, by the complexity of Lincoln's personality: "Occupied all day with matters of vast moment, deeply anxious about the fate of the greatest army in the world, with his own fame & future hanging on the events of the passing hour, he yet has such a wealth of simple bonhommie & good fellow ship that he gets out of bed & perambulates the house in his shirt to find us," in order to share the pleasure he was taking in one of Hood's little jokes.

During that first week in May, Lincoln scarcely slept. There were black rings under his eyes. "I *must* have some relief from this terrible anxiety," he said, "or it will kill me." He went to the opera and sat in his box "either enjoying the music or communing with himself," one reporter observed. In the middle of the night he read Shakespeare, or Thomas Hood.

The "Wilderness" was aptly named, a thirty-mile-long stretch of woods, thorny underbrush, and swampland below Culpeper. Grant hoped to move his army swiftly through the forest and attack Lee's forces on open ground north of Richmond. But knowing that the density of thickets, second-growth trees, and the uneven ground would countercheck Grant's greater numbers, Lee decided to ambush the Federals in the Wilderness on May 5.

For two days and nights the armies struggled savagely in the gloom. Gun smoke mixed with the haze of brushfires ignited by red-hot bullets made it impossible for soldiers to see more than a few yards ahead. They fired and hacked away blindly, often killing their own men. The stench of burning flesh filled the air. Sparks from the flaming tinder caused cartridge bandoliers to detonate, sending shells slicing through the torsos of the men wearing them. Rather than dying from the flames that engulfed them, wounded fighters took their own lives. One Confederate soldier called it "a butchery pure and simple." Grant's aide-de-camp wrote, "It seemed as though Christian men had turned to fiends and hell itself had usurped the place of earth."

Twenty-two thousand men were killed and wounded in the battle. The only welcomed news that reached the telegraph office was Grant's resolution not to give up. "I propose to fight it out on this line if it takes all summer," he stated. When Lincoln read this telegram to a crowd outside the White House, people did not know whether to cheer or weep. As Grant marched on to Spotsylvania, some (including Mary Lincoln) called the cigar-chewing General a butcher.

Ambulances jammed the highways heading for Falmouth. Whistling steamers arrived every hour at the Sixth Street wharves with their gruesome cargo of dead and wounded men.

"The arrivals, the numbers, and the severity of the wounds, outvied anything that we had seen before," Whitman wrote. "For days and weeks the melancholy tide set in upon us. The weather was very hot; the wounded had been delayed in coming, and much neglected. Very many of the wounds had worms in them. An unusual portion mortified [became gangrenous]."

Whitman continued to report on Oscar Cunningham and the soldier who was wasting away from dysentery—as if his own fate was somehow bound up in theirs. "The poor fellow . . . with diarrhea . . . is only partly conscious, is all wasted away to nothing, & lies most of the time in half stupor, as they give him brandy copiously—yesterday I was there by him a few minutes, he is very much averse to taking brandy . . ." The man was painfully dehydrated; naturally the last thing he wanted was the fiery liquor, and he fought the medics who tried to make him drink it. "He is almost totally deaf the last five or six days—there is no chance for him at all." On May 6 the soldier was still alive, "but O what a looking object, death would be a boon to him, he cannot last many hours . . ."

At last Oscar had his leg amputated, high up on the thigh. He "has picked up beyond expectation, now looks altogether like getting well," Whitman noted. But on May 10 Whitman wrote: "the poor diarrhea man died, & it was a boon—Oscar Cunningham, 82nd Ohio, has had a relapse, I fear it is going bad with him—lung diseases are quite plenty—night before last I staid in hospital all night tending a poor fellow . . ."

Whitman was pushing himself. On May 18 he admitted, "I am pretty tired, & my head feels disagreeable, from being in too much." He took comfort in the good news from a wounded man in his brother's regiment that George was unhurt. Then Walt learned that the house where he had been living had been sold and he would have to move. He hastily rented a third-story hall bedroom at 502 Pennsylvania Avenue, near the Capitol. Unfortunately the new dwelling stood near the fetid canal that ran along the mall and into a ditch of stagnant water at Third Street. Soon Whitman was complaining of the bad air and spending a lot of time writing his letters in the lobby of the Willard Hotel.

"Mother, it is just the same old story," he wrote wearily on May 25, "poor suffering young men, great swarms of them come up here, now, every day, all battered and bloody . . . 4000 arrived here this morning, & 1500 yesterday." Oscar Cunningham was sinking rapidly. "Said to me yesterday, O if he could only die."

"One new feature," the poet observed, "is that many of the poor afflicted young men are crazy, every ward has some in it that are wandering—they have suffered too much, & it is perhaps a privilege that they are out of their senses."

"Mother, it is most too much for a fellow, & I sometimes wish I was out of it—but I suppose it is because I have not felt first rate myself," he had written on May 7. On May 30 Whitman complained of a headache, a fullness in the skull he often felt in hot weather, and four days later he told his mother, "if this campaign was not in progress I should not stop here, as it is now beginning to tell on me, so many bad wounds, many putrified, & all kinds of dreadful ones, I have been rather too much with . . ."

He had just come from Cunningham's bedside. The soldier was dying, beyond hope. The smiling, golden-haired giant of a man Whitman had thought fit for a sculptor's model was "all wasted away to a skeleton, & looks like some one fifty years old." And now he was always petulant, or angry with everyone but Whitman. Congressman Martin Kalbfleisch walked into the ward where Whitman was writing a letter, looked around him at the human wreckage, trembled, and burst into tears.

Oscar died at two o'clock in the morning, Sunday, June 5. "It was a blessed relief, his life has been misery for months—the cause of death at last was the system absorbing the pus . . ."

On June 10 the doctors told Whitman he had spent too much time in Armory Square, where the worst wounds were, and had, Whitman wrote, "absorbed too much of the virus in my system." Four days later they asked him to stay out of the hospitals for the time being—advice he evidently did not heed. By June 17 he was so stricken, the ward master ordered him to return to Brooklyn for a fortnight. Whitman never mentions a diagnosis, but the physicians told him he must leave town, that he needed "an entire change of air, & c."

He would not return to Washington for six months. By that time the war would be almost over.

WHY LINCOLN LAUGHED

The picture of the President in his nightshirt on the eve of the Battle of the Wilderness, convulsed with laughter, bursting to share with his overworked secretaries Thomas Hood's joke, is a staple of Lincoln biographies. Curiously, no account of the incident mentions which of Thomas Hood's myriad stories and poems Lincoln read aloud to Nicolay and Hay—what at that critical moment the sleep-deprived President found so funny. In his diary Hay refers to the piece as "An Unfortunate Bee-ing." Is there such a story?

Thomas Hood (1799–1845) was an English poet and humorist whom laughter served as the best medicine against the depredations of poverty and consumption. He was also an ingenious illustrator who drew hilarious double-entendre caricatures for his own stories. Some of these featured an honest, well-intentioned yeoman who stumbles into preposterous disasters.

There is no *tale* in Hood's eight-volume *Complete Works* called "An Unfortunate Bee-ing." Hay, in his description of the event in his diary, seems to have mistaken the caption to an illustration for the story's title.

On page 531 of an 1860 collection, *The Choice Works of Thomas Hood,* the mystery is solved: there is the illustration and story that Lincoln found so amusing. It shows a man who has knocked over a beehive. His back is to us, his fists are raised skyward in imprecation, his right knee is lifted as if by an antic dance he might shake off the bees that pour from the broken hive and surround him. The caricature illustrates "The Scrape-Book," a story first published in a comic annual in 1831. Under the title is the epigram "Luck's All!"

> Some men seem born to be lucky. Happier than kings, Fortune's wheel has for them no revolutions . . . At games of chance they have no chance; but what is better, a certainty. They get windfalls, without a breath stirring—as legacies. Prizes turn up for them in lotteries. At the very worst in trying to drown themselves, they dive on some treasure undiscovered since the Spanish Armada; or tie their halter to a hook, that unseals a hoard in the ceiling. That's their luck.
>
> There is another kind of fortune, called ill-luck; so ill, that you hope it will die;—but it don't. That's my luck.
>
> Other people keep scrap-books; but I, a scrape-book.

The next three pages take the form of a fictional diary (coincidentally for April and May, when Lincoln was reading it), narrating the mishaps and calamities of Hood's "Unfortunate" and his long-suffering bride, Belinda. These include being run down in a rowboat by a coal-brig, and then "providentially picked up by a steamer that burst her boiler . . . Saved to be scalded!" Throwing a punch at a thief attempting to snatch Belinda's purse, the man misses the thief and blackens Belinda's eye, whereupon "Belinda's part is taken by a big rascal, as deaf as a post, who wanted to fight me for striking a woman." Then his number comes up in the lottery—but he loses the ticket.

The centerpiece of this catalog of misadventures concerns the week of the protagonist's wedding day, April Fools' Day, when he stumbles over his father-in-law's beehives.

> He has 252 bees: thanks to me he is now able to check them. Some of the insects, having an account against me, preferred to *settle* on my calf. Others swarmed on my hands. My bald head seemed a perfect hummingtop! . . . Rushed bee-blind into the horsepond, and *torn out* by Tiger, the housedog. Staggered incontinent into the pigsty, and collared by the sow . . . for kicking her sucklings.

Wanting oil for his wounds, he finds only "lamp-oil"—the irritant kerosene.

> Relieved of the stings at last—what luck!—by 252 operations.

The novelist William Makepeace Thackeray said that "humor is the mistress of tears," and Lincoln himself excused one of his laughing fits with the comment "I laugh because I must not cry; that is all; that is all." But "The Scrape-Book" and Thomas Hood's drawing of "An Unfortunate Bee-ing" are so relevant to Lincoln's own predicament in 1864 that the emblem warrants close examination. As fancifully rendered by Hood, the ovoid hive is broken in half; the top half rests on a bench, like a little igloo, while the bottom is turned up, on the ground next to the unfortunate victim's feet. Bees rush from both hemispheres to attack the hapless bridegroom.

An Unfortunate Bee-ing

A more perfect caricature of the broken Union of States, the furious citizens of the North and South, and Lincoln's ill luck in happening upon the presidency at this moment could scarcely be devised. Will Rogers said that "everything is funny as long as it's happening to someone else," but the more familiar the fool, the more disposed we are to laugh, relieved that this time we have escaped his folly and torment. Lincoln delighted in wordplay and the reductio ad absurdum. For these reasons and others he laughed that night as he read aloud, to John Hay and John Nicolay, Thomas Hood's story "The Scrape-Book."

There were a few more days left in 1864 than there were bees in Hood's story. The President was stung most days, especially during the summer by the members of his own party. Lincoln's problem—fortunately for posterity—was that he kept doing what he thought was right, often with flagrant disregard for public sentiment and party politics. Grant's pursuit of Lee that spring from the inferno of the Wilderness to a crushing defeat at Cold Harbor had cost the Union fifty thousand men. Mary Lincoln complained: "Grant is a butcher and not fit to be at the head of an army. He loses two men to the enemy's one. He has no management, no regard for life . . ." At the height of widespread antiwar demonstrations in the North and South, and appeals to Lincoln to negotiate for peace, the President stood behind Grant and issued a call for five hundred thousand more volunteers. It seemed that the entire Union was tilting toward Virginia and men were spilling into a deep ditch near Richmond, where Grant smoked cigars and whittled, waiting for the abyss to fill so he could march across it and finish the horrid war.

Disapproval of Lincoln was so widespread that a week before the National Union Convention in Baltimore, which would nominate him for a second term, a group of disgruntled Republicans held a rump convention in Cleveland. On May 31 many liberals, including Elizabeth Cady Stanton, William Cullen Bryant, and radical followers of Wendell Phillips, convened to protest "the imbecile and vacillating policy of the present Administration in the conduct of the war" and to nominate their handsome hero John C. Frémont for president.

Frémont might represent a serious threat, Hay confided to Lincoln, if he had more ability.

"Yes," said Lincoln, "he is like Jim Jett's brother. Jim used to say that his brother was the damnedest scoundrel that ever lived but in the infinite mercy of Providence he was also the damnedest fool."

The Ohio convention fizzled, as newsmen like Greeley, who at first welcomed the movement, withdrew their support. Prominent Eastern Republicans like Sumner stayed away, fearful of permanently alienating Lincoln. Nevertheless, the Frémont candidacy might divide the party sooner or later, depending upon Grant's performance on the battlefield. Frémont continued to challenge Lincoln long after the Baltimore convention of the National Union (Republican) Party. There, on June 7, Abraham Lincoln and Andrew Johnson were unanimously nominated to run on a ticket whose platform included a constitutional amendment abolishing slavery.

In Baltimore there was agreement but little enthusiasm; a sense of inevitability in the nomination—almost resignation. Illinois Republican Clark Carr murmured that the people "think that God tried his best when he made Mr. Lincoln and they are all for his re-election." Lincoln's campaign manager David Davis told him, "the opposition is so utterly beaten that the fight is not even interesting." In fact, there was no prominent Republican other than Frémont—and the invalidated Chase—who wanted Lincoln's job during that terrible time. It looked doubtful that any Republican could win the office, and it seemed only fitting and just that Lincoln should be the man to lose it.

He occupied a lonely height where he saw dangers invisible to others. Knowing the precarious balance of politics in New York, he fought Salmon Chase's appointment of an incompetent Radical for the important position of assistant treasurer of the United States in New York City. Chase had grown accustomed, when crossed, to expressing his indignation by formally tendering his resignation, ever confident the President would not accept it. This time, the fourth, Lincoln stunned the Secretary and outraged the liberal Senators—not only by accepting Chase's resignation, but by naming a successor within hours.

A deputation of Chase's friends scurried to the White House, demanding an explanation for the change in the cabinet. Lincoln described his disagreement with Chase over the New York appointment; then he told them what he had written to Chase the day before: "You and I have reached a point of mutual embarrassment in our official relation which it seems cannot be overcome, or longer sustained." The President was not about to imperil the Union Party's power in New York State for the sake of Salmon Chase's delicate pride.

In late June the thermometer climbed into the nineties and hovered there as Congress remained in session long after adjournment time. In withering heat they had been debating a Reconstruction bill, drafted by Maryland Congressman Henry Winter Davis and Senator "Bluff" Ben Wade of Ohio, two radicals sworn to derail Lincoln's own moderate plans for Reconstruction, already under way in Louisiana and Tennessee. The Wade-Davis Bill passed narrowly in the Senate by an 18–14 vote on July 2. The congressional plan was more stringent than Lincoln's: it required a majority of voters—swearing allegiance to the Union—to set up a new state government, rather than 10 percent; it barred most former secessionist leaders from voting and office holding, rather than a few; and it refused to pay the Confederacy's war debts. The central point of the bill, however, was the immediate emancipation of slaves in all the states. On July 4, the document lay on Lincoln's desk in his grand office in the Capitol, and the weary legislators were waiting for him to sign it, so they could go home.

He would not sign the bill, though he carefully read and signed others. When the Radical Senator Zachariah Chandler from

Michigan peevishly pointed out, "the important point is *that* one prohibiting slavery in the reconstructed states," Lincoln coolly replied: "That is the point on which I doubt the authority of Congress to act." The lawyer in Lincoln was speaking, and so was the political visionary. Abolition was not a matter for Congress to decide by legislation. Nothing short of an amendment to the Constitution, or the slow deliberation of the separate states, would put an end to slavery.

When Chandler fumed, "It is no more than you have done yourself," the President replied, "I may in an emergency do things on military grounds which cannot be done constitutionally by Congress."

Lincoln's pocket veto of the Wade-Davis Bill was one of the most courageous uses of executive power in American history, and certainly the most contentious. "I am inconsolable," Charles Sumner lamented. Lincoln knew he was in for trouble, but explained to John Hay, "At all events, I must keep some consciousness of being somewhere near right: I must keep some standard of principle fixed within myself." He could not have foreseen the virulence of the backlash in his own party.

In August, Ben Wade asked Horace Greeley to publish a manifesto attacking Lincoln for the pocket veto of Congress's plan for Reconstruction. Greeley, long exasperated with the President, and freshly piqued by his own failure to negotiate peace with the Rebels at a conference in Niagara Falls, was only too happy to give two and a half columns of the *Tribune* to Wade and Davis's proclamation, "To the Supporters of the Government."

The Congressmen wrote: "A more studied outrage on the legislative authority of the people has never been perpetrated." Charging Lincoln with "dictatorial usurpation" and calling his veto a "rash and fatal act . . . a blow at the friends of his Administration, at the rights of humanity, and at the principles of republican government," the two Republicans menaced Lincoln's renomination.

"If he wishes our support," they wrote, "he must confine himself to his executive duties—to obey and execute, not make the laws—to suppress by arms armed Rebellion, and to leave political reorganization to Congress."

The document was unique in the annals of American history, shocking to all who read it, regardless of their politics. Nicolay and Hay would call the Wade-Davis manifesto "the most vigorous attack that was ever directed against the President from his own party during his term." It was clearly a maneuver to destroy Lincoln's candidacy. James Gordon Bennett, writing for the *New York Herald*, predicted that the manifesto would bring about a new convention that would annul the nominations of both Frémont in Cleveland and Lincoln in Baltimore and replace them with a ticket of "acknowledged ability and patriotism." Bennett called for Lincoln to withdraw voluntarily. Thurlow Weed, who had done so much for Lincoln in New York, told Benjamin Butler: "Lincoln is gone, I suppose you know as well as I. And unless a hundred thousand men are raised sooner than the draft, the country's gone too."

As if on cue, in the midst of the Wade-Davis fracas, Rebel forces under General Jubal A. Early had stolen upon Harpers Ferry and crossed the Potomac to attack Washington. How could such a large Confederate army have gotten so far north as to threaten the capital itself? It had been bad enough that Grant's siege of Petersburg had failed to dislodge Lee from his labyrinth of trenches. Now Lincoln had to suffer the embarrassment of an invasion. If Early occupied Washington for forty-eight hours, the Union would be disgraced and the Confederacy recognized abroad.

In his long frock coat and stovepipe hat Lincoln stood on the parapet of Fort Stevens and watched the Confederate soldiers approach, overwhelming the Union pickets, until the Rebels came within shooting distance. A man standing near the President was shot in the leg. Worse things could befall the President than being shot by an enemy soldier on the earthworks of Fort Stevens. Small wonder that Lincoln stood defiantly, spyglass in hand, remaining a conspicuous target until General Horatio Wright warned he would have him forcibly removed. At least the raiders weren't Republicans. As Lincoln confessed to Noah Brooks, "To be wounded in the house of one's friends is perhaps the most grievous affliction that can befall a man." He had been made to suffer more keenly at the hands of Ben Wade and Horace Greeley than he had been thus far by the Democrats or the Rebels.

Early's troops retreated, but General Wright did not pursue them. So the President had one more military fiasco to add to his political humiliations. Only laughter could relieve him. As groups of Radical Republicans were meeting in Boston, Cincinnati, and New York to discuss replacing Lincoln, he joked:

> It reminds me of an old acquaintaince, who, having a son of a scientific turn, bought him a microscope. The boy went around, experimenting with his glass upon everything that came his way. One day, at the dinner table, his father took up a piece of cheese. "Don't eat that, father," said the boy; "it is full of wrigglers."
>
> "My son," replied the old gentleman, taking at the same time, a huge bite, "let 'em *wriggle;* I can stand it if they can."

New York moderate Thurlow Weed believed that Lincoln's insistence on making the abolition of slavery a condition for any peace negotiations was extreme. "As things stand now Mr. Lincoln's re-election is an impossibility. The people are wild for Peace." Even Weed had begun flirting with the Democrats, who were willing to give up the cause of abolition to preserve the Union.

A week before the Democratic Convention, Henry Raymond, chairman of the executive committee of Lincoln's party, warned him: "The tide is setting strongly against us."

Not the least of Lincoln's liabilities was his wife, shuttling to and from New York on shopping sprees and secret, quixotic missions to garner political support from the likes of Thurlow Weed and the hostile newspaperman James Gordon Bennett, meanwhile renegotiating her bills with the Broadway merchants. A two-thousand-dollar lace shawl. Two diamond-and-pearl bracelets. Commissioner of public buildings Benjamin French knew of "rumors that Democrats are getting up something in which they intend to show up Madame Lincoln." This would not be difficult. She had run up personal debts of twenty-seven thousand dollars. Mary was more concerned about the coming election than was her husband, upon separate grounds: "If he is elected," she told Elizabeth Keckley, "I can keep him in ignorance of my affairs, but if he is defeated, then the bills will be sent to him."

On August 23, as the cabinet members arrived for their meeting at the long table under the glass-globe chandelier, Lincoln presented the men with a folded paper, its edges pasted so that the contents could not be read. He asked each man in turn—Stanton, Welles, Usher, Fessenden, and so on—to write his name across the back of the paper. When all had signed, Lincoln closed the endorsed document in his desk drawer. He would say no more about it until after the election. He had written:

Executive Mansion
Washington, August 23, 1864

This morning, as for some days past, it seems exceedingly
probable that this Administration will not be re-elected. Then
it will be my duty to so cooperate with the President elect, as
will save the Union between the election and the inauguration;
as he will have secured his election on such ground that he can
not possibly save it afterwards.

He meant that if General George McClellan won on a platform that
permitted slavery, the peculiar institution would continue to divide
the nation as it had all along. Did Lincoln intend to cooperate with
McClellan by *not* cooperating with him? We will never know. No
sooner had the President filed this curious document (now in the
Library of Congress) than the tide began to turn in his favor.

It was the Democrats' turn to show their hand. On August 30
in Chicago they nominated Lincoln's old nemesis, General
McClellan, on a "peace platform," a condemnation of the war and
a plea for peace that would prove an albatross for the candidate.
The public soon called it "the Chicago Surrender." The humor of
McClellan's predicament did not escape Lincoln or his Secretary
of the Navy, Gideon Welles, who said, "there is fatuity in nomi-
nating a general and a warrior in time of war on a peace platform."
Folly was no Republican monopoly. It was far easier to attack an
incumbent President in wartime than to unseat him.

While admitting that he sought a second term in part from
"personal vanity, or ambition," Lincoln explained that he had
higher motives: "God knows I do not want the labor and responsibility of the office for another four years. But I have the common

pride of humanity to wish my past four years Administration endorsed." Far more was at issue than his pride; democracy itself was at stake. If Americans voted for the Union, for Lincoln, they would be working "for the best interests of their country and the world, not only for the present, but for all future ages."

A White House visitor asked Lincoln how it felt to be president. He laughed. "You have heard about the man tarred and feathered and ridden out of town on a rail? A man in the crowd asked how he liked it, and his reply was that if it wasn't for the honor of the thing, he would much rather walk."

Lincoln may have laughed because he acknowledged the whimsical, freakish workings of Fortune. As if fate had designed to cancel the Democrats' claim that the war was a lost cause, on September 4 Sherman wired the President, "Atlanta is ours, and fairly won." Lincoln called the victory a gift from God and declared Sunday, September 4, a national day of thanksgiving. He directed that hundred-gun salutes should be fired in every major city. Success on the battlefield was one benefit the electorate never questioned, and this candidate would not neglect the opportunity for good press. Great Atlanta, the railroad center and freight entrepôt, the chief seat of power in the deep South, was now under Federal control.

———

Saturday night, a week later, Walt Whitman sat with friends "of the Fred Gray association" drinking beer in a dive on the Lower East Side of Manhattan. They had started in the larger saloons and gradually worked their way down to this "crowded, low, most degraded place . . . one of those places where the air is full of the scent of thievery, druggies, foul play, & prostitution gangrened."

A poor bleary-eyed girl brought their beer to the table. Whitman noticed that she was wearing a McClellan campaign medal on her breast.

"Barmaid," he called to her. Pointing out the medal he asked, "Are the other girls here for McClellan too?"

"Yes, every one of them, and they won't tolerate a girl in the place who is not. And the *fellows* are too," she added proudly.

Whitman counted. "There must have been twenty girls, sad, sad, ruins . . ." This was the city where the draft rioters had burned down a Negro orphanage. Working-class women, and their men, had yet to warm to Lincoln. Whitman observed: "I should think nine tenths, of all classes, are Copperheads here, I never heard before such things as I hear now whenever I go out— then it seems tame & indeed unreal here, life as carried on & as I come in contact with it & receive its influences."

"I go out regularly," he wrote to O'Connor, "sometimes out on the bay, or to Coney Island, & occasionally a tour through New York Life, as of old"—the circuit of beer halls and low taverns such as the one infested with Copperheads. One would think that New York and Brooklyn had not heard the hundred-gun salutes celebrating the fall of Atlanta; New Yorkers were still under the influence of Greeley's anti-Lincoln publications and the wrath of the Radicals. They were still seething over the draft, putting their faith in handsome George McClellan and his "peace platform." Meanwhile, Greeley, Weed, Sumner, and even "Bluff" Ben Wade, who had stirred such opposition, had begun to beat the drum for Lincoln, in the wake of Union victories.

The poet's health had recovered, but for "a lingering suspicion of weakness now and then." He had begun visiting the sick in Brooklyn City Hospital; in leisure hours he went out horseback riding and fishing. *Drum-Taps,* his book of war poems, had failed to find a publisher. He resolved to publish the poems himself, when he could find the funds, just as he had brought out *Leaves of Grass.*

It was a strange time for a Lincolnite to be in New York. Until now the poet had been uncertain of his plans, although he wrote to Nellie O'Connor, "I think it quite possible I shall be in Washington again this winter." That Saturday night, drinking lager in the nest of Copperheads, he seems to have made up his mind to return to the Federal City, drawn by the same affinity that had led him there in the first place.

———

Victory followed upon victory in the Shenandoah Valley, where Grant had ordered Major General Philip Sheridan to destroy Jubal Early's Rebel army. Grant told General Sheridan to pillage the region "so that crows flying over it for the balance of the season will have to carry their provender with them." In late September Sheridan triumphed at Winchester and Fisher's Hill, finally crushing Early's army in mid-October.

Now Republicans of every stripe—Radical, Moderate, and Conservative—hit the campaign trail in support of the Union Party, if not Lincoln himself, trumpeting the valor of Sherman and Sheridan, and attacking McClellan's peace-at-any-price platform. Even Salmon Chase joined the canvass. The Radical John Frémont dropped out, having cut a deal with Lincoln to withdraw if the hated Conservative Montgomery Blair, Postmaster General, was dropped from the cabinet.

Near Election Day, on the night of October 21, 1864, a crowd gathered outside the White House. A torchlight parade, with rockets and Roman candles, brightened the sky. In an upper window under the portico Lincoln stood, smiling, with eleven-year-old Tad at his side. The people serenaded the President and his son, and then called loudly for a speech.

"I was promised not to be called upon for a speech tonight," Lincoln responded, "nor do I propose to make one. But, as we have been hearing some very good news for a day or two, I propose that you give three cheers for Sheridan."

The crowd noisily obliged. There was warm respect for Sheridan, a small wonder in the Union army, an American Napoleon, a bandy-legged cavalry officer who stood five feet five inches tall.

"While we are at it," the President continued, with a twinkle in his eye, "we may as well consider how fortunate it was for the Secesh [Secessionists] that Sheridan was a very little man. If he had been a large man, there is no knowing what he would have done with them." This brought peals of laughter and applause.

Lincoln was too wise to be confident he would win the coming election. But he had grounds for optimism.

Election night was warm and rainy. As Lincoln sat in the cipher room with John Hay, Thomas Eckert (chief of the telegraph office), Gideon Welles, and others, the dispatches soon quelled the last of his doubts. He sent Mary word of the triumphant early returns.

"She is more anxious than I," Lincoln said.

It was a landslide. Toward midnight Eckert ordered out for a pan of fried oysters, and coffee. "The President went awkwardly and hospitably to work shovelling out the fried oysters. He was most agreeable and genial all the evening in fact," Hay recalled. Hay and Lincoln went home.

At 2:30 A.M. a band serenaded the President at the White House, and he "answered from the window with rather unusual dignity and effect."

"I am thankful to God for this approval of the people. But

while deeply grateful for this mark of their confidence in me, if I know my heart, my gratitude is free from any taint of personal triumph. I do not impugn the motives of any one opposed to me. It is no pleasure for me to triumph over any one; but I give thanks to the Almighty for this evidence of the people's resolution to stand by free government and the rights of humanity."

When Hay and Lincoln came upstairs, Ward Hill Lamon was waiting for them. He refused Hay's offer of a bed, but accepted a glass of whiskey and some blankets. When Lincoln closed the door to his bedroom, Lamon rolled himself up in his cloak and the blankets and lay down there with his arsenal of bowie knives and pistols around him. Thus he passed the night, Hay recalled, "in that attitude of touching and dumb fidelity," certain that the President was in more danger now than ever.

SPRING, 1865

*I*t was a season rich in promises and startling reversals of fortune, as changeable as the Maryland weather. Returning to Washington in the bitter cold and dusk of late winter, Whitman had been pleased by his prospects: a job in the Department of the Interior; new lodgings on higher ground, a mile north of the fetid canal; and his health restored. At the same time he was haunted by the fate of his brothers. At last, sadly, he had committed Jesse to the Kings County Lunatic Asylum. And Captain George Whitman, captured by Rebels at Poplar Grove Church, Virginia, had languished in a Petersburg camp for four months, a prisoner of war.

Whitman's new job, as a copyist in the Office of Indian Affairs, came to him by way of his old friend William O'Connor, now head of the Light House Board, and Assistant Attorney General J. Hubley Ashton, whose office was directly beneath O'Connor's in the Treasury building. Ashton, highly placed in Lincoln's administration, had long been a friend and admirer of the poet and his work. For a year or more O'Connor had been lobbying to find

Whitman a comfortable job in the government. That he was at last successful, with Ashton's help (Ashton petitioned William Otto, of the Interior, on Whitman's behalf), bespeaks no change in Whitman's qualifications but rather a subtle shift in the political climate after Lincoln's reelection. Lincoln, overwhelmed by office seekers, each of whom he felt "darted at him, and with thumb and finger carried off a portion of his vitality," decided to change as few functionaries as possible. "To remove a man is very easy, but when I make a go to fill his place, there are *twenty* applicants, and of these I must make *nineteen* enemies." Now that men like the Assistant Attorney General and the Assistant Secretary of the Interior were more secure in their own positions, they were less fearful of taking on cases like Walt Whitman's.

The job was a plum, as O'Connor had described it, "an easy berth, a regular income [twelve hundred dollars per annum] . . . leaving you time to attend to the soldiers, to your poems, & c." Whitman's desk was in the basement of the Patent Office, a room in the northeast corner, across the street from Gardner's Gallery, and Shepherd & Riley's Bookstore, where the poet liked to browse. He wrote to his brother Jeff: "It is easy enough—I take things very easy—the rule is to come at 9 and go at 4—but I don't come at 9, and only stay until 4 when I want . . . I am treated with great courtesy . . ." In this same letter he says, "I feel quite well, perhaps not as completely so as I used to, but I think I shall get so this spring . . ."

He had directed much of his energy toward getting George out of prison. In a dispatch to the *New York Times*, Whitman attacked the administration's "cold-blooded policy" concerning the exchange of prisoners, while grandiloquently absolving Lincoln of responsibility. "Under the President (whose humane, conscientious, and fatherly heart I have abiding faith in) the control of exchange has remained with the Secretary of War [Stanton], and also with Major-General Butler." Stanton's logic was unassailable to anyone not himself a prisoner, the kin of a prisoner, or a moralist. To wit: "It is not for the benefit of the Government of the United States that the power of the Secessionists should be repleted by some fifty thousand men in good condition [Confederate POWs] now in our hands, besides getting relieved of the support of nearly the same number of wrecks and ruins, of no advantage to us, now in theirs." George was among those "wrecks and ruins," but Lincoln, ruled by logic rather than sentiment, would not cross his Secretary of War. Whitman begged his friend John Swinton, editor of the *New York Times,* to write to General Grant requesting "one of the special exchanges . . . in favor of my brother George," pleading "the deep distress of my mother whose health is getting affected, & of my sister—& thinking it worth the trial myself." Swinton wrote to Grant, and the slow wheels of a prisoner exchange began to turn.

In the meantime Whitman made himself at home. He liked his new room at 468 M Street, second door west of Twelfth, very near the house he had shared with the O'Connors when he first arrived in Washington. There was an open-air market nearby where the carts would arrive laden with fruits, vegetables, and flowers. He had a good big bed, an iron stove, and a pile of firewood in his room. He was particularly pleased with his landlady, Mrs. Edward Grayson, her Southern sympathies notwithstanding—her husband and son were both fighting in Confederate gray. She was "very obliging, starts my fire for me at 5 o'clock every afternoon, & lights the gas, even, & then turns it down to be ready for me when I come home."

He spent evenings and weekends in Armory Square Hospital, but he assured his brother Jeff he "need not be afraid about my overdoing the matter. I shall go regularly enough, but shall be on my guard against trouble." Whitman meant to defend himself against disease as well as emotional involvement with the soldiers, a devotion that had cost him "days and nights of unutterable anxiety: sitting there by some poor devil destined to go: always in the presence of death."

Spring struggled fitfully against a winter as cold and cruel as any in memory, and the violent changes in weather mirrored Whitman's moods of hope and despair about George's release. "Such caprices, abruptest alternations of frowns and beauty, I never knew."

Whitman wondered if the heat and cold, the rain and snow, "and what underlies them all," were not somehow influenced by the passions of humankind, "strain'd stronger than usual, and on a larger scale than usual." He was not the first to observe that for two years there had been remarkable expressions "of the subtle world of the air above us and around us. There, since this War . . . strange analogies, different combinations, a different sunlight, or absence of it . . . After every great battle, a great storm."

Now there came evenings of supreme beauty, when Venus shone large and bright in the Western sky, hanging close to the moon in its first quarter. "The sky, dark blue, the transparent night, the planets, the moderate west wind, the elastic temperature, the unsurpassable miracle of that great star, and the young and swelling moon swimming in the west, suffused the soul." Out of the silence Whitman heard the clear, slow notes of a bugle sounding taps in one of the military hospitals.

On such evenings the poet liked to stroll with the crowds up Pennsylvania Avenue toward the lighted rotunda of the Capitol. He stood for a long while gazing up at the illuminated slits in the dome. ("It comforts me somehow.") Then he would mount the steps, look in upon the members hard at work in the Hall of Representatives, and wander through long frescoed corridors beneath the Senate. This old habit now afforded him more satisfaction than ever. In a few days Lincoln would stand on the East Portico, take the oath of office, and deliver his Second Inaugural Address.

One block north of the Capitol, in a quaint red-brick house on an acre of ground, Whitman's friend John Burroughs lived with his wife, Ursula. Burroughs had a broad forehead, a pointed black beard, and keen, kind eyes. Like several of Whitman's friends, he worked in the Treasury building; but after hours he enjoyed hoeing his potatoes, tending his chickens, and looking after his cow Chlöe, who grazed on the common near the Capitol. The twenty-eight-year-old Burroughs idolized Whitman, who would serve as the subject of the naturalist's first book, *Notes on Walt Whitman, as Poet and Person* (1867). Whitman was a regular guest for breakfast on Sundays, often testing Ursula's patience by arriving so late she would have to reheat the food.

Their mood in that generous household on the eve of Lincoln's inauguration is well expressed in Burroughs's invitation to a friend: "We have a spare bed and would be delighted to have you come. Walt is here, Spring is here, the Bluebird and Robin are here. The Spirit says Come, the flesh says Come, Wife says Come, 'Abe' says Come, *so Come!*"

The weather remained capricious. One night, after a visit with Burroughs on Capitol Hill, a storm blew out of the northwest. Whitman, who had to work the next day, threw a blanket around his shoulders and hurried down Delaware Avenue, past the Senate wing of the Capitol, to meet the Union Line horsecar on Pennsylvania Avenue.

The horses pulled a fifteen-foot-long omnibus, seven feet wide. It halted, and Whitman entered through the rear. He gave his nickel to the red-haired conductor and took a seat on one of the long benches that ran along the sides of the car, twenty vacant seats covered in silk and velvet lighted by a pink-glass-globe oil lamp that hung in the center.

The conductor, twenty-one-year-old Peter Doyle, would never forget that night, or the impression Walt Whitman made upon him as he came in out of the rain: "We felt [drawn] to each other at once."

The storm was awful. Walt had this blanket—it was thrown round his shoulders—he seemed like an old sea-captain. He was the only passenger, it was a lonely night, so I thought I would go in and talk with him. Something in me made me do it and something in him drew me that way. He used to say there was something in me had the same effect on him.

Anyway, I went into the car. We were familiar at once—I put my hand on his knee—we understood.

When the horsecar reached its terminus in Georgetown, Whitman did not get out. He rode all the way back with his new comrade, to Doyle's home near the Navy Yard in the Southwest section of the city.

Like other lovers stunned by the phenomenon of love at first sight, the two men may have been sparing of words during that rainy night. But they had a great deal to talk about. Doyle reminded Whitman in many ways of Fred Vaughan, his lover in the 1850s, muse of his "Calamus" poems.

> One flitting glimpse, caught through an interstice,
> Of a crowd of workmen and drivers in a bar-room, around the stove,
>   late of a winter night—And I unremarked seated in a corner;

Of a youth who loves me, and whom I love, silently approaching,
*   and seating himself near, that he may hold me by the hand;*
A long while, amid the noises of coming and going—of drinking
*   and oath and smutty jest,*
There we two, content, happy in being together, speaking little,
*   perhaps not a word.*

Like Vaughan, Doyle was Irish; he was baptized in Limerick City, in Ireland, on June 16, 1843. And like Vaughan, Doyle was, at the time he met Whitman, a transit worker, much younger than the poet.

Peter George Doyle stood straight as a soldier, making the most of his five feet eight inches. He had a jaunty air about him, too much humor to be vain about his good looks—merry blue eyes wide-set above high cheekbones, a sharp nose and jutting chin, clean-shaven except for a fair, drooping mustache. He had grown up with his three brothers and a sister in Alexandria, Virginia, where the family immigrated in 1852. In 1858 they moved to Richmond, where Doyle's father worked in an iron foundry.

A week after Virginia left the Union, seventeen-year-old Peter joined the Richmond Fayette Artillery. During eighteen months of service the adolescent soldier survived a series of violent engagements, including the rear-guard Battle of Williamsburg and the Battle of Seven Pines. During the Penninsula Campaign, half of his company was lost. His tour of duty culminated on September 17, 1862, at Antietam, the bloodiest single-day battle ever fought in America. Whitman's brother George stood on the opposite side of the barricades from Private Doyle—they might have fired at each other.

Doyle was badly wounded there. While recuperating in a Richmond hospital, the war-weary youth petitioned the Confederate

Secretary of War for a discharge. Protesting that he was not a citizen of the Confederate States but a British national, he declared his intent to return to his native country at the first opportunity. The discharge was granted on November 7.

As the Union Line horsecar passed the belfry of the Central Guard House at Ninth Street, Doyle recalled how in April 1863 he had ended up in prison by a series of mishaps that might have been comical if they had befallen somebody else. First, after leaving the hospital, he was arrested for desertion, as if he had not been discharged, and ordered to return to duty with his company, then stationed in Petersburg. He preferred not to rejoin his outfit. Instead, Doyle decided to quit the Confederate States. He crossed enemy lines, and was captured by Federal soldiers who took him to Washington, where he was charged with "entering & attempting to enter our lines, from the insurgent states, without a permit."

Confined to a squalid annex of the Old Capitol Prison near Duff Green Row, Doyle rattled his chains, insisting that he was a British subject in flight from the wreckage of Virginia. On Monday, April 20, 1863, Doyle's name appeared in the *Washington Star* in the list of prisoners; the next day his sister-in-law Ellen Doyle visited him in his cell. The family must have petitioned the British consul. On May 2, Secretary Seward inquired after Doyle on behalf of the British minister Lord Lyons. Judge Levi Turner concluded that Doyle, and some other prisoners, were "poor Irishmen who fled from Richmond to avoid starvation." On May 11, having taken an oath not to support the Rebellion, the nineteen-year-old fugitive was set free.

He took a job as a smith at the Navy Yard, near the house in Southeast Washington where he lived with his brother Francis and his wife. He moonlighted as a horsecar conductor with the Washington & Georgetown Railroad Company. Peter Doyle was a survivor. His impish smile as it appears in photographs is the expression of a man who has suffered, endured, and arrived at a state of ironic merriment.

His extended Catholic family in Washington was large and affectionate. Like Whitman, Doyle had assumed responsibility for his widowed mother and his younger siblings. Although he had only a rudimentary "Jesuit education," Doyle loved the theater and opera and would soon become an enthusiastic audience for his new friend's recitations of Shakespeare, Tennyson, and *Leaves of Grass.*

For the next eight years the two men were comrades, companions, lovers. Just as the poet Thomas Gray speculated that the country churchyard might contain "Some mute inglorious Milton," so John Burroughs found in the trolley conductor "a mute inglorious Whitman." And the two made up a whole, the tall, heavy-set poet and the slight, unlettered workingman who loved limericks. The men complemented—"completed"—each other. The playful, affectionate Rebel was so handsome that a Dr. William Tindall, observing him on the horsecar, called him "the young Apollo." Watching Whitman and Doyle on the omnibus platform, Dr. Tindall called it "the most taciturn mutual admiration society I ever attended," and remarked upon "the restfulness which genius sometimes finds in the companionship of an opposite type of mentality."

Doyle remembered, "It was our practice to go to a hotel on Washington Avenue after I was done with my car." This was the Union Hotel, near the Georgetown terminus of the route, a four-story whitewashed inn and tavern with a little portico and a dormered roof, at the corner of Washington and Bridge Streets. Late at night they would call for beer and a light supper. "Like as not I would go to sleep—lay my head on my hands on the table. Walt would sit there, wait, watch, keep me undisturbed—would wake me when the hour of closing came." Under the stars the lovers would cross the M Street bridge over Rock Creek, toward Whitman's rooms, a fifteen-minute walk away.

On Sundays they would sometimes take long hikes along the Potomac, all the way to Alexandria. They crossed the Navy Yard bridge, heading south along the Maryland side of the river, then took the ferry to Virginia. They would return via the Virginia banks, crossing Long Bridge onto "the Island," the neighborhood bounded by the city canal and the Eastern Branch, where Peter lived with his family.

On these outings, Doyle recalled, Whitman was "always whistling or singing. We would talk of ordinary matters. He would recite poetry, especially Shakespeare—he would hum airs or shout in the woods."

William O'Connor marked the transformation in his friend that spring, after he met the young Irishman. "A change had come upon him. The rosy color had died from his face in a clear splendor, and his form, regnant and masculine, was clothed with inspiration, as with a dazzling aureole . . ." Whitman explained to O'Connor what had made the difference: "Love, love, love! That includes all. There is nothing in the world but that—nothing in all the world. Better than all is love."

In love with Peter Doyle that spring and summer, Whitman would recover his full powers of creativity. During this period he would write what Algernon Swinburne called "the most sweet and sonorous nocturn ever chanted in the church of the world," his elegy, "When Lilacs Last in the Dooryard Bloom'd."

It rained steadily for five days before Lincoln's second inauguration, on March 4, 1865. On the main thoroughfares of Washington the mud measured from five inches on uptown streets to fifteen inches or more on Pennsylvania Avenue.

The night before the ceremony the torches of a firemen's procession lit up the fog on Pennsylvania Avenue with a silvery haze. Over the Capitol dome the roof lights of the House and Senate in session crowned the cloudy skies with a radiant halo that could be seen for miles. That glow emblazoned the Stars and Stripes floating over the dome, bringing out every fold in the ensign in brilliant relief.

Hundreds of strangers who had come to see the President sworn in wandered dazed, forlorn, with carpetbags and blanket-rolls strapped to their backs, and many found their way to the well-lighted and comfortably heated Capitol, thinking of spending the night there. Hotels were overbooked; the proprietors of the Willard and the National placed cots and mattresses in the parlors and halls.

Restless with excitement, Walt Whitman must have been up all night on Friday the third; or perhaps Peter Doyle drove him up to the park in front of the Capitol on the first morning horsecar from the Navy Yard.

At dawn Whitman was seated in the dim light of the Hall of Representatives, in the crowded gallery, scribbling in pencil in his homemade notebook, observing "the members nervous from long drawn duty, exhausted, some asleep, and many half-asleep." The members debated appropriation bills, one for the army being the most hotly contested because so many legislators refused to pay any money to the Illinois Central Railroad. Mr. Robert Schenk of Ohio requested that the President repeal the regulation requiring colored persons to obtain passes before leaving the city. Then there was a brawl over whether civilians might still be tried by military tribunals.

"The gas-light, mix'd with the dingy day-break produced an unearthly effect. The poor little sleepy, stumbling pages, the smell of the Hall . . . the strong hope that the War is approaching its close—the tantalizing dread lest the hope may be a false one . . . the grandeur of the Hall . . . all made a mark'd combination," Whitman wrote.

Suddenly there burst upon the dome a heavy gale of rain and wind out of the south. "It beat like a deluge on the heavy glass roof of the Hall, and the wind literally howled and roared." The sleepers woke in pop-eyed fear, some bolted for the doors, some gaped at the roof, and some of the pages began to cry. But soon after the drowsing men awakened they recovered their composure and went on with their business, while the storm raged on. "Perhaps," Whitman considered, surveying the motley Thirty-eighth Congress, "the shock did it good."

He reported on the inaugural events for the *New York Times,* whose editor John Swinton welcomed him as an "Occasional Correspondent." Weather would be a dramatic aspect of the story. "The elements, all the meteorological influences, have run riot for weeks past," the poet observed.

Chief among those influences, at first, was the "Mud, (and such mud!) amid and upon which streaming crowds of citizens; lots of blue-dressed soldiers; any quantity of male and female Africans; horrid perpetual entanglements at the crossings, sometimes a dead lock; more mud, the wide street black, and several inches deep with it." The Engineer Corps considered laying pontoons from the White House to the Capitol, but discovered the bottom was too soft to hold the anchors of the pontoons. Police ordered all those who could not swim to stay on the sidewalks. The *Evening Star* reported on March 4: "No one is believed to have been lost." The muck particularly tested the mettle of the ladies, whose shawls were drenched, crinolines smashed, their silk and velvet, their antique lace and moiré skirts spattered and draggled with mud.

In the early morning the poet observed "the wide Avenue, its vista very fine, down at one end closed by the Capitol, with milky bulging dome, and the Maternal Figure over all, (with the sword by her side and the sun glittering on her helmeted head;) at the other, the western end, the pillared front of the Treasury Building, looking south." He watched as the grand vista filled with "the oceanic crowd, almost equal to Broadway," as the procession of soldiers, bands, floats, and dignitaries left their various rendezvous spots on Seventeenth and Nineteenth Streets on the far side of the White House to begin their parade through the slough of Pennsylvania Avenue.

The President came first, in mid-morning, riding alone in his plain two-horse barouche, at a sharp trot. With the top folded down, the barouche looked like a black slipper. Whitman saw him going out well ahead of the parade, and thought Lincoln "wished to be on hand to sign bills, & c, or to get rid of marching in line with the muslin Temple of Liberty, and the pasteboard Monitor [the bands and floats]." In fact, Lincoln had a number of bills to sign before appearing in the Senate chamber before 11:45 to take his seat in time for the swearing in of Vice President Andrew Johnson. Mrs. Lincoln, in a white silk dress with a shoulder cape of point lace, sat next to Rhode Island Senator Henry Anthony in the diplomatic gallery.

Outside, on the Avenue, tens of thousands of people stood on the sidewalk and on the balconies of houses and public buildings. The national flag in all sizes waved from windows, carriages, carts, and horse-harnesses. Whitman later wrote of the "clattering groups of cavalrymen out there on a gallop," the firemen with their engines, and "a regiment of blacks in full uniform, with guns on their shoulders." He was eager to correct any impression that the parade was orderly, military. No, said the poet, the different groups "were characterized by a charming looseness and independence." From the thirteen marshal's aides wearing cherry-colored scarves with white rosettes and yellow gauntlets to the National Union College Band; from floats and fifers to the sashay of the drunken Washington Press Corps, the various military officers, and the Masons and Odd Fellows bringing up the rear—this was more like a Mardi Gras jamboree than a Grand Review. "Each went up and down the Avenue in the way and at the time which seemed convenient, and was a law unto itself."

Just after midday the gray clouds began to stir and scud, for moments uncovering patches of blue. Whitman saw, directly overhead, "our heavenly neighbor Hesperus, the star of the West," Venus. Trudging on toward the inaugural platform that stretched out from the east steps of the Capitol, the poet paused with the crowd to admire Venus until the leaden clouds covered the "star" again.

As the President stepped out from behind the columns of the crowded portico, leading senators, Supreme Court justices, and cabinet members, "a tremendous shout, prolonged and loud, arose from the surging ocean of humanity around the Capitol building," wrote journalist Noah Brooks, Lincoln's friend. Trumpets played fanfares; flags waved over the sea of heads in the great plaza, and as far as the eye could see. As the tall, gaunt President advanced, and unfurled his address, printed in two columns upon a single sheet of paper, waves of applause swept through the crowd to its distant fringes.

"A curious little white cloud," Whitman noted, "the only one in that part of the sky, appeared like a hovering bird, right over him." Brooks saw that the sun suddenly "burst forth in its unclouded meridian splendor, and flooded the spectacle with glory and with light." Many took it as an omen, and "prayed that so might the darkness which had obscured the past four years be now dissipated by the sun of prosperity."

Whitman did not comment on the 703-word speech, one of the shortest inaugural addresses in American history, notable that day more for its restraint than for its eloquence. If former Rebel Peter Doyle was at his side (the horsecars were sidetracked), Doyle would have been the more relieved that in Lincoln's account of the war's beginnings, the President did not blame either the North or the South outright for the tragedy.

"All dreaded it—all sought to avert it . . . Both parties deprecated war; but one of them would *make* war rather than let the nation survive; and the other would *accept* war rather than let it perish. (Long applause.) And the war came."

The President now conceded that "all knew" that slavery had been "the cause of the war," and he brooded over the ensuing ironies of war between the states. "Both read the same Bible, and pray to the same God; and each invokes His aid against the other. It may seem strange that any men should dare to ask a just God's assistance in wringing their bread from the sweat of other men's faces; but let us judge not that we be not judged."

Below Lincoln on the platform was the black suffragist Frederick Douglass, who called the speech "a sacred effort." Above the President stood the actor John Wilkes Booth. He had gotten an inauguration-stand ticket from Miss Lucy Hale, who lived with her father, Senator John P. Hale of New Hampshire, in the National Hotel, where Booth stayed. He was secretly engaged to the girl.

Less than five minutes later Lincoln would conclude his speech with these generous words: "With malice toward none; with charity for all; with firmness in the right, as God gives us to see the right, let us strive on to finish the work we are in; to bind up the nation's wounds; to care for him who shall have borne the battle, and for his widow, and his orphan—to do all which may achieve and cherish a just, and a lasting peace, among ourselves, and with all nations."

Whitman described the effect the President's wise speech appeared to have upon the weather: "a forenoon like whirling demons, dark with slanting rain, full of rage; and then the afternoon, so calm, so bathed with flooding splendor from heaven's most excellent sun, with atmosphere of sweetness; so clear it showed the stars, long, long before they were due." Others praised the speech. Charles Francis Adams Jr. wrote to his father, minister to England: "This inaugural strikes me in its grand simplicity and directness as being for all time the historical keynote of this war . . . Not a prince or minister in all Europe could have risen to such an equality with the occasion."

Six months after Salmon Chase's ignominious departure from the cabinet, Lincoln had rehabilitated him by naming him chief justice of the Supreme Court. Now the man who had worked hardest to undo Lincoln was swearing him in as President. Who can imagine what emotions surged in Chase's breast? Lincoln kissed the Bible amid deafening applause and cheers and a salvo of artillery. Later Lincoln said to Brooks, "Did you notice that sunburst? It made my heart jump."

As members of the crowd went their ways Whitman hung back so he could get a good view of the President returning to the White House in his barouche. It was a little after three o'clock. Whitman said that Lincoln looked very tired: "The lines, indeed, of vast responsibilities, intricate questions, and demands of life and death, cut deeper than ever upon his dark brown face." Yet underneath the furrows the poet was moved to recognize "all the old goodness, tenderness, sadness and canny shrewdness."

Whitman felt as he had on those summer evenings in 1863 when the President waved from his carriage, and on that Halloween when he had seen Lincoln in the White House: "I never see that man without feeling he is one to become personally attached to, for his combination of purest, heartiest tenderness, and native Western even rudest forms of manliness."

Tad, and Senator Lafayette Foster of Connecticut, returned with Lincoln. Around their carriage rode the marshal on horseback, in an orange-colored scarf, and his thirteen aides, all wearing yellow gloves and bearing blue batons with gilt tips. All wore dark civilian clothes. Following the President came Senator Anthony and Mrs. Lincoln in her carriage, Robert Lincoln in his, and the foreign ministers in two more. Then came the civic procession, on foot, not so much a parade as a victory dance, with cheers and shouting.

That afternoon, returning to his room to bathe and to change his muddy clothing, Whitman received the longed-for news of his brother George's release from the Danville prison. He had been exchanged on February 22 and had notified his mother immediately. Thinking Walt would have seen George's name in the list of exchanged prisoners in the newspapers, Mrs. Whitman waited a week before writing to him in Washington: "George has come home came this morning he looks quite thin and shows his prison life but feels pretty well considering what he suffered he was very sick at one time i think it was in January with lung fever he was six weeks in the hospital so bad that the doctor thought he would die."

There was a good deal for Whitman to celebrate on that beautiful evening in March as he strolled down Thirteenth Street in his fine black frock coat, linen shirt, and black tie, turning west on New

York Avenue, sidestepping puddles, passing the Treasury on the way to the White House. It promised to be a pleasant part of his day's work of journalism, attending the President's eight o'clock levee. But the event would get few words in his dispatch. "I ought to mention the President's closing Levee . . . Never before was such a compact jam in front of the White House, all the grounds filled, and away out to the spacious sidewalks." That is all he wrote to the *Times,* although he observed far more that evening. Swept along with the crowd, he passed through the columns under the portico, "surged along the passage-ways, the Blue and other rooms, and through the great East room." There the President stood, flanked by Ward Hill Lamon and Tad. "Crowds of country people, some very funny," Whitman wrote. He said the room was "upholstered like a stage parlor," which did not go unnoticed by the rustics, who were ripping away little pieces of the carpet and draperies for souvenirs. In a corner, the Marine Band was diligently playing.

"I saw Mr. Lincoln, drest all in black, with white kid gloves, and a claw-hammer coat, receiving, as in duty bound, shaking hands, looking very disconsolate, and as if he would give anything to be somewhere else."

The reception was unusually large, and Lincoln is supposed to have shaken hands with nearly six thousand persons. As far as we know Walt Whitman did not shake Lincoln's hand, although from only a few feet away he watched the President intently. Perhaps the poet did not wish to add to the President's duty; perhaps Whitman imagined a more favorable occasion, in the future, for them to become acquainted.

He would not be seeing Lincoln at the inaugural ball on Monday night, either, although it would be held in the great Doric edifice where Whitman now worked, the Patent Office building. His reasons for forgoing the festivities he makes clear in his *Times* dispatch: "I could not help thinking of the scene of those rooms, where the music will sound and the dancers feet presently tread— what a different scene they presented to my view a while since . . .

"Tonight, beautiful women, perfumes, the violin's sweetness, the polka and the waltz; but then, the amputation, the blue face, the groan, the glassy eye of the dying, the clotted rag, the odor of old, wounds and blood, and many a mother's son amid strangers, passing away untended there, (for the crowd of the badly hurt was great, and much for nurse to do, and much for Surgeon.)"

When he finished his copy work at the Office of Indian Affairs, in the basement, at about five o'clock, Whitman climbed the marble steps to the great central hall, the "Salle des Beaux Arts," to view the preparations for the ball. The huge room—264 feet long, 62 feet wide, with arched ceilings 30 feet in height—was itself dazzling. Nowhere else but in Paris and Munich was there such artful polychromy—the cornices, ceilings, and compartments all painted with combinations of red and yellow, and red intermingled harmoniously with blue and green. The enormous pillars stood out in bold relief, colored a brilliant ultramarine. Light from hundreds of gas jets lent the tones an additional richness.

The dining table was set up in the west wing, which was the same size as the room just described. This board took up the entire length of the hall but for 20 feet at either end reserved for the pantries and steam tables. The chef had prepared supper for five thousand. The centerpiece was an exact model of the Capitol, and the culinary adornments included pyramid confections of coconut, chocolate, nougat, macaroon, *croquant*, and caramel with fancy cream candy. The bill of fare listed sixty-six items, including four different beef dishes; others of veal, pheasant, quail, and venison; and thirty desserts, among them charlotte russe, blancmange, maraschino ice cream, *crème napolitane,* and *crème du Chateaubriand.*

Whitman reminded his readers how different these same rooms appeared to him, "a while since, filled with a crowded mass of the worst wounded of the war." He cautioned:

"Think not of such grim things, gloved ladies, as you bow to your partners, and the figures of the dance this night are loudly called, or you may drop on the floor, that has known what this one knew, but two short winters since." The poet means, of course, that the ballroom *floor* remembers the human blood shed upon it, in case the dancers should forget. This bitter warning appeared in the *New York Times,* days after the ball. Whitman deleted it from the reprint of the article in his book *Memoranda During the War* (1875).

For weeks after the inauguration Lincoln was ill. He was thirty-five pounds underweight and so weak he sometimes permitted his driver to help him out of his barouche. While journalists reported that the President suffered from the flu, he had no symptoms other than weight loss, fatigue, and a chill in his hands and feet. He would prop his damp stockinged feet on a hassock so near the hearth they would steam.

Surgeon General Joseph Barnes suspected that Lincoln was on the verge of a nervous breakdown. "Poor Mr. Lincoln," Mary Todd told Elizabeth Keckley, "he's looking so broken-hearted, so completely worn out. I fear he will not get through the next four years." To Noah Brooks, Lincoln admitted, "nothing touches the tired spot."

On Tuesday, March 14, the President was so weak he could not rise from the bed. Mrs. Lincoln, called from her bedroom, summoned the family physician, Dr. Robert K. Stone, who, after a thorough examination, concluded that the case was one of "complete exhaustion." That day the cabinet met in Lincoln's bedroom.

The next morning, though still shaky, Lincoln returned to his office for a full day's work. This included receiving the credentials of the Austrian ambassador and interviewing a delegation from Louisiana about the restructuring of the state's government. That night, in the company of Mrs. Lincoln, Senator Ira Harris, and Harris's daughter Clara, the President attended Mozart's opera *The Magic Flute* at Grover's Theatre.

And sometime that day or the next, Lincoln had to find time to write a speech of some length and great wit to be delivered on Friday, March 17, St. Patrick's Day. The occasion was the presentation of a Confederate flag—captured by the 140th Indiana Regiment at Fort Anderson, North Carolina—to Indiana's governor, Oliver Morton. The platform for the ceremony was the balcony over the portico of the National Hotel on the north side of Sixth and Pennsylvania.

The National, a red-brick, five-story hotel with ten parlors and fifty-eight rooms, was the traditional gathering place for Southern leaders and sympathizers. John Wilkes Booth now occupied room 231 on the second floor rear, overlooking the livery stables on C Street. This weekend, the newspapers announced, "the celebrated young American Tragedian has kindly volunteered his valuable services" in a benefit performance as Pescara in *The Apostate* at Ford's Theatre. Booth was taking every opportunity to act in Washington, where he could be near the President. Sherman's successes in South Carolina and Sheridan's thrashing of Jubal Early in the Shenandoah Valley meant that time was running out for the

Confederacy. Gold had fallen to $163 an ounce—a sure harbinger of peace. The South was so near collapse that any conspiracy to abduct or assassinate the President would soon be pointless.

So, that Friday, Booth had scheduled a midnight meeting of all six of his conspirators, engaging a private dining room at Gautier's Restaurant two blocks from the National.

At four o'clock in the afternoon Whitman left his office and walked down Seventh Street toward the National Hotel to hear the President. Saloons near the teeming Center Market, and at Brown's Hotel on the corner of Pennsylvania, were full of Irishmen and others in green toasting St. Patrick, singing "Tara's Harp" and the Irish national hymn. As Whitman neared the telegraph office at the corner of Sixth Street, the mounted police, expecting the President, were holding up traffic around the hotel. Lincoln drew up in his carriage, and as he limped toward the portico the Marine Band played "Hail to the Chief." Loud and prolonged cheers welcomed the President as he entered the National with Governor Morton, Colonel W. T. Dennis, and four officers of the nineteenth Indiana Regiment who had been held in Rebel prisons for twenty months.

The cheering reached its crescendo as the party appeared on the balcony. When the applause dwindled, the Colonel was first to speak. He read a letter on behalf of other officers of the Nineteenth Indiana, expressing their honor in "presenting to your Excellency a rebel garrison flag." Then the large flag, of the finest bunting, was hung from the balustrade: two blue bars crossed from corner to corner upon a red ground; fifteen stars clustered upon the bars.

The display of the magnificent flag drew another round of applause. The Governor thanked the people, then expressed his gratitude to the soldiers for their gallantry. He congratulated one and all on "the speedy end of the rebellion." He said, "I have seen dark hours, but my faith in the success of the cause has never been depressed."

Governor Morton then introduced the President, "whose purity and patriotism was confessed by all, even the most violent agitators." There was hearty applause from almost everyone but the skulking John Wilkes Booth, who had gone from scheming to kidnap Lincoln to wanting to shoot him. Whitman was gratified to hear Lincoln prophetically praised:

> His Administration will be recognized as the most important epoch of history. It struck the death blow to slavery [applause] and built up the Republic with a power it had never before possessed. If he had done nothing more than put his name to the emancipation proclamation, that act alone would have made his name immortal. [Applause.]"

Lincoln then stepped to the front of the balcony. As cheering reached a climax and then died away, Whitman looked at the President through the budding branches of the sapling elm trees that grew from the sidewalk spaces between the streetlamps. The President was ill—emaciated and pale. Yet now, on this afternoon in early spring, he would draw himself up to his full height and summon that radiant smile that had disarmed the rustic crowds during the debates with Douglas in 1858 and captivated New York's intelligentsia at Cooper Union in 1860. This was a joyous occasion. In this address, his next to last major public speech, Lincoln would charm and entertain the crowd with his indomitable humor.

The subject was serious: a recent proposal by the Confederates to enlist Negroes in their army—offering freedom to every slave agreeing to fight. The idea infuriated Lincoln. On St. Patrick's

Day he decided to break his silence on the subject, and make it a laughingstock.

At least four newspaper accounts of the speech have survived. The one below, from the *Washington Star,* appears to be the most accurate, in capturing Lincoln's wording as well as the audience's response.

"It will be but a very few words that I shall undertake to say. I was born in Kentucky, raised in Indiana, and live in Illinois [laughter], and I now am here where it is my business to be, to care equally for the good people of all the states." Lincoln expressed his pleasure that the Indiana soldiers had triumphed, but he was not disposed "to make a distinction between the states, for all have done equally well." For this consideration he received another round of applause.

Approaching his theme, Lincoln allowed there was hardly an aspect of the war upon which he had not made his views public. And yet, "There is one: the recent attempt of our erring brethren, as they are sometimes called, [laughter] to employ the negro to fight for them . . . that was their business and not mine; and if I had a wish upon the subject, I had not the power to introduce it or make it effective."

The shadows lengthened; a light breeze unfurled the Stars and Stripes that flew from an upright pole at the peak of the hotel's cornice, above Lincoln's head. Whitman recalled: "His face was lighted up: it seemed removed, beyond, disembodied." The crowd listened in suspense, spellbound.

"The great question with them was, whether the negro, being put into the army, will fight for them." Now it was the orator's understanding of the mordant humor ingrained in the question that furrowed his brow and curled the corner of his mouth. He would play upon the irony to perfection. "I do not know, and therefore cannot decide."

The shrugging protest brought peals of laughter from Pennsylvania Avenue.

They ought to know better than we, and do know. I have in my lifetime heard many arguments why the negro ought to be a slave; but if they fight for those who would keep them in slavery it will be a better argument than any I have yet heard. [Laughter and applause.]

He who will fight for that ought to be a slave. [Applause.] They have concluded, at last, to take one out of four of the slaves and put him in the army; and that one out of four, who will fight to keep the others in slavery, ought to be a slave himself, unless he is killed in a fight. [Applause.]

While I have often said that all men ought to be free, yet I would allow those colored persons to be slaves who want to be; and next to them those white men who agree in favor of making other people slaves. [Applause.] I'm in favor of giving an opportunity to such white men to try it on for themselves.

Walt Whitman, surrounded by this cheering, laughing crowd, admired Lincoln's folksy employment of the ancient rhetorical trick, the reductio ad absurdum.

"I will say one thing with regard to the negro being employed to fight for them that I *do* know," Lincoln continued, wryly. "I know he cannot fight and stay home and make bread too. [Laughter and applause.] And as one is about as important as the other to them, I don't care which they do. [Renewed applause.]"

On second thought, the President admitted: "I am rather in

favor of having them try them as soldiers. [Applause.] They lack
one vote of doing that [in the Confederate Congress] and I wish I
could send my vote over the river, so that I might cast it in favor of
allowing the negro to fight. But they cannot fight and work both.

"We must now see the bottom of the enemy's resources . . . I
am glad to see the end so near at hand. [Applause.] I have said now
more than I intended to, and will, therefore, bid you good bye."

A burst of handclapping, cheers, and huzzas, and as the Marine
Band tootled a spirited air the President waved and left the balcony. It was the last time Whitman would ever see him.

In the hotel parlor Lincoln received the greetings of a few
friends before leaving for the White House. Outside, the throng
sent up three cheers for the flag, three for the President, and three
for the Governor, and then dispersed. Whitman was carried along
with the crowd up the Avenue past the Center Market, then over
the Seventh Street Bridge to Armory Square Hospital. He would
check up on his soldiers before meeting up with Peter Doyle to celebrate St. Patrick's Day. Whitman had received a two-week leave
of absence from work so that he could return to Brooklyn. His
train would be leaving in the morning.

That Saturday night John Wilkes Booth opened at Ford's Theatre
in one of his most famous roles, the obsessed villain Pescara in
Irish playwright Richard Lalor Shiel's melodrama *The Apostate*.
Pescara, Governor of Granada, so hates the dark Moors that he
mounts a genocidal attack upon them. Booth had gotten tickets for
his coconspirators John Surratt, David Herold, Louis Weichmann,
and George Atzerodt, in the President's box, so they might become familiar with its access and defenses.

Seated near the stage, Booth's friends watched their illustrious leader as he strutted and rolled his eyes and dispatched one hapless Moor after another, crying, "What if I rush and with a blow strike life from out his heart?"

That night and the next the conspirators drank brandy and champagne at Gautier's, and at Taltavul's Restaurant, which adjoined the theater. Booth, who had been a moderate drinker, was now consuming astonishing amounts of brandy, as much as a quart in two hours. The men heatedly contested the risky plan to "capture" Lincoln; by the end of the weekend it dawned upon Booth that he might have to go it alone. He realized that in the absence of several stouthearted collaborators he would have to give up his own life to take President Lincoln's.

Lincoln had shared with Congressman Cornelius Cole his confidence that "one man's life is as dear to him as another's, and he [an assassin] could not expect to take my life without losing his own." Booth had become the unlikely fanatic, one ready to lose his own life if he could take the President down with him. That Sunday, as Booth swilled brandy three blocks away, Lincoln attended Gounod's *Faust* at Grover's Theatre. Later that night the President dreamed of his assassination.

Whitman went to Brooklyn in late March on a two-week furlough to visit his brother George, who was convalescing from his prison ordeal. Walt stayed on an extra two weeks to oversee the production of his new book of poetry.

Book publishing was slow during the war years, but even so the delays in *Drum-Taps*'s debut were extreme. Whitman's patience was admirable. There are at least seventeen known references by Whitman and his friends in their general correspondence to the imminent appearance of *Drum-Taps*, beginning in May 1863, when one friend, E. M. Allen, wrote to John Burroughs, "He has a volume coming out soon called 'Drum Taps.' " On November 17, 1863, Whitman wrote to Charles Eldridge, "I must bring out Drum Taps. I *must* be continually bringing out poems." On March 2, 1864, Whitman wrote to his mother that he would soon be in New York to bring out *Drum-Taps*, and during that spring and summer he told his brother and Burroughs the same thing. In July, sick, bedridden, he told William O'Connor, "I intend to move heaven & earth to publish my 'Drum Taps' as soon as I am able to go around."

By 1865 Whitman had resolved to publish the book himself rather than wait any longer. While friends urged him to get the support of an established publisher such as G. W. Carlton in New York, Whitman told Nellie O'Connor, "I feel it is best for me to print my books myself." Perhaps he feared rejection; certainly Whitman wanted the finest paper and binding, and type set to his own specifications, and he was willing to pay for these things out of his own pocket rather than relinquish control to a publisher.

He thought these were the finest poems he had ever written. In a letter to William O'Connor at the beginning of 1865 he declared the book "superior to *Leaves of Grass*—certainly more perfect as a work of art, being adjusted in all its proportions & its passion having the indispensible merit that though to an ordinary reader let loose with wildest abandon, the true artist can see that it is yet under control." He believed he had expressed the "large conflicting fluctuations of despair & hope . . . the unprecedented anguish of wounded & suffering, the beautiful young men in wholesale death & agony, everything sometimes as if blood-color, & dripping blood. The book is therefore unprecedently sad . . . but it also has the blast of the trumpet . . . then an undertone of sweetest

comradeship and human love . . . Truly also, it has clear notes of
faith & triumph."

Regrettably, the success of *Drum-Taps* as a work of art is
known only to a few people who have read the rare early editions
of the volume. Whitman later dissolved the book and scattered
most of its poems throughout the final editions of *Leaves of Grass*.
What survives in his collected works under the subtitle "Drum-
Taps" is a ghost of the book's original living form.

Whitman staunchly believed in these poems. By now he also
knew he was the man to oversee their printing and distribution to
the public, probably by subscription. The most likely reason the
book had been delayed this long was for lack of funds. His salary
of $100 a month now made it possible for the poet to make a down
payment for stereotyping the verses. Although printers advised
him that the cost of paper and printing would be much lower if he
waited a few weeks, he couldn't wait. On April Fools' Day he
signed a contract with Peter Eckler to stereotype five hundred
copies of *Drum-Taps* for $254. He probably borrowed some of the
money from John Burroughs.

On that same day, Major General Philip Sheridan, leading the
charge in the Appomattox campaign, succeeded in turning Robert
E. Lee's flank at the Battle of Five Forks. The Rebel army began a
frantic retreat to the west. Sheridan, in hot pursuit with infantry
and cavalry, closed off Lee's escape route beyond Appomattox
Courthouse. Confederate President Jefferson Davis and his cabinet fled Richmond.

Three days later, on April 4, Abraham Lincoln arrived near
Richmond on the flagship USS *Malvern*, with his son Tad and his
bodyguard William Crook. They walked to downtown Richmond, surrounded by black people shouting "Glory, glory!"

Thousands of white citizens watched the entourage in sullen silence from the windows of those homes and shops that had survived the torches. Some bridges and warehouses were still ablaze, others smoking. When Lincoln reached the former Confederate executive mansion, now the Union military headquarters, he sat in Jefferson Davis's chair, and the soldiers cheered.

"Thank God I have lived to see this," Lincoln said. "It seems to me that I have been dreaming a horrid dream for four years, and now the nightmare is gone."

Lee surrendered to Grant on April 9. The Union rejoiced. Crowds and bands surrounded the White House, serenading the happy President and his family at all hours.

In New York, Whitman labored over *Drum-Taps*. The foremost authority on the printing of this book, F. DeWolfe Miller, has written that the poet "had, we can be quite sure, hovered over the galley proofs at Eckler's between April 1 and 15."

Back in Washington, on the evening of April 14, Whitman's friend Peter Doyle hung up his conductor's uniform and put on his best clothes: a double-breasted frock coat with satin edging on the lapels, and a white lace tie and matching pocket handkerchief. It had been a fine spring day, with clouds hiding the sun now and then. Lilacs scented the air, and the dogwood and Judas trees were blooming. In the afternoon the wind came up, and now there was a damp chill in the air. Doyle swung aboard the horsecar at the Navy Yard, enjoying his status as a passenger, on his way up to Ford's Theatre.

The President and his wife had gone out on a carriage ride late that afternoon. They ended up at the Navy Yard, where Lincoln chatted with the sailors and boarded one of the ironclads that had been hit at Charleston harbor. Mary later recalled that he was "cheerful—almost joyous." Maybe Doyle had seen the crowd gathered around Mr. and Mrs. Lincoln, so near his home at 62 M Street South, and this prompted him to attend the comedy at Ford's Theatre—knowing that the President would be there. The newspapers, especially the *Evening Star*, had interlarded the entertainment ads with the announcement: *The President and his Lady will be at the Theatre this evening*—as if to say that the theater was *the* place to be tonight.

"I heard that the President and his wife would be present and made up my mind to go," Doyle recalled. The sun set at 6:45. As the streetcar headed north on Eighth Street and then west on Pennsylvania Avenue, the lamplighters were at work with their ladders and wicks; the mist made halos around the lanterns. Although it was Good Friday, the last full day of Lent, the saloons were booming with revelers celebrating the peace. Alone that evening, Peter Doyle would celebrate victory just as Whitman might have done if he had been in town, by seeing, and applauding, the President in Ford's Theatre.

Doyle got off at Tenth Street near the Canterbury Music Hall, a corner theater that featured bawdy shows. As he walked up Tenth, the traffic thickened and slowed. Gilded carriages and coaches were parked on both sides of the street, their black reinsmen at ease in the driver's boxes. A wooden ramp ran the length of the theater to protect the ladies' dresses from the mud. Gentlemen in woolen overcoats and shawled ladies with small fur muffs poured into the brick theater through the arched doorways. There was a queue at the box office. In the windows of the houses across the street, people had opened their curtains, hoping for a glimpse of the President.

Peter Doyle gave his ticket to the usher, removed his hat, and mounted the stairs to the second gallery. He took a seat on a straight-backed chair on the left side of the theater, across from the State Box. He waited. At last the conductor tapped his baton and lifted it to begin the overture, and two black boys in scarlet breeches drew back the curtain. The President's box, decked with silk flags festooning a painting of George Washington, was still empty at 8:15 when the actress Laura Keene made her entrance in *My American Cousin.* At 8:30 the patrons in the dress circle began to rise from their seats and clap, first a few and then all, craning their necks as the President led his party down the right side aisle and up to the State Box. Laura Keene stopped the action onstage to join in the ovation. Peter Doyle stood up with the rest of the audience to welcome the President and his wife, as the orchestra played "Hail to the Chief." The clapping continued awhile after the band played its last notes, and the Lincolns settled in to enjoy the play.

"There was nothing extraordinary in the performance," Doyle remembered. "I saw everything on the stage and was in a good position to see the President's box." Lincoln sat in a rocking chair. Draperies partly concealed him from the curious crowd. At approximately 10:10 John Wilkes Booth stole into the State Box, put his derringer to the back of Lincoln's head between his left ear and his spine, and pulled the trigger.

"I heard the pistol shot," Doyle recalled years later. A laugh line in the play muffled the little explosion, so he was not immediately sure what it meant. "I really knew nothing of what had occurred until Mrs. Lincoln leaned out of the box and cried, 'The President is shot!' I needn't tell you what I felt then, or saw. It is all put down in Walt's piece—that piece is exactly right." (Doyle refers to Whitman's amplified narrative in his famous speech on Lincoln.) "I saw Booth on the cushion of the box, saw him jump over, saw him catch his foot, which turned, saw him fall on the stage. He got up on his feet, cried out something which I could not hear for the hub-hub and disappeared."

There had been 1,675 people in the theater, not counting Booth, the first to depart. Doyle recalled: "I suppose I lingered almost the last person. A soldier came into the gallery, saw me still there, called to me: 'Get out of here! We're going to burn this damned building down!' I said: 'If that is so I'll get out!' "

Doyle, like everyone else, was in shock—disoriented by the sudden loss of the government's conscience, its guiding principle embodied in a mortal. The nation spun, temporarily rudderless.

WHEN LILACS LAST IN
THE DOORYARD BLOOM'D

*W*hitman wrote to William O'Connor that he was "mainly satisfied with Drum-Taps because it delivers my ambition of the task that has haunted me, namely, to express in a poem . . . the pending action of this *Time & Land we swim in*, with all their large conflicting fluctuations of despair & hope, the shiftings, masses, & the whirl & deafening din, (yet over all, as by invisible hand, a definite purport and idea) . . ." His satisfaction with *Drum-Taps* came to an abrupt and unseasonable end.

Word of Lincoln's death at 7:22 A.M. on April 15 arrived in New York with the morning newspapers. The tolling of church bells awakened many Brooklynites, including Whitman and his mother.

"Mother prepared breakfast—and other meals afterward—as usual," he recalled, "but not a mouthful was eaten all day by either of us. We each drank half a cup of coffee; that was all. Little was said. We got every newspaper morning and evening, and the frequent extras of that period, and pass'd them silently to each other."

In late morning the sky darkened; by noon it was raining. Whitman walked out toward the docks, notebook and pencil in hand. "When a great event happens," he jotted, "or the news [of] some signal solemn thing spreads out among the people, it is curious to go forth and wander awhile in the public ways." All the shops were closed, "business public & private all suspended." Along the crowded wharves the ships' flags were at half-mast, and many spars were flying black pennants. Looking at the sky the poet saw long black clouds "like great serpents slowly undulating in every direction."

"Lincoln's death—black, black, black . . . ," he wrote in his notebook. And on people's faces he noted a "strange mixture of horror, fury, tenderness, & a stirring wonder brewing."

At four in the afternoon he took the paddlewheel Fulton Ferry across the East River so he could walk up Broadway. "The scene was solemn & most eloquent—I had so often seen Broadway on great gala days . . . deck'd with rich colors jubilant show crowds, & the music of a hundred bands with marches & opera airs—or at night with processions bearing countless torches & transparencies & gas lanterns . . ."

But now, "the stores were shut, & no business transacted, no pleasure vehicles, & hardly a cart—only the rumbling base of the heavy Broadway stages incessantly rolling." The columns of some buildings had spiral windings of black and white crape. Groups gathered around bulletin boards, talking in hushed tones. The poet struggled to find words to describe the weather, "sulky, leaden, & dripping continually moist tears—" He noted that one fashionable art dealer, having closed his doors, exhibited in the plate glass window a lone picture frame, hauntingly empty. "In this death the tragedy of the last five years has risen to its climax—the blood of Abraham Lincoln has—" he wrote in his notebook. But then his pencil could not keep pace with his feelings.

Whitman realized that the assassination was a watershed in American history and the nation's consciousness. "Time & Land" had changed forever. Overnight the book that Whitman prized for its timeliness had become a dated relic. Even as printer Peter Eckler was pulling the first proofs of *Drum-Taps*, America had undergone its greatest trauma since the first Battle of Bull Run, Whitman believed, and the "invisible hand" that had given it a definite purport and idea was stilled forever. Whitman prophesied that "the tragic splendor of his death, purging, illuminating all, throws round his form, his head, an aureole that will remain and grow brighter through time," and when future historians would seek an event to summon up "this turbulent nineteenth century of ours," they would "seek in vain for any point to serve more thoroughly their purposes than Abraham Lincoln's death."

This Saturday, stunned and grief-stricken as he was, the poet realized that his book had fallen behind the action of the times: *Drum-Taps* must reckon with the death of the President.

> *Hush'd be the camps to-day;*
> *And soldiers, let us drape our war-worn weapons;*
> *And each, with musing soul retire, to celebrate,*
> *Our dear commander's death . . .*

On Monday, April 17, the newspapers announced that Lincoln would be buried on Wednesday in the Congressional Cemetery. That day and the next, the poet was in New York writing the poem "Hush'd Be the Camps To-Day," which bears the subcaption

"A. L. Buried April 19, 1865." Whitman ordered Peter Eckler to stop the press and insert the new poem on page 69 of the seventy-two-page book.

> *No more for him life's stormy conflicts;*
> *Nor victory, nor defeat—No more time's dark events,*
> *Charging like ceaseless clouds across the sky.*
>
> *But sing, poet, in our name;*
> *Sing of the love we bore him—because you,*
> *dweller in camps, know it truly.*
>
> *Sing, to the lowered coffin there;*
> *Sing, with shovel'd clods that fill the grave—a verse*
> *For the heavy hearts of soldiers.*

On such short notice this was the best the poet could do to bring his book up to date. The next day, it was announced that the funeral plans were changed: the chief obsequies would be held on the nineteenth in the capital. Then the funeral train would begin its sad twelve-day journey north, to Baltimore, Harrisburg, Philadelphia, New York, then west to Albany, Cleveland, Columbus, Indianapolis, and Chicago en route to Springfield, where Lincoln would be interred in May.

That week Whitman had agonizing decisions to make. He seems to have been bewildered by the events, and perplexed by the status of *Drum-Taps*. Should he withdraw the book and rewrite it to reflect the recent tragedy? Should he halt publication, or finish what he had begun? Would the public want the book in its present state? The binder's cost would be eighteen cents per volume. All the money Whitman had been able to save or borrow was riding on the decision.

Mourning Lincoln, grieving over his blighted book, sometime that week Whitman compromised. Before leaving New York, on April 21, he ordered the Bradstreet Bindery to sew up a hundred copies of *Drum-Taps*. He returned to Washington on April 22 with the full printer's copy, which he later presented to Peter Doyle.

According to the terms of his extended furlough, Whitman was supposed to return to Washington on Monday, April 17, where he would have witnessed the funeral rituals he later commemorated in "When Lilacs Last in the Dooryard Bloom'd." For nearly a century, until the publication of F. DeWolfe Miller's study of the receipts and letters concerning the printing of *Drum-Taps* in the Charles E. Feinberg Collection in the Library of Congress, scholars assumed that Whitman based "When Lilacs Last in the Dooryard Bloom'd" upon his personal experience of Lincoln's funeral, or the torchlit night procession of the funeral train, or possibly both. A careful reading of the exchanges among Whitman, Eckler, and the bindery reveals that Whitman instead gathered his imagery from reading newspaper accounts. Passing from printer to binder in Manhattan, or from the Patent Office to Gardner's Gallery and newsstand on D Street in Washington, Whitman studied the black-bordered morning and evening editions covering the funeral train's progress. He devoured the language of grief he found in the papers hawked on street corners.

He was with the printer and binder in New York when the civic procession escorted the hearse from the White House to the Capitol, as the bands played the dead march. He was traveling south about the time the funeral train took its slow course north (he may actually have *passed* the coffin going the other way), arriving in Washington just as Lincoln's remains were placed in the rotunda of New York's City Hall for viewing.

The dark cortege as it moved from City Hall up Fifth Avenue

to the Hudson River Depot—twenty thousand Union troops in blue, and eighty thousand civilian mourners of every race, religion, and political persuasion—was witnessed by more than a million people. Whitman was far away.

"New York never before saw such a day," said the *New York Herald*. "Rome in the palmiest days of its power never witnessed such a triumphal march . . ." The funeral train continued its journey to Illinois, as every major city on the route arranged its own elaborate ceremonies, described in detail in newspapers that sold almost as fast as they could be printed. In Washington, Whitman mourned quietly, introspectively, alone or in the company of Burroughs, O'Connor, and Doyle. He returned to his copy work and his visits to the hospitals.

Sometime in late April Whitman began, in black pencil on white-woven paper, to make notes for a formal elegy for Lincoln. He noted: "As to the other Presidents, in life & death, they have had their due in formal & respectful treatment, in life & death. But this one alone has touch'd the popular heart to its deepest. For this one alone, through every City, every Country farm, the untouch'd meal, the heavy heart & moistened eye and the song in private chambers[.]" He resolved to "make a list of things, sights, scenes, landscapes, rivers . . . and bring it in / also in dim perspective, the large and varied future /

> *No mourning drape hang*
> *I about my song*
> *But these I hang &*
> *plant about my*
> *song.*

He started his list with the words of mourning, probably gathered from newspapers or from a thesaurus:

> Sorrow   grieve   sad   mourn (I use) *mourn*ing   *mourn*ful
> melancholy   dismal   heavy-hearted   tears   black
> sobbing   sighing   funereal   rites   wailing
> lamenting . . .

This is clearly a cathartic free-association meant to generate the funereal language for his elegy. The vocabulary list, more than a hundred words in three columns, evolves from terms of extroverted grieving to:

> depression   pain of mind   passionate regret   afflicted with
> grief   cast down   downcast   gloomy   serious   Sympathy
> moving compassion   tenderness   tender-hearted   full of
> pity . . .

Several of these phrases, such as "passionate regret," reveal Whitman's feelings about losing this compatriot with whom he had felt such an affinity, one he had often praised as "tender-hearted" and "full of pity," this nodding acquaintance he had wished might someday become a friend.

From the simple listing of elegiac words in his notebook, Whitman advanced to the description of the hermit thrush, which became the symbol for his poetic expression of grief:

> Hermit Thrush / Solitary Thrush / moderate sized grayish
> brown bird / sings oftener after sundown sometimes quite in
> the night / is very secluded / likes shaded, dark places in
> swamps—is very shy / song clear and deliberate—has a
> solemn effect—his song is a hymn / real, serious sweet . . .

—only those that frequent the deep remote dark woods hear it— ...

—it is perhaps all the more precious, because it is only sung in secluded places—he never sings near the farm houses—never in the settlement / is the bird of the solemn primal woods & of Nature pure & holy—

A letter from John Burroughs to Myron Benton (a friend of Whitman's) that summer comments that Whitman "is deeply interested in what I tell him of the Hermit Thrush, and says he has used largely the information I have given him in one of his principal poems." Burroughs called the hermit thrush's song "The finest sound in Nature. It is not a proud, gorgeous strain like the tanager's or the grosbeak's . . . it suggests no passion or emotion—nothing personal, but seems to be the voice of that calm, sweet solemnity one attains to in his best moments. It realizes peace and a deep, solemn joy that only the finest souls may know." The picture of that great naturalist leading the "Good Gray Poet" through swamps at midnight to hear the thrush is an appealing bit of lore attached to the story of the poem's genesis. But Whitman may not have heard the elusive thrush, any more than he had seen the funeral train.

To be sure, there were lilacs in abundance that spring, with their purple, drooping panicles, their heady scent; and there was the "western star," Venus, low in the sky in the evenings. But this is more a poem of deep imaginative reflection than of immediate experience. "Lilacs" is one of the most self-consciously literary, deliberately constructed poems Whitman ever wrote. So much of his verse, particularly the war poetry of *Drum-Taps,* has the immediacy of an eyewitness account. This poem, probably Whitman's greatest, does not. It is an uncommonly long and complex lyric of more than two hundred lines, with epic qualities. And unlike many of Whitman's long poems, its twenty-one sections are in continuous development from the first sight of the fragrant flower to the sound of the thrush in the woods at the close.

> *I give you my sprig of lilac.*

> *(Nor for you, for one, alone;*
> *Blossoms and branches green to coffins all I bring . . .*

Although Whitman still visited wounded and dying soldiers every afternoon after a day's work in the Patent Office building, his other activities slowed. His notebook entries and correspondence dwindled, as he spent more and more of his lamplit hours in his room writing, mining the imagery of the Washington spring and his memories of Lincoln.

> *And how shall I deck my song for the large sweet soul that has gone?*
> *.   .   .*

> *O what shall I hang on the chamber walls?*
> *And what shall the pictures be that I hang on the walls,*
> *To adorn the burial-house of him I love?*

> *Pictures of growing spring, and farms, and homes . . .*

His meditation would lead him ultimately to "the knowledge of death as walking one side of me / And the thought of death close-walking the other side of me, / And I in the middle, as with companions, and as holding the hands of companions . . ." The poet would serve as a ferryman, a guide to the river of the dead, one who understands the healing power of death.

The richness of the poem comes from Whitman's skillful braiding of the strands of three major images—blossom, star, and bird—throughout an epic drama, whose suspense is prolonged until the final verses. The setting is the geography of the nation, as the funeral train passes through cities and towns, farms and fields. But the scene has a metaphysical dimension, opening into the realm of death—which perhaps no poet has ever known so intimately—and the future "ever-returning spring," where he, and his poem, will mourn perennially.

The dramatic situation is straightforward: the grieving poet, trapped in the "harsh surrounding cloud that will not free my soul," desires to offer a fitting tribute to the man he loves, the President he reveres. The question is this: What could possibly suffice, for a hero so grand and bereavement so profound? The answer may be found in the poem's panoramic sweep.

1

When lilacs last in the door-yard bloom'd,
And the great star early droop'd in the western sky in the night,
I mourn'd . . . and yet shall mourn with ever-returning spring.

O ever-returning spring! trinity sure to me you bring;
Lilac blooming perennial, and drooping star in the west,
And thought of him I love.

2

O powerful, western, fallen star!
O shades of night! O moody, tearful night!
O great star disappear'd! O the black murk that hides the star!
O cruel hands that hold me powerless! O helpless soul of me!
O harsh surrounding cloud that will not free my soul!

3

In the door-yard fronting an old farm-house, near the white-wash'd
    palings,
Stands the lilac bush, tall-growing, with heart-shaped leaves of rich
    green,
With many a pointed blossom, rising, delicate, with the perfume
    strong I love,
With every leaf a miracle . . . . . . and from this bush in the
    door-yard,
With its delicate-color'd blossoms, and heart-shaped leaves of rich
    green,
A sprig, with its flower, I break.

4

In the swamp, in secluded recesses,
A shy and hidden bird is warbling a song.

Solitary, the thrush,
The hermit, withdrawn to himself, avoiding the settlements,
Sings by himself a song.

Song of the bleeding throat!
Death's outlet song of life——(for well, dear brother I know,
If thou wast not gifted to sing, thou would'st surely die.)

5

Over the breast of spring, the land, amid cities,
Amid lanes, and through old woods, (where lately the violets peep'd
    from the ground, spotting the gray debris;)
Amid the grass in the fields each side of the lanes——passing the
    endless grass;

Passing the yellow-spear'd wheat, every grain from its shroud in the
    dark-brown fields uprising;
Passing the apple-tree blows of white and pink in the orchards;
Carrying a corpse to where it shall rest in the grave,
Night and day journeys a coffin.

6

Coffin that passes through lanes and streets,
Through day and night, with the great cloud darkening the land,
With the pomp of the inloop'd flags, with the cities draped in black,
With the show of the States themselves, as of crape-veil'd women,
    standing,
With processions long and winding, and the flambeaus of the night,
With the countless torches lit—with the silent sea of faces, and the
    unbared heads,
With the waiting depot, the arriving coffin, and the sombre faces,
With dirges through the night, with the thousand voices rising strong
    and solemn;
With all the mournful voices of the dirges, pour'd around the coffin,
The dim-lit churches and the shuddering organs—Where amid these
    you journey,
With the tolling, tolling bells' perpetual clang;
Here! coffin that slowly passes,
I give you my sprig of lilac.

7

(Nor for you, for one, alone;
Blossoms and branches green to coffins all I bring:
For fresh as the morning—thus would I chant a song for you, O sane
    and sacred death.

All over bouquets of roses,
O death! I cover you over with roses and early lilies;
But mostly and now the lilac that blooms the first,
Copious, I break, I break the sprigs from the bushes:
With loaded arms I come, pouring for you,
For you and the coffins all of you, O death.)

8
O western orb, sailing the heaven!
Now I know what you must have meant, as a month since we
     walk'd,
As we walk'd up and down in the dark blue so mystic,
As we walk'd in silence the transparent shadowy night,
As I saw you had something to tell, as you bent to me night after
     night,
As you droop'd from the sky low down, as if to my side, (while the
     other stars all look'd on;)
As we wander'd together the solemn night (for something I know not
     what, kept me from sleep;)
As the night advanced, and I saw on the rim of the west, ere you
     went, how full you were of woe;
As I stood on the rising ground in the breeze, in the cool transparent
     night,
As I watch'd where you pass'd and was lost in the netherward black of
     the night,
As my soul, in its trouble, dissatisfied, sank, as where you, sad orb,
Concluded, dropt in the night, and was gone.

9
Sing on, there in the swamp!
O singer bashful and tender! I hear your notes—I hear your call;

I hear—I come presently—I understand you;
But a moment I linger—for the lustrous star has detain'd me;
The star, my comrade, departing, holds and detains me.

10

O how shall I warble myself for the dead one there I loved?
And how shall I deck my song for the large sweet soul that has gone?
And what shall my perfume be, for the grave of him I love?

Sea-winds, blown from east and west,
Blown from the eastern sea, and blown from the western sea, till there
*   on the prairies meeting:*
These, and with these, and the breath of my chant,
I perfume the grave of him I love.

11

O what shall I hang on the chamber walls?
And what shall the pictures be that I hang on the walls,
To adorn the burial-house of him I love?

Pictures of growing spring, and farms, and homes,
With the Fourth-month eve at sundown, and the gray-smoke lucid
*   and bright,*
With floods of the yellow gold of the gorgeous, indolent, sinking
*   sun, burning, expanding the air;*
With the fresh sweet herbage under foot, and the pale green leaves of
*   the trees prolific;*
In the distance the flowing gaze, the breast of the river, with a wind-
*   dapple here and there;*
With ranging hills on the banks, with many a line against the sky,
*   and shadows;*

And the city at hand, with dwellings so dense, and stacks of
   chimneys,
And all the scenes of life, and the workshops, and the workmen
   homeward returning.

12

Lo! body and soul! this land!
Mighty Manhattan, with spires, and the sparkling and hurrying
   tides, and the ships;
The varied and ample land—the South and the North in the light—
   Ohio's shores, and flashing Missouri,
And ever the far-spreading prairies, cover'd with grass and corn.

Lo! the most excellent sun, so calm and haughty;
The violet and purple morn, with just-felt breezes:
The gentle, soft-born, measureless light;
The miracle, spreading, bathing all—the fulfill'd noon;
The coming eve, delicious—the welcome night, and the stars,
Over my cities shining all, enveloping man and land.

13

Sing on! sing on, you gray-brown bird!
Sing from the swamps, the recesses—pour your chant from the
   bushes;
Limitless out of the dusk, out of the cedars and pines.

Sing on, dearest brother—warble your reedy song;
Loud human song, with voice of uttermost woe.

O liquid, and free, and tender!
O wild and loose to my soul! O wondrous singer!

You only I hear . . . . . . yet the star holds me, (but will soon depart;)
Yet the lilac, with mastering odor, holds me.

14

Now while I sat in the day, and look'd forth,
In the close of the day, with its light, and the fields of spring, and
    the farmer preparing his crops,
In the large unconscious scenery of my land, with its lakes and
    forests,
In the heavenly aerial beauty, (after the perturb'd winds, and the
    storms;)
Under the arching heavens of the afternoon swift passing, and the
    voices of children and women,
The many-moving sea-tides,—and I saw the ships how they sail'd,
And the summer approaching with richness, and the fields all busy
    with labor,
And the infinite separate houses, how they all went on, each with its
    meals and minutia of daily usages;
And the streets, how their throbbings throbb'd, and the cities pent,—
    lo! then and there,
Falling among them all, and upon them all, enveloping me with the
    rest,
Appeared the cloud, appear'd the long black trail;
And I knew Death, its thought, and the sacred knowledge of death.

15

Then with the knowledge of death as walking one side of me,
And the thought of death close-walking the other side of me,
And I in the middle, as with companions, and as holding the hands of
    companions,
I fled forth to the hiding receiving night, that talks not,

Down to the shores of the water, the path by the swamp in the
    dimness,
To the solemn shadowy cedars, and ghostly pines so still.

And the singer so shy to the rest receiv'd me;
The gray-brown bird I know, receiv'd us comrades three;
And he sang what seem'd the song of death, and a verse for him I
    love.

From deep secluded recesses,
From the fragrant cedars, and the ghostly pines so still,
Came the singing of the bird.

And the charm of the singing rapt me,
As I held, as if by their hands, my comrades in the night;
And the voice of my spirit tallied the song of the bird.

16
Come, lovely and soothing Death,
Undulate round the world, serenely arriving, arriving,
In the day, in the night, to all, to each,
Sooner or later, delicate Death.

Prais'd be the fathomless universe,
For life and joy, and for objects and knowledge curious;
And for love, sweet love—But praise! O praise and praise,
For the sure-enwinding arms of cool-enfolding Death.

Dark Mother, always gliding near, with soft feet,
Have none chanted for thee a chant of fullest welcome?
Then I chant it for thee—I glorify thee above all;

I bring thee a song that when thou must indeed come, come
　　unfalteringly.

Approach, encompassing Death—strong Deliveress!
When it is so—when thou hast taken them, I joyously sing the dead,
Lost in the loving, floating ocean of thee,
Laved in the flood of thy bliss, O Death.

From me to thee glad serenades,
Dances for thee I propose, saluting thee—adornments and feastings
　　for thee;
And the sights of the open landscape, and the high-spread sky, are
　　fitting,
And life and the fields, and the huge and thoughtful night.

The night, in silence, under many a star;
The ocean shore, and the husky whispering wave, whose voice I
　　know;
And the soul turning to thee, O vast and well-veil'd Death,
And the body gratefully nestling close to thee.

Over the tree-tops I float thee a song!
Over the rising and sinking waves—over the myriad fields, and the
　　prairies wide;
Over the dense-pack'd cities all, and the teeming wharves and ways,
I float this carol with joy, with joy to thee, O Death!

17
To the tally of my soul,
Loud and strong kept up the gray-brown bird,
With pure, deliberate notes, spreading, filling the night.

Loud in the pines and cedars dim,
Clear in the freshness moist, and the swamp-perfume;
And I with my comrades there in the night.

While my sight that was bound in my eyes unclosed,
As to long panoramas of visions.

18

I saw the vision of armies;
And I saw, as in noiseless dreams, hundreds of battle-flags;
Borne through the smoke of the battles, and pierc'd with missiles, I
*   saw them,*
And carried hither and yon through the smoke, and torn and bloody;
And at last but a few shreds of the flags left on the staffs, (and all in
*   silence,)*
And the staffs all splinter'd and broken.

I saw battle-corpses, myriads of them,
And the white skeletons of young men——I saw them;
I saw the debris and debris of all dead soldiers;
But I saw they were not as I thought;
They themselves were fully at rest——they suffer'd not;
The living remained and suffer'd——the mother suffer'd,
And the wife and the child, and the musing comrade suffer'd,
And the armies that remain'd suffer'd.

19

Passing the visions, passing the night;
Passing, unloosing the hold of my comrades' hands;
Passing the song of the hermit bird, and the tallying song of my
*   soul,*

Victorious song, death's outlet song, (yet varying, ever-altering song,

As low and wailing, yet clear the notes, rising and falling, flooding
  the night,

Sadly sinking and fainting, as warning and warning, and yet again
  bursting with joy,)

Covering the earth, and filling the spread of the heaven,

As that powerful psalm in the night I heard from the recesses.

20

Must I leave thee, lilac with heart-shaped leaves?

Must I leave thee there in the door-yard, blooming, returning with
  spring?

Must I pass from my song for thee;

From my gaze on thee in the west, fronting the west, communing with
  thee,

O comrade lustrous, with silver face in the night?

21

Yet each I keep, and all;

The song, the wondrous chant of the gray-brown bird, I keep,

And the tallying chant, the echo arous'd in my soul, I keep,

With the lustrous and drooping star, with the countenance full of
  woe;

With the lilac tall, and its blossoms of mastering odor;

Comrades mine, and I in the midst, and their memory ever I keep—
  for the dead I loved so well;

For the sweetest, wisest soul of all my days and lands . . . and this
  for his dear sake;

Lilac and star and bird, twined with the chant of my soul,

With the holders holding my hand, nearing the call of the bird,

There in the fragrant pines, and the cedars dusk and dim.

As in the great English elegies that served as Whitman's models—Milton's "Lycidas," and Shelley's "Adonais"—the true name of the deceased is never mentioned. This is wholly fitting here because "Lilacs" honors not just the President but all "the dead I loved so well," hundreds of soldiers Whitman had attended in the hospitals. Lincoln becomes the "powerful, western, fallen star," one of the "trinity" of symbols that includes lilacs, with their fragrance an emblem of breath (spirit) and regeneration, and the thrush, representing in turn "the thought of him I love" and "Death's outlet song of life," before becoming the poet's voice and the very elegy he is creating.

To these three symbols Whitman adds a fourth major trope, the allegorical figure of Death, the veiled "Dark Mother" he summons in the sublime section 16 of his poem: "Come, lovely and soothing Death, / Undulate round the world, serenely arriving . . . Have none chanted for thee a chant of fullest welcome?" She is reminiscent of "the Maternal Figure over all," shining at the top of the Capitol dome Whitman admired.

In the drama of the poem the poet moves from the bedrock of the present moment, where he asks his central question, What is the fitting tribute for such a man?, to the realms of revery and vision—the beautiful American landscape in spring (sections 11, 12, and 14) and the nightmare memories of war (section 18). Although he does not find his answer in either realm, the journey is intrinsically valuable, as it yields poetic imagery—and it is in the poetry itself that the mourner will find consolation at last.

Whitman identified his poetry with his ideal of the democratic nation, a nurturing Union that sanctified human love, of man for man, man for woman, mother for child, etc. He believed he had been born of this ideal Union, and he regarded it as the end to which he was inevitably and appropriately consecrated. America had made him, and America would reclaim him. Poetry had blessed him, and poetry would forever enfold him. No wonder he wanted to make his own books! In the infirmity of old age he would take great pains to design his own mausoleum, at a fabulous cost.

The demise of his democratic hero, Lincoln, provided the poet with an occasion to celebrate Death as the "Dark Mother," the "strong Deliveress," to link death boldly with birth. Whitman's death song, often called the "Death Carol," in section 16, is his most precious gift for the slain hero—and for himself as well—for it frees both the President and the poet from the bonds of the grave. It is the peaceful absolution of a soldier's missionary, one who had sat at so many bedsides and watched so many a young man peacefully breathe his last in the arms of the "strong Deliveress." In his earlier poem "The Dresser," he first calls upon Her: "Come sweet death! be persuaded O beautiful death! In mercy come quickly." In that poem and others in *Drum-Taps* Whitman's intimacy with maternal Death is so complete he appears to embody it himself: "Many a soldier's loving arms about this neck have cross'd and rested, / Many a soldier's kiss dwells on these bearded lips."

"I knew Death, its thought, and the sacred knowledge of death," he says in section 14 of "Lilacs." It is not the dead who suffer, but the survivors. In section 15 Whitman makes the subtle and wise distinction between the "knowledge of death," which walks on one side of him, and the "thought of death close-walking the other side," producing one of the most magical group portraits in poetry since Dante. The "knowledge of death" is a sacred comfort; the common "thought of death," one's own extinction, is an especially unsettling mystery. The poet walks between them, but it is the menacing comrade who comes closest. They are a powerful trio descending into the dark and silent swamp, where the thrush will sing for them the song that the poet lacks the art, or the hubris, to sing himself.

Whitman's choice of the hermit thrush, the shy "singer bashful and tender," to represent the poet, to sing "what seem'd the song of death, and a verse for him I love," underscores Whitman's resolve to subjugate his own voice. The poet whose exaltation of personality revolutionized the medium of poetry was chastened by his experience in the hospitals. In the War for the Union, and in human suffering, Whitman had found something larger and more important than the vaunting Self in *Leaves of Grass*. He assured O'Connor that his new book was superior because it was free of the "perturbations" of his earlier works. By this he meant erotic turmoil, certainly; but he also recognized that his war experience had subdued his personal ambitions for fame and distinction. Whitman had not wholly conquered his inner "perturbations." He would struggle with them all his life. But, as Gay Wilson Allen has written, "one means by which he controlled them in his *Drum Taps* poems was through the transmutation of his private yearnings for affection into *a universal philosophy of love as a social force*." This sublimation is one of the triumphs of *Drum-Taps* as a whole, and of "Lilacs" as the masterwork of the collection.

The dramatic progress of the poem gives the spotlight to the thrush for the climactic hymn "Come, lovely and soothing Death," as the poet (in section 17) stands back in awe: "While my sight that was bound in my eyes unclosed, / As to long panoramas of visions."

The apostrophe to the "western orb, sailing the heaven," in section 8 of the poem, affectionately recalls Whitman's personal encounters with the President, particularly during the summer of

1863. "Now I know what you must have meant ... / As we walk'd in silence in the transparent shadowy night, / As I saw you had something to tell, as you bent to me night after night, / As you droop'd from the sky low down, as if to my side, (while the other stars all look'd on;) / ... how full you were of woe ..." As Whitman personifies Venus, which shone so brilliantly during February and March, he is also recollecting his evening interactions with the President in his carriage on Vermont Avenue, when Lincoln met his gaze and nodded to him, en route to the Soldiers' Home.

The poem develops an intimacy between Whitman and Lincoln that transcends social contact. The famous dedication in the last stanza, "for the dead I loved so well; / For the sweetest, wisest soul of all my days and lands ..." echoes the diary entry of November 1, 1863 ("his face & manner ... were inexpressibly sweet"), after Whitman had visited the White House and watched Lincoln through the doorway, thinking, "I love the President personally." Even on that Halloween, and on other days when he might have been introduced to Lincoln, Whitman hung back in awe and from a keen artistic instinct. As the poem reaches its resolution, joining lilac, star, and thrush with the chant of the poet's soul, it becomes clear that Lincoln occupied a unique place in Whitman's cosmos. Some people we see daily, but we never know them. Others we may know more by reputation and aura than by association; yet with these, on the basis of infrequent eye contact, we may feel a spiritual bond. The avatar of Democracy, the Commander-in-Chief, was an almost fantastic blend of the real and the ideal, the semidivine hero and the earthy pioneer. Had Whitman ever become well acquainted with Lincoln it is possible that the love that called his great poem into being, the mastering

passion that made him play second fiddle to a thrush, would have
been dulled by custom.

———

No one knows what became of the hundred copies of *Drum-Taps*
that Whitman had ordered bound in April 1865. A few of them
arrived in Washington, fittingly, in late May during the days of the
Grand Review of the Union armies, another great event of that
season. "The long and glittering wide ranks—will they never
stop? For two whole days [May 23–24] commencing early in the
morning and continuing long into the night," Whitman wrote in
his journal. He informed his mother that he had seen President
Johnson, Generals Grant, Meade, and Sherman, and, most important of all, his brother George, marching with his New York regiment.

Mary Lincoln, undone by grief as well as her change in status,
chose the first day of the Grand Review to leave Washington. She
had stayed in the White House longer than was deemed appropriate, because no one had the temerity to ask her to leave. "I go
hence brokenhearted with every hope in life almost crushed," she
said, boarding the train. She could not be persuaded to return to
Springfield, which was the only place she could now reasonably
afford to live. She had too many enemies there, the widow said.
With her sons she took up residence in a Chicago hotel that was far
beyond her means.

The Bradstreet Bindery sent out five copies of *Drum-Taps* to
Louisa Whitman, a copy to Emerson, and a bundle that arrived on
Whitman's desk in time for his forty-sixth birthday, May 31. The
book was a slender duodecimo, bound in liver-maroon cloth,
4½ by 7⅞ inches. On the front was stamped a round medallion

Drum Taps in gold leaf, one word below the other in a circle of gold; on the back the same device was blind-stamped. The spine was unmarked. Whitman gave a copy each to William and Nellie O'Connor; and copies to his immediate superior, Assistant Secretary of the Interior William Otto, and to incoming Secretary of the Interior James Harlan. It would have been better not to give a copy to Harlan, thus calling attention to himself and his poetry, which the new Secretary disliked.

Before Lincoln's death Whitman had prepared a broadside for advertising *Drum-Taps*, and fifty copies of the broadside were printed for use in bookstores. After April 15, there is no evidence of further promotion. As of 1959, Whitman scholar F. DeWolfe Miller could locate only eighteen copies of *Drum-Taps*, none of which appeared to have been sent out for review. Miller writes: "Anyone slightly familiar with Whitman's promotional activities will conclude immediately that he would not have released it for sale without seeing to it that some sort of notices appeared." It is possible that Whitman reduced the binding order; it is certain that, considering the book inadequate, he quietly, passively suppressed it.

Whitman's abandonment of the first edition of *Drum-Taps* appears to coincide with his progress on "When Lilacs Last in the Dooryard Bloom'd" and the other poems for the second edition—such poems as "O Captain! My Captain!" and "Spirit Whose Work Is Done."

At first glance it may seem hard to believe that the poet who wrote "Lilacs" also wrote "O Captain! My Captain!" Yet his letter of March 19, 1863, compares the head of state to a ship's captain, and doubtless Whitman had seen the newspaper story that the night before the assassination the President dreamed of a ship about to enter port under full sail. Nevertheless, after the sweeping, complex prosody of "Lilacs," the meter and rhyme of "O Captain! My Captain!" seem uncharacteristically mechanical, formulaic.

1

O CAPTAIN! my captain! our fearful trip is done;
The ship has weather'd every rack, the prize we sought is won;
The port is near, the bells I hear, the people all exulting,
While follow eyes the steady keel, the vessel grim and daring:
    But O heart! heart! heart!
      Leave you not the little spot,
        Where on the deck my captain lies,
          Fallen cold and dead.

2

O captain! my captain! rise up and hear the bells;
Rise up—for you the flag is flung—for you the bugle trills;
For you bouquets and ribbon'd wreaths—for you the shores a-
    crowding;
For you they call, the swaying mass, their eager faces turning;
    O captain! dear father!
      This arm I push beneath you;
        It is some dream that on the deck,
          You've fallen cold and dead.

3

My captain does not answer, his lips are pale and still;
My father does not feel my arm, he has no pulse nor will:
But the ship, the ship is anchor'd safe, its voyage closed and done;
From fearful trip, the victor ship, comes in with object won:
    Exult, O shores, and ring, O bells!
      But I, with silent tread,

> *Walk the spot my captain lies,*
> *Fallen cold and dead.*

This is the original form of the poem as published. In later editions line 6 becomes "O the bleeding drops of red," line 14 becomes "This arm beneath your head," and the penultimate verse will read "Walk the deck my Captain lies"——changes for the better.

The author of *Leaves of Grass* was so much the poetic revolutionary that sometimes one might forget he was a Victorian, with debts to his colleagues across the ocean. The three sections of the piece, and the arrangement of the verses on the page, thinly disguise the very conventional form: it is actually a ballad of nine quatrains rhythmically similar to Coleridge's stanzas in "The Rime of the Ancient Mariner," as well as to many of Tennyson's ballads, including "New Year's Eve" and "The Talking Oak."

The literary medium that links Whitman's most famous poem with his greatest is Alfred, Lord Tennyson's celebrated elegy for Arthur Hallam, *In Memoriam A. H. H.*, published in 1850. Whitman's feelings for Tennyson's poetry were volatile but intense. He kept up with the English poet's work from the time *Maude* was jointly reviewed with *Leaves of Grass* in 1855. Whitman regarded the older writer with a mixture of affection and competitive envy. He began by calling Tennyson's poetry "tedious and affected, with some sweet passages," but by the 1860s he admitted Tennyson's mastery, memorized and recited his verses, and followed his career with more faithful attention than he allowed other contemporaries. Tennyson sent Whitman money when he needed it; Whitman sent Tennyson a signed portrait of himself. He was flattered when somebody said he looked like Tennyson.

Whitman would have been keenly interested in *In Memoriam*, one of the most popular poems of the time, printed in lavishly

illustrated editions, with its many "sweet passages" and its undercurrent of homoerotic passion for "My Arthur, whom I shall not
see / Till all my widow'd race be run . . ."

> *Tears of the widower, when he sees*
> *A late-lost form that sleep reveals,*
> *And moves his doubtful arms, and feels*
> *Her place is empty, fall like these;*
> . . .
>
> *Which weep the comrade of my choice,*
> *An awful thought, a life removed,*
> *The human-hearted man I loved,*
> *A Spirit, not a breathing voice.*
>
> —TENNYSON, *IN MEMORIAM*, XIII

"The seasons bring the flowers again," Tennyson sings, but "not
for thee the glow, the bloom." In his long suite of interwoven
quatrains the English poet struggles like his American counterpart
to find verses worthy of his theme. "I brim with sorrow drowning
song," he laments. Then, like Whitman commiserating with the
thrush ("dear brother I know, / If thou wast not gifted to sing,
thou would'st surely die"), Tennyson joins the Old World finch,
or linnet: "I do but sing because I must, / And pipe but as the lin-
nets sing . . ."

Whitman's "Lilacs" benefited from Tennyson's architecture
and handling of themes in *In Memoriam*, and his "O Captain! My
Captain!" profited from the English poet's nautical figures and
quatrain structure. It is ironic that "O Captain! My Captain!"
became Whitman's most popular poem in his lifetime. (During the
twentieth century it became one of the ten most widely known
poems in the language.) This was the piece everyone asked him to

read aloud in public long after he was sick of its singsong cadences. "I say, Damn My Captain . . . ," he told his friend Horace Traubel. "I'm almost sorry I ever wrote the poem."

Whitman was not writing in a vacuum, literary or personal. The chief fact of his existence during that spring and summer was that he was in love with Peter Doyle. Burroughs and Dr. Tindall saw the lovers together on the streetcar and elsewhere, and remarked upon their obvious joy in each other's company. Whitman was content in what we would now call a stable relationship. This buffered him from the inevitable tremors of misfortune.

On June 30, 1865, a Friday, Whitman arrived in his basement office and was handed this notice: "Services of Walter Whitman of New York as a clerk in the Indian Office will be dispensed with from and after this date." Stunned by the sudden dismissal, panicked at the loss of his salary so near the completion of *Drum-Taps*, he walked the seven blocks through the dust on G Street to the colonnaded Treasury building. He mounted the stairs to O'Connor's office and showed him the pink slip. O'Connor, furious, stormed downstairs into the office of Assistant Attorney General J. Hubley Ashton and accused Whitman's boss, Secretary of the Interior James Harlan, who was a Methodist deacon, of singling the poet out for persecution.

Ashton, who liked Whitman, bearded Secretary Harlan in his den the next morning. While Harlan publicly would insist he had based his decision on his budget, he confided to Ashton that he had discovered a corrected proof of *Leaves of Grass* in the clerk's desk drawer, and that he would not have the author of such a book in his department even if the President himself should order his reinstatement.

During the months and years following, the infamous pink slip became a cause célèbre, as English, French, and American readers chose sides for and against the "persecuted" author. O'Connor himself published the keynote defense, *The Good Gray Poet*, in January 1866, six months after the incident.

But that June the dismissal caused little more than a ruffle in Whitman's composure as he worked on his poetry and visited his soldiers in the evenings. He had experienced a weekend of anxiety, but thanks to O'Connor's swift intervention, on Monday morning Whitman was at a new desk, in the Attorney General's Office, under Ashton's protection. This was the most comfortable job he would ever have, in a well-lighted office with a southern view of the Arlington Hills across the river; he could even purchase books and charge them to the departmental library.

By September Whitman had written enough new poetry and culled enough verse from old manuscripts to fill a twenty-four-page duodecimo signature. He arranged with the Washington printers Gibson Brothers to print one thousand copies of the *Sequel to Drum-Taps* (for a cost much less than the New York printer's), and ordered the New York binder Abraham Simpson to stitch up five hundred copies of the old sheets and the new ones together. The enlarged *Drum-Taps* was launched on the market in October, and the official publication date, announced in the *New-York Tribune*, was October 28, 1865.

As always, the reviews of Whitman were mixed. There were a dozen or more. Young Henry James attacked the volume, implying that Whitman had exploited the nation's trauma for his own selfish purposes. William Dean Howells, personally devoted to Whitman, allowed that "the poet conveys to the heart certain emotions which the brain cannot analyze, and only remotely perceives." Yet he denied that *Drum-Taps* was literary art, declaring, "He [Whitman] cannot be called a true poet."

In a comprehensive review, "The Poetry of War," published in the *New York Times,* Oliver Wendell Holmes, who certainly knew of *Drum-Taps,* made no mention of Whitman's book. And so it fared for this great volume. The publishers Bunce and Huntington, who had offered to distribute the book, withdrew their support. Three months later a reviewer remarked that it "could scarcely be got at a bookstore."

All but forty copies have vanished without a trace, and now you could not purchase one for any amount of money. The first edition of *Leaves of Grass* frequently comes on the market; but *Drum-Taps,* almost never.

The brown cloth binding and gold-leaf medallion on the cover were the same as had been designed before Lincoln's funeral. An alert bibliophile, holding the closed volume, would notice a subtle change in the cut and stained paper: the paper's edge, which had been plain white, now was flecked with brown, like the breast of the hermit thrush.

part four

EPILOGUE:
NEW YORK, 1887

MADISON SQUARE THEATRE:
NEW YORK, APRIL 14, 1887

The "mast-hemm'd" Manhattan of Whitman's youth had become a behemoth, the international center of financial and industrial power. It was evident in the view of the shoreline from the Navy Yard to Red Hook, where the poet's beloved ferryboats plied the East River. Where sailing ships had once anchored, now multistoried warehouses of iron and brick ranged along the waterfront, beneath the gleaming stone towers and steel span of the "eighth wonder of the world," the new Brooklyn Bridge.

Since the beginning of the Civil War the population had almost doubled, to a million and a quarter, the result of surging immigration. As Germans, Italians, and Russian and Polish Jews fled Europe to work in lumber and coal yards near the Hudson River, or toil in the garment and shoe factories southwest of Broadway, Greenwich Village changed almost beyond recognition. The old New York Hospital on Pearl Street had closed its doors long since. The Astor House, where Whitman first saw Lincoln, was in decline, as hotels with elevators, like the marble Fifth Avenue

Hotel at Twenty-fourth Street, attracted the well-heeled guests. The colorful Bowery theaters Whitman once frequented could not compete with the fancy playhouses of Union Square. The Bowery now featured minstrels, sword swallowers, snake charmers, and bawdy shows in the shadow of the ugly, noisy Third Avenue elevated line.

As newcomers crowded into tenements and once-elegant apartment houses, downtown real estate values plummeted. The glamorous blocks of lower Broadway that Whitman once admired from the top of a bone-rattling omnibus had lost their charm. Horse-drawn streetcars ran smoothly on tracks. Fashionable retailers kept moving north along Broadway in pursuit of the rich, who were building mansions farther and farther uptown. Charley Pfaff had closed his rathskeller, trying his luck in a tavern on Twenty-fourth Street for a while, but failed. Now Pfaff was dead, and so were Henry Clapp and Ada Clare.

Walt Whitman's dream of America's momentous destiny had come true in ways that did, and did not, please him. The triumph of the North in the war had hastened change that was no doubt inevitable: greater industrialism (commanded by capital), finer technology in the service of industry, Federalism, and the concentration of political and economic power in the hands of a few. Nowhere were these developments more conspicuous than in the New York of the Gilded Age, when the Tweed Ring controlled City Hall for the convenience of businessmen, and the income gap between the rich and the poor was about to inspire an effective uprising of organized labor. For as long as Whitman could recall, Manhattan had been a bustling borough; but the population boom brought a new intensity. Now there was a sense of urgency, sometimes desperation, in the streets, as men and women hurried about their business.

Twenty-two years after the assassination, Abraham Lincoln had become a perplexing memory that was, like the terrible war over which he had presided, for most people best forgotten. Five Presidents had come and gone since Lincoln's murder, and now the anniversary of the tragedy was no longer noted in the newspapers except on rare occasions such as this one advertised in the *New York Times* theater section:

MADISON SQUARE THEATRE
A. M. PALMER . . . . Manager
THURSDAY AFTERNOON
April 14, at 4 o'clock
Complimentary Testimonial to Mr.
WALT WHITMAN
on which occasion he will deliver a lecture on
ABRAHAM LINCOLN
it being the 25th anniversary of the assassination
Tickets $1.50 and $1. For sale at Brentano's, at
the theatre, and by J. B. Pond, Everett House

It is proof of the public's short memory that Albert Marshman Palmer, who had helped Whitman during the war, and J. B. Pond, the impresario with imperial whiskers who was promoting the event, were trumpeting it as the "silver" anniversary of the assassination, which was three years off. Couldn't people count, or had they really forgotten the year of the calamity? Well, this was show business. Sarah Bernhardt was in town, playing in *Theodora*, and Augustin Daly's company was celebrating its one-hundredth performance of *Taming of the Shrew* starring Ada Rehan, John Drew, and Otis Skinner. So if a slight inaccuracy in the display ads might bring luster to the event and fill a few more seats, what was the

WALT WHITMAN
on
ABRAHAM LINCOLN

Major Pond has the pleasure of announcing a lecture on Abraham Lincoln to be delivered on the 22nd Anniversary of the Assassination, Thursday, April 14th, at 4 o'clock P. M., in the

MADISON SQUARE THEATER
NEW YORK

Reserved Seats $1.50, Admission $1.00. Tickets for sale at the Theater. Orders may be sent to Maj. J. B. Pond, Everett House; E. C. Stedman, 66 Broadway-44 E. 26 St.; J. H. Johnston, Lotus Club; R. W. Gilder, 33 E. 17th St.: Brentano's, Union Square.

harm in it? A. M. Palmer was not wholly above such sleight-of-hand dealings.

The years after the war had not been kind to Whitman, although he looked, in repose, like a god. Reporters routinely used "Jovian" to describe his head, images of which appeared everywhere, from signed photos sold in souvenir shops to the embossed lid on the box of the cigars named after him. The looks were deceiving. In 1873 a stroke deprived him of the use of his left arm and leg, only a few months before his mother's death, which he called "the great dark cloud of my life." He had to give up his government job in 1874. For a while he moved into her rooms in Camden, New Jersey, where she had gone to live with George, preserving them just as they had been when she was alive. In 1875 another stroke damaged his right side, and chronic rheumatism left Whitman—according to Burroughs—"a mere physical wreck" at fifty-six.

Nevertheless, through his writings, self-promotion, the pitting of friends against enemies and even friends against friends, he developed uncanny power, the mystical authority of a vain invalid. Dr. Silas W. Mitchell, the eminent neurologist who diagnosed Whitman's vascular pathology, recalled: "He was the most innocently and entirely vain creature I ever knew. The perfect story of his vanity will, I fancy, never be written. It was past belief." The Whitman of Camden was not the angel of Armory Square Hospital. Now he was a man on a very different kind of mission—to ensure his immortality. He burnished his image until it shone, widespread and inextinguishable.

Dependent upon his family and friends for financial and physical support, Whitman mustered his remaining energies to cultivate the power of his personality. He wrote poems and memoirs, and devoted much of his time to fueling international debate over *Leaves of Grass*. In this he was highly successful. Attacks came regularly—in 1881, Anthony Comstock's Society for the Suppression of Vice banned his book—and Whitman prevailed upon friends worldwide to defend him. He never lost the potent charisma that pervaded the world through *Leaves of Grass* and the appealing portrait photos that he had printed by the gross, signed, and sold or gave away to a growing coterie. Proselytes came from all over the world to visit the eminence in his cluttered study, shake his feeble hand, and wait for any words of wisdom that might fall from his lips in desultory conversation. He covered his knees with a wolf-skin robe. With his cane he pointed to a photo of Lincoln on the wall. Visitors went away spreading the gospel of Whitman.

In his youth he had pursued the world through the medium of

poetry. Now the literary world came to him: Oscar Wilde, Edward Carpenter, Joaquin Miller, Moncure Conway, Bram Stoker, Henry Wadsworth Longfellow, and many more, made the pilgrimage to Camden to honor the author of *Leaves of Grass*. Others from across the sea paid their respects by mail: Tennyson, William Michael Rossetti, Edward Dowden, and John Addington Symonds. Swinburne praised Whitman in the early 1870s, then later recanted, writing, "Mr. Whitman's Eve is a drunken apple-woman, indecently sprawling in the slush and garbage amid the rotten refuse of her overturned fruit-stall . . ." It was all one. As Henry Clapp had taught him: "Better to have people stirred against you if they can't be stirred for you." For Whitman the waters of reputation would never be still. The same year that Emerson left him out of his anthology *Parnassus* (1875), the Irish critic Standish O'Grady, in a review in *Gentleman's Magazine,* called Walt Whitman "the noblest product of modern times."

Peter Doyle had faded from his life, a sad, inevitable loss. The two men had changed greatly since their meeting in 1865, when Whitman was healthy and Doyle was just a youth. They never lost their fondness for each other. But the relationship could not survive the difference in ages, the separation, and the poet's severe illness. In June 1875 Whitman wrote to Doyle, from Camden to Washington, that he thought it was unlikely he would recover from his strokes. Whitman was giving the young man permission to get on with his life.

They continued to visit each other, at longer and longer intervals. The pain of losing Doyle was assuaged somewhat when, in 1876, Whitman met and befriended a seventeen-year-old typesetter, Harry Stafford. Stafford's parents owned beautiful farmland near the healing waters of Timber Creek, New Jersey. There, from 1876 to 1884, the poet spent much of his time in good weather refreshing his health and spirits.

When Harry Stafford married Eva Wescott in 1884, his place in Whitman's affections and business affairs was soon filled by young William Duckett, a long-faced, gangly boy from the Camden neighborhood. That year Whitman purchased a little house on Mickle Street, and Duckett moved in with him. In 1885 the Philadelphia lawyer Thomas Donaldson, at whose home the poet was a frequent guest, raised the funds to buy Whitman a horse and buggy, so he would not feel so confined. Donors such as Mark Twain, John Greenleaf Whittier, Edwin Booth, and Oliver Wendell Holmes contributed a total of $320, enough to purchase a sleek two-seater phaeton with leather upholstery, a sorrel named Frank, a halter, and a buggy-whip. Thereafter Bill Duckett was known as Whitman's driver. The old man's relationship with the youth, as with his other paramours, was shrouded in secrecy.

By the 1880s the poet had become not so much a literary lion as an object of adoration and awe. The inner circle of devotees was a curious mix of old friends, physicians, lawyers, wealthy capitalists, writers, and intellectual eccentrics. The old friends included William O'Connor, despite their decade of estrangement over Negro suffrage (Whitman had thought the Fifteenth Amendment premature), and the faithful John Burroughs. Dr. Richard Maurice Bucke, a Canadian who first visited Whitman in 1877, wrote a biography of him in 1883, and later authored the classic study of genius and mysticism *Cosmic Consciousness* (1901), in which Whitman joins Jesus Christ, Muhammad, St. Paul, Dante, and Blake as an exhibit.

Orator Robert Ingersoll (the Great Agnostic) and poet and publisher Richard Watson Gilder beat the drum for Whitman in

New York. From England came Anne Gilchrist (the widow of William Blake's biographer Alexander Gilchrist), hopelessly in love with Whitman, and writers Edward Carpenter and Oscar Wilde, both plying Whitman for a confession of his homosexuality, which he refused. There was the American lawyer Thomas B. Harned, who would amass a priceless collection of Whitman manuscripts and relics, and several would-be Boswells. Foremost among these was the indefatigable Horace Traubel, who shadowed the poet, interviewing him by the hour and recording his every word, producing at last the mammoth nine-volume *With Walt Whitman in Camden*.

From this hub radiated countless patrons, philanthropists, portrait artists, supernumeraries, cranks, imitators, and the merely curious, wanting a brush with fame. Some idea of the climate in Camden was expressed by Traubel in conversation with the poet: "I don't worship the ground you tread on or kiss the hem of your garment . . . . But I think I know how you are bound to be regarded in the future . . ." Others showed less restraint. The journalist and ex-Harvard-divinity-student William Sloan Kennedy wrote to Burroughs in 1880: "*As a man and friend I think Whitman as near perfect as it is possible to be.* I think him the equal, and in many respects the superior of the much misunderstood Jesus . . ."

For such a phenomenon to spring up, and flourish, several conditions usually obtain. First, the hero's achievements must inspire the adoration of a number of susceptible persons. Second, the hero, if alive, must desire and foster that devotion. Whitman did so. Preferring private to public charity, when a Massachusetts Congressman introduced a bill that would have granted the poet $125 monthly as a pension for his hospital work, Whitman squelched the movement, announcing, incredibly, "I do not deserve it." His devotees became more devoted than ever. Third, the hero must promise the faithful salvation in the glow of his not-too-available presence, and reward or punish followers by indulgence and excommunication, creating a hierarchy of intimates.

Finally, the hero must have secrets—at the core of his charisma dwells a sacred mystery, personal, artistic, or religious. If the mystery has an erotic component, so much the better, and if the hero or heroine is a person of extraordinary beauty, better still.

"The full beauty of his face and head did not appear till he was past sixty," wrote Burroughs. After that, the naturalist insisted, there was no comparable specimen to be found under heaven: the high arching brows, the straight nose, the heavy-lidded gray eyes, the symmetrical head, the soft, long white beard. "Time depleted him in just the right way—softened his beard and took away the too florid look . . . The expression was full of pathos, but it was as grand as that of a god." Dr. Bucke wrote: "No description can give any idea of the extraordinary physical attractiveness of the man."

As for his secrets: there was the lasting mystery of *Leaves of Grass,* a masterpiece with no evident antecedents, a work of genius that defied conventional analysis. There was also the riddle of Whitman's sexuality, endlessly intriguing. Finally there loomed the abiding question of his mystical, and his real, connection with Abraham Lincoln. This last was of the greatest interest to the American public. It was the Lincoln connection that the New York crowd had been invited to witness and celebrate on April 14, 1887, in the Madison Square Theatre.

The theater's manager, A. M. Palmer, who had provided Whitman with train tickets back in 1863, had recovered from his youthful embarrassments as "the collector de facto" of the Port of New York after confessing to accepting bribes. After years of doing penance as an obscure drudge in the Mercantile Library, he was launched on an illustrious career as a producer, an occupation less vulnerable to the moral sensitivities of the public. He had grown long sideburns—dundrearies—and was as handsome as ever. For three years now, he had been the sole manager and proprietor of the successful Madison Square Theatre. Once again, at the bidding of John Hay and other friends of Whitman, Palmer was pleased to help the poet, leasing his auditorium during an idle afternoon, upon generous terms, for Whitman's Lincoln lecture.

The Madison Square Theatre was fit for the greatest diva's vanity. Of all the "jewel box" theaters of the Gilded Age, this small, lofty playhouse on West Twenty-fourth Street near Fifth Avenue was the nonpareil. Here dramatist Steele MacKaye had invented an "elevator stage," two stages one atop the other switched through a counterweighted system of ropes and pulleys. The basket-handle proscenium arch was so high that the orchestra sat in its own pillared balcony up there, *above* the stage.

The house seated 688 on a steep slope from the low dress circle to the horseshoe of the two upper galleries, so no one sat more than ninety feet from the footlights, and most of the audience seemed to be right "on top" of the actors.

And it glittered like the inside of a Fabergé egg. The walls gilded in arabesque patterns, the scrolled brackets, the double columns framing the stage, the fanlight over the orchestra box were designed by Louis Comfort Tiffany, as were the coffered ceiling, the circular stained-glass skylight, and the drop curtain embroidered with trees and flowers. The boxes to the right and left of the stage were like little bronzed, gem-studded turrets, with cut-glass chandeliers glowing deep within.

On the stage of this resplendent theater, the Good Gray Poet was slated to address the most distinguished audience that would ever hear him, and a subject the years were backlighting with an eerie mystique—the passion and cult of Abraham Lincoln.

Whitman had arrived at the Westminster Hotel the night before. He had traveled on a 4:30 P.M. train out of Camden via Trenton and Jersey City, convoyed by patron Robert Pearsall Smith and accompanied by his companion William Duckett. Smith, a glass manufacturer from Philadelphia, had collaborated with New York jeweler John Johnston and other Whitman friends in arranging the lecture. It was Smith who had booked the rooms at the Westminster, a stately hotel on the northwest corner of East Sixteenth Street and Irving Place, four blocks south of Gramercy Park. Though past its prime, the hotel had a literary tradition; Smith made sure that Whitman got the same rooms, all "en suite," with private door and staircase, which Charles Dickens had occupied in 1842. The newspapers linked the names, and this guaranteed the lead notice in the "Personal Intelligence" column of the *New York Times*, which announced the illustrious visitors to the city each day.

That morning, while Duckett was helping Whitman with the ritual of his ablutions in the Westminster Hotel, the painful limbering of his body on a day when much would be expected of it, another ritual was unfolding far off, near Springfield, Illinois. The body of Abraham Lincoln was being exhumed and reburied, whether for the seventh or the eighth time no one is quite certain. The body could not seem to stay put; or rather, people would not let it rest.

Sometime between 1876 and 1878, grave-robbers had broken into the monument at Oak Ridge where the President had been entombed, and nearly succeeded in snatching away Lincoln's remains. They meant to hold the body for ransom, and might have carried it off if an undercover agent of the Secret Service had not infiltrated the gang. For reasons of security, John C. Power, the custodian of the burial site, was evasive about the dates and details.

The plot was foiled, but it struck fear into the heart of John Stuart, head of the Lincoln National Monument Association. He ordered custodian Power to remove the body from its crypt and hide it somewhere else, in the catacomb beneath Memorial Hall. Marble-worker Adam Johnson and his assistants lifted Lincoln's five-hundred-pound casket from the sarcophagus, and Johnson cemented the lid back in place. That night Johnson, Power, and three members of the Lincoln National Monument Association carried the coffin around an obelisk, through the hall, and into the labyrinth. Unable to bury the coffin without attracting attention, they covered it over with old boards, in the darkness. There it lay for years while pilgrims to the cemetery wept over the empty sarcophagus above.

But word got out that Lincoln's body was not where it was supposed to be. John Power still doubted that the coffin would be safe in its proper sarcophagus, yet he feared the scandal that would erupt if Lincoln were to be found where he had been unceremoniously stowed—under the lumber pile. The custodian confided in two distinguished friends, Major Gustavus Dana and General Jasper Reece. Recognizing the weight of their responsibility, and the sheer physical challenge of burying the heavy coffin secretly, these gentlemen called upon six others to form the brotherhood of the Lincoln Guard of Honor. The nine men had badges designed for their lapels and swore a blood oath of silence. Wielding shovels and pickaxes, by lantern light they buried Lincoln deep in the earth at the far end of the labyrinth.

Mary Lincoln had died in 1882, ending a sad and tortuous odyssey that had led her in and out of poverty and disgrace; in and out of Bellevue Hospital for the insane, in Batavia, Illinois, where her son Robert had had her committed. Tad had died of TB in 1871 at age eighteen. She had no one left but the heartless Robert, who, until the day she died, Mary believed was after her money. Someone, of course, would have had to inform Robert where his father's body had been hidden; then Robert insisted that the custodians remove his mother there too, in equal secrecy.

So now, for five years, the visitors to Oak Ridge's Lincoln Memorial had been paying their respects to two vacant crypts, although rumors of subterfuge persisted. In the spring of 1887, the Lincoln National Monument Association decided that the time had come to provide a burglarproof new tomb deep in the center of the floor of the North Hall. On the morning of April 14, according to the *New York Times,* "the members of the Guard of Honor and the Lincoln Monument Association, including many men who knew Mr. Lincoln . . . saw masons hew away the stones over the hidden grave. The two coffins were brought out and that of Mr. Lincoln opened."

———

No more rattling omnibuses for Walt Whitman. This afternoon Robert Pearsall Smith would see to it that the poet and his young companion rode uptown in a carriage.

From the porte cochere of the Westminster Hotel they glided west on East Sixteenth Street through blooming Union Square, then followed Broadway seven blocks north toward Madison Square and Twenty-fourth Street, where Broadway and Fifth Avenue converged. How the city had changed since the Pfaffians held their revels on lower Broadway, and as Manhattan grew northward and skyward! On the right at Nineteenth Street they passed W. & J. Sloane, where colorful Persian rugs hung in the wide showcases, then on the left Lord & Taylor, displaying sleek, bustled gowns and spring bonnets. Whitman admired the cast-iron palaces of the Ladies' Mile shopping district, the slender columns of the tall buildings. Brooks Brothers was coming up, at the corner of Twenty-second. Maybe he would make enough money from the lecture to buy new shirts.

The light summer suits in shopwindows seemed out of place to the travelers on this unseasonably chilly afternoon. The thermometer at Hudnut's Pharmacy, 218 Broadway, stood at 48 degrees, and though the breeze was at their backs, out of the south, it would get no warmer.

William Duckett had a toothache. He wore a bowler hat that made his long face look longer, and a swallowtail coat whose sleeves his arms had outgrown, so that his pale hands dangled. He tenderly stroked his jaw, looking up at the buildings in wonder. As the reinsman turned the horses left onto Twenty-fourth Street around the grand Corinthian portico of the Fifth Avenue Hotel, the poet held the binding of papers from which he would read his lecture on Lincoln.

The lecture notes had become a palimpsest of scribbled paragraphs, pages clipped and edited from *Memoranda During the War*, and newsprint clippings, all pasted up, curiously, upon the leaves of a little book called *The Bride of Gettysburg*, a narrative poem by J. D. Hylton published in 1878. That was the year that John Burroughs and Richard Watson Gilder first proposed "a benefit be got up for you in N.Y. and that you be asked to lecture on Lincoln."

Whitman had glued the end papers of *The Bride* together, and also pasted yellow glazed paper over the covers. In the back of his makeshift book were several poems he might choose to recite after the lecture, including his "O Captain! My Captain!," Anacreon's "The Midnight Visitor," and Robert Burns's "John Anderson, My

Jo." The speech itself Whitman had first delivered in Steck Hall on Fourteenth Street, on April 14, 1879. Since then he had given the same address, with slight variations, in Association Hall, Philadelphia (1880); the St. Botolphe Club in Boston (1881); the Pythian Club in Elkton, Maryland; Morgan Hall, Camden; Chestnut Street Opera House, Philadelphia; and a church in Haddonfield, New Jersey, all in 1886; and he had delivered it for the eighth time just a week and a half earlier for the Unitarian Society in Camden. The speech was always a success, and in major cities it seldom failed to reap columns of publicity in the newspapers. On this afternoon, the occasion of the ninth lecture on Lincoln, as Whitman approached the grand brick theater with its high arched doors, its Victorian cornice braced with ogee moldings, he had every reason to be confident.

Major James B. Pond, promoter of "Concerts, Lecturers, and All Description of Musical, Lyceum and Literary Entertainments," as his letterhead stated, had been engaged to ballyhoo the event and sell tickets. But as might have been expected, the winning and influential John Hay stood at the epicenter of this distinguished sociodrama. It was Hay who would deliver the audience that mattered.

———

Mark Twain was staying next door to the theater, in his suite at the white marble Fifth Avenue Hotel. He was slowly recovering from the glasses of Château d'Yquem Sauternes that had flowed at the all-night gala after the hundredth dazzling performance of Augustine Daly's production of *The Taming of the Shrew*. At fifty-one Twain was much in demand at events like this one (a landmark in American theater history), where his name and wit added distinction—the press followed him. He was a sturdy man with a thick neck, trim wavy hair going gray at the temples, and a brown, down-turned mustache. In those days the author did not affect white outfits; in public he wore a dark three-piece suit and a straight black bow tie.

The marathon celebration started just after midnight, and did not break up until 5:00 A.M. Mark Twain ate terrapin and pâté de foie gras in the company of the glamorous thespians, and guests who included painter Elihu Vedder; the great actor Wilson Barrett, Whitman's friend, now playing *Hamlet* at the Star Theatre; and General and Mrs. William Tecumseh Sherman. Daly gave General Sherman the place of honor and made him toastmaster. When the time came for speech making, the soldier who had destroyed much of Georgia spoke with surprising eloquence and wit about the arts in general and Shakespeare in particular. Twain could add little to the warrior's remarks.

Daly had produced two of Twain's plays, and Twain was hopeful the director would stage another. Twain drawled: "I have been counting the roses on the table—9,000 roses. This is the hardest theatre in New York to get into, and I'm glad I've got so far in at last."

He would have no difficulty getting a good seat in the Madison Square Theatre, although it was much smaller than Daly's on Broadway. With all of Major Pond's exertions, about half the seats had been sold—not a bad advance for an afternoon lecture. The size of the audience did not matter so much as its character, to which the author of *The Prince and the Pauper* and *Adventures of Huckleberry Finn* had agreed to lend a share of prestige. Important friends—John Hay, William Dean Howells, and Richard Watson Gilder, among others—would be expecting him.

Twain's feelings about Whitman were complex. Shakespeare aside, poetry bewildered him. Often these days he was hearing his name linked with Whitman's, as a species of indigenous genius, which may not have pleased him. Also, Twain had followed Whitman's lead in the art of self-promotion, which may have led to uneasiness on the younger man's part, the desire to avoid guilt by association. Yet he never refused to contribute to Whitman's welfare—when money was needed for the carriage, for instance, or when mutual friends solicited funds to keep food on the poet's table. "What we want to do is to make the splendid old soul comfortable," he would tell the *Boston Herald* on May 24, 1887. Perhaps the stories of Whitman's work in the hospitals moved Twain; maybe he admired some of Whitman's verses. We will never know, because Mark Twain strictly refrained from comment upon *Leaves of Grass* or judgments of Whitman's literary stature.

As Twain joined the crowd passing under the filigreed marquee, it became clear that this lecture on Lincoln was a literary occasion of unique importance. William Dean Howells thought so.

There was no American writer Twain admired and loved more than Howells. Howells corrected Twain's manuscripts, favorably reviewed most of his novels, and more than any other person saw to it that Twain was taken seriously as an artist rather than regarded as a travel writer or joker. In turn, Twain praised Howells as one of the finest writers in the language. As friends of twenty years' standing they had shared many joys and sorrows. Now here was Howells, flush with the success of *The Rise of Silas Lapham* and *Indian Summer*, tearing tickets in the archway of the theater lobby—having been pressed into service as a gate man for Walt Whitman.

As Twain entered the theater, he joined the other patrons in their wonder at the beauty of Tiffany's muted colors and ornate design. It made Daly's very fine theater look like a barn. John Hay greeted him warmly, grateful for his attendance. Twain had known

Hay since 1871, when Hay was an editorial writer for the *New-York Tribune*, and they had become intimate friends. Hay helped Twain get a novel published in 1880. Nobody but Lincoln had ever made Hay laugh like Twain: one Sunday afternoon in Hay's house the two men fell to laughing so hysterically that Mrs. Hay, a devout Presbyterian, frowned upon them for desecrating the Sabbath.

Since his years in the White House, Hay had held diplomatic posts in Paris, Vienna, and Madrid and served as assistant secretary of state under Rutherford B. Hayes. But he was known foremost as the author of *Pike County Ballads* and *Castilian Days*. For the past two years he had been living in Washington, D.C., again, working with an ailing John Nicolay on the ten-volume *Abraham Lincoln: A History;* some of the volumes were already in print. The last volume would be published in 1890.

Hay was pleased to see how many celebrities had made the scene: the popular fiction writer Frank ("The Lady or the Tiger?") Stockton and his wife; the sculptor Augustus Saint-Gaudens; the eminent art critic Mariana Griswold Van Rensselaer; the clergymen-writers Henry Van Dyke, author of the controversial *The Reality of Religion,* Edward Eggleston, author of *The Hoosier Schoolmaster,* and Moncure Conway. Alongside Daniel Coit Gilman, president of Johns Hopkins University, there was the czar of New York literary society, Edmund C. Stedman, poet, critic, and anthologist, sitting with his family in a private box on the far side of the stage. Five-year-old Laura Stedman, the poet's granddaughter, was excited about the part she had been asked to play at the end of the afternoon's program.

Mark Twain knew most of these men and women, and most knew one another. The poet Richard Watson Gilder, editor of the *Century* magazine, who had been publishing Twain's stories since 1881, was there with his wife as well as his sister Jeannette and brother Joseph, coeditors of the journal of arts and culture the *Critic*. Richard Gilder had dined with Whitman, Stedman, Johnston, and Burroughs the night before at the Westminster, as Whitman noted in his diary.

Here was the author of *Hans Brinker, or The Silver Skates*, Mary Mapes Dodge, now editor of *St. Nicholas Magazine*, where *Tom Sawyer Abroad* would be serialized, and their young friend the incredibly successful Frances Hodgson (*The Secret Garden*) Burnett, who had recently had *Little Lord Fauntleroy* serialized in Dodge's journal. The ladies, their hair tightly curled, frizzy-fringed, packed close to the head, wore high-necked velveteen day-dresses with bustles. Miss Burnett knew this theater well— one of her own plays, *Esmeralda*, had played here to packed houses for 350 nights. Twain had sent her an affectionately inscribed copy of *The Prince and the Pauper*.

General Sherman and his wife shared a box with the Gilders. Andrew Carnegie, who considered Whitman the greatest poet in America, occupied his own box (for which he paid $350 to supplement the proceeds). The industrialist was making an unusual public appearance, harried as he was by questions about the stove molders' strike that had moved from Chicago to Detroit and now threatened Pittsburgh. Mark Twain did not yet know Carnegie, who would play an important role in his financial affairs in the decade to come. Hay was close to Carnegie, and it is possible this was the afternoon that Twain first met the philanthropist. The stove molders' strike was a lively topic of conversation in the dim, chilly theater stalls; so was yesterday's lynching of John Thomas from the ceiling joist of a courtroom in Union City, Tennessee. Accused of raping a ten-year-old white girl, the black man was summarily judged guilty by three justices of the peace, whereupon the mob rushed the defendant with cries of "Hang him!," threw a rope over the beam, noosed the doomed man, and lifted him high in the air.

In the turret-shaped box to the left of the stage, John Burroughs, the naturalist who introduced Whitman to the hermit thrush, sat with the Boston Brahmins of literature, James Russell Lowell and Charles Eliot Norton. Now that Emerson and Longfellow were dead, Lowell was America's most respectable poet-critic, having succeeded Longfellow to the chair of modern languages at Harvard. He also had served as minister to Spain and England. His presence here with Norton, his Harvard colleague and coeditor of the *North American Review,* bestowed upon the event the benediction of the highest culture. Professor Norton recalled with satisfaction how he had been one of the first critics to praise *Leaves of Grass* in print, writing in *Putnam's,* in 1855, "aside from America, there is no quarter of the universe where such a production could have had a genesis."

And somewhere in the scattered audience in the dress circle sat the Cuban exile poet and founder of the Cuban Revolutionary Party, thirty-four-year-old José Martí, who soon would export the gospel of Whitman to South America.

At four o'clock the bustling, chatty ticket-holders took their seats. The houselights dimmed, in anticipation of Walt Whitman's entrance.

Backstage smelled of gas jets, pomade, roses, and sawdust. The poet checked his image in the mirror. His trousers and waistcoat were made of dark gray wool; his sack coat was darker, almost black. He wore dove-gray hand-knitted stockings and low-cut shoes. Nowadays Whitman never wore a tie. His snow-white beard served for a neckcloth. The most outstanding feature of his outfit was his fancy linen shirt, which looked like it might have come from Oscar Wilde. The wide white collar was loose, the cuffs turned over the sleeves, revealing the edging of lace.

William Duckett handed Whitman his cane, shaped like a shepherd's crook and so weathered the varnish was worn away.

The curtain rose upon the elaborate drawing room set from Palmer's production of *Jim, the Penman,* with a few adjustments. A small table had been placed downstage center; to the audience's left of it was an armchair, and to the left of that stood another chair, on the back of which hung a laurel wreath streaming ribbons of red, white, and blue. Wilson Barrett had sent it. He had an eight o'clock curtain for *Hamlet,* and after partying with Twain all night he could not possibly attend his friend's lecture.

In Philadelphia the orchestra had played a prelude—Franz von Suppé's "The Poet's Dream," then a little serenade by Schubert; even in Camden, the week before, a contralto had sung a few popular tunes to settle folks into their seats. Now there was nothing to warm up the audience but their own sotto voce chatter. It was time to go on.

Putting his arm through Duckett's, and leaning on his cane, Whitman, blinking, slowly made his way into the illumination cast by fifty or more gas jets. Painfully he made his way to the table, sat down in the chair, and laid his cane on the floor. Duckett exited.

"The audience gave him the greeting of friends to a friend," said the *New York Times,* suggesting that the applause was warm rather than strident. Many called Walt by name from here and there in the triple-tiered hall. Smiling, he thanked them. "He fumbled a little as his hand sought his glasses and adjusted them."

Whitman began to read from "papers which he hardly touched, allowing himself to slowly improvise," Stuart Merrill, a young poet, recalled. Jeannette Gilder, reporting for the *Critic,* wrote, "His voice is somewhat nasal in quality, but so high and clear that, without being raised above a conversational pitch, it was distinctly audible in all parts of the little theatre." She compared his appearance, the ruddy cheeks and white hair, to that of the late William Cullen Bryant, who in his last years realized the conventional ideal of Father Time.

Whitman began:

How often since that dark and dripping Saturday, that chilly April day now twenty-two years agone, my heart has entertained the dream, the wish to give of Abraham Lincoln's death its own special thought and memorial. Yet, now the sought-for opportunity offers, I find my notes incompetent, and the fitting tribute I dreamed of seems as unprepared as ever. As oft, however, as the rolling years bring back the hour, I would that it might be briefly dwelt upon. And it is for this, my friends, that I have called you together.

What followed was fifty minutes of drama the *Times* called "impressive in the extreme," as Whitman sat almost motionless at the table, using his voice and eyes to channel the spirit and presence of Lincoln into the jewel-like theater.

I shall not easily forget the first time I ever saw Abraham Lincoln. It must have been about the eighteenth or nineteenth of February, 1861. It was rather a pleasant afternoon in New York City, as he arrived here from the West, to remain a few hours, and then pass on to Washington, to prepare for his inauguration. I saw him in Broadway, near the site of the present Post-Office. He came down, I think, from Canal Street, to stop at the Astor House . . . From the top of an omnibus, (driven up one side, close by, and blocked by the curbstone and the crowds) I had, I say, a capital view of it all, and especially of Mr. Lincoln, his look and gait—his perfect composure and coolness, his unusual and uncouth height, his dress of complete black, stovepipe hat pushed back on his head, his dark complexion, seamed and wrinkled, yet canny-looking face, his black, bushy head of hair, disproportionately long neck, and his hands held behind as he stood observing the people.

In the audience, the painter Francis B. Carpenter was half lost in reverie. Privileged in 1864 with six months' access to the White House to render the President's portrait, he had grown to love Lincoln, but could not paint him convincingly. John Hay recalled John Nicolay's observation that there were many photographs of Lincoln but no portrait of that face that could move through a dozen gradations of light and shade, line and contour, humor, sympathy, sadness, and fury—all in a matter of minutes. To these men who had known Lincoln intimately, Whitman's voice recalled him more vividly than the photographs.

As I sat on the top of my omnibus . . . the thought, dim and inchoate then, has since come out clear enough, that four sorts of genius—four mighty and primal hands, will be needed to the complete limning of this man's future portrait—the eyes and brains and fingertouch of Plutarch and Aeschylus and Michael Angelo, assisted by Rabelais.

. . . Now the rapid succession of well-known events, (too well known—I believe, these days, we almost hate to hear them mentioned)—the national flag fired on at Sumter—the uprising of the North, in paroxysms of astonishment and

rage—the chaos of divided councils—the call for troops—
the first Bull Run—the stunning cast-down, shock, and dis-
may of the North . . . Four years of lurid, bleeding, murky,
murderous war.

Jeannette Gilder observed the "almost unbroken silence in
which [the speech] was given." There was hardly a soul in the
audience who had not lost a friend or close relative in the conflict.

"Even yet too near us," Whitman speculated,

its branches unformed yet, (but certain,) shooting too far into
the future . . . A great literature will yet arise out of the
era . . . for all future America—far more grand, in my opinion, to the hands capable of it, than Homer's siege of Troy, or
the French wars to Shakspere [sic].

He was setting the stage for his own contribution to that literature.

I must leave these speculations, and come to the theme I have
assign'd and limited myself to. Of the actual murder of President Lincoln . . .

Now Whitman became actor and playwright, confident in the
audience's willing suspension of disbelief. There was every reason
to believe him: Whitman had witnessed all but a few of the events
he brought to life, and almost no one living knew which of the
scenes he was describing secondhand.

John Hay, John Burroughs, and a few others knew that this well-
worn script depended upon artifice. All accepted this for what it
was. The night Lincoln was shot, Whitman had not been in Ford's
Theatre, as his publicity claimed. But Peter Doyle had, and in order

to bring his audience to the time and place, the poet would use Doyle's eyewitness account, which now seemed Whitman's own.

———

At Oak Ridge Cemetery that afternoon the North Hall of the Lincoln Monument was closed to the public and the press. Inside, all those who had shared the secret of the tomb, the Lincoln Guard of Honor and eighteen persons who had known the President, stood by in silence as the plumber Leon P. Hopkins of Springfield chiseled an opening in the lead of the casket.

The casket rested upon sawhorses. This was a specialty of the plumber's, one that guaranteed him an odd immortality, hammering out the peephole in Lincoln's coffin, and then soldering it shut again. This was the third time he had been called to the task in twenty-two years (and it would not be the last). Now he went about his work with a sure hand. The purpose of the ritual was to ascertain if Lincoln's corpse was in the coffin where it belonged.

When the plumber had put down his tools and lifted away an oblong piece of the casket above Lincoln's head, the twenty-seven witnesses filed past to get a "last" look at the great man's features. According to the *New York Times* reporter, who later interviewed members of the secret brotherhood, "the body was found to be in a remarkable state of preservation and easily recognizable." As the headrest of the casket had collapsed, Lincoln's head was slightly tilted back. Lincoln's features, framed by the coarse black hair and perfectly trimmed beard, remained stunningly lifelike.

What had made the face always interesting, if not beautiful, was the vivid play of light and shadow upon its spare Gothic architecture. If, in his final years, he had wasted away to a figure that looked like the spectre of death, now in death he had suffered the least diminution of mortality. Of course, there was the very pecu-

liar matter of the President's skin. As the funeral cortege had
passed through Harrisburg and Lancaster, coal country, Lincoln's
face had turned, curiously, black. It would have been unseemly for
the President to appear in the rotunda of New York's City Hall as
the silent interlocutor of a minstrel show. So the morticians had
covered the President's face with a paste of white chalk. Now this
had dissolved, leaving the dark lineaments dusted with a faint
white powder.

"The deed hastens," Whitman continued from his armchair in the
opulent stage parlor. The *Times* noted, "as his words touched any
part of the theatre, he would look up at it in a way that was better
than any gesture and impressive in the extreme."

Whitman recalled Lincoln's passion for the theater: "I have
myself seen him there several times. I remember thinking how funny
it was that he, in some respects, the leading actor in the stormiest
drama known to history's stage, should sit there and be so completely
interested and absorbed in those imaginary doings.

"On this occasion the theatre was crowded. There were many
ladies in rich and gay costumes, officers in their uniforms, many
well known citizens, young folks, the usual clusters of gaslights,"
the poet recalled, as his eyes rested warmly on these similar characters and props before him, "the usual magnetism of so many
people, cheerful and talkative, with perfumes and the music of vio-
lins and flutes in the air. And over all, and saturating all, that vast,
vague, yet realistic wonder, victory, the Nation's victory, the triumph of the Union, filling the air . . .

"The President came betimes, and with his wife witnessed the
play from the large stage boxes of the second tier . . . The acts and
scenes of the piece, ('Our American Cousin') one of those singu-

larly written compositions"—and Whitman waxed droll—"which have at least the merit of giving entire relief to an audience engaged in mental action or business excitements and cares during the day, as it makes not the slightest call on either the moral, emotional, pathetic, or spiritual nature—"

Now they laughed—Twain, Hay, Palmer, and the dozens of literati—at the moment of comic relief before disaster would strike. All welcomed Whitman's satire of the shallow comedy, which "had progressed through perhaps a couple of its acts, when in the midst of it came a scene not really or exactly to be described at all . . . a passing blur in which two ladies are informed by an impossible Yankee that he is not a man of fortune. The dramatic trio made their exit, leaving the stage clear for a moment. At this period came the murder of Abraham Lincoln.

"Great as that was, with all its manifold train circling around it, and stretching into the future for many a century in the politics, history, and art of the New World, the main thing, the actual murder, transpired with the quiet and simplicity of any commonest occurrence—the bursting of a pod in the growth of vegetation, for instance." The poet's simile was surprising and adept. He spoke slowly, making every word tell.

. . . Came the muffled sound of a pistol shot, which not one hundredth part of the audience heard at the time. There was a moment's hush, a vague, startled thrill, and then, through the ornamented, draperied, starred and striped spaceway of the President's box, a man raises himself . . . leaps below to the stage, a distance of perhaps 14 or 15 feet, falls out of position, catching his boot heel in the drapery of the American flag, but quickly rises and recovers himself as if nothing had happened—Booth, the murderer, dressed in plain black broadcloth, bareheaded, with raven glossy hair and eyes, like some mad animal, flashing with light and resolution, yet with a certain calmness, holds aloft a large knife. He walks along, not much back from the footlights, turns fully toward the audience his face of statuesque beauty, lit by those basilisk eyes . . . and launches out in a firm and steady voice these words: "Sic Semper Tyrannis." [Thus always to tyrants.] Then he walks with pace neither slow nor rapid diagonally across the back of the stage and disappears.

Twenty-three-year old Stuart Merrill, an aspiring poet listening that afternoon, was utterly transported. It was "as though the event had taken place the evening before," he wrote. "Not a gesticulation, no raising of the voice. *I was there; everything happened to me.* His address was as gripping as the reports of the tragedies of Eschylus."

Walt Whitman continued:

A moment's hush—a scream—the cry of "Murder!" and Mrs. Lincoln leans out of the box with ashy cheeks and lips, and pointing to the retreating figure cries: "He has killed the President." There is a moment's strange, incredulous suspense, and then—the deluge. The mixture of horror and uncertainty, a rising hum . . .

Ford's Theatre is in chaos. Women faint. People in flight break chairs and railings, trample one another.

The screams and confused talk redouble, treble; two or three manage to pass up water from the stage to the President's box; others try to clamber up . . .

The President's soldiers burst into the theater with fixed bayonets, ordering the hysterical crowd to clear out.

———

Little Laura Stedman, being led from the theater box where she had been sitting with her grandfather, the distinguished poet Edmund C. Stedman, and their family, had butterflies in her stomach as she thought of her role in the play. Through a warren of passages down and underground and then up into the glow of gaslights that spilled over from the radiant stage set to the wings Laura made her way. She stood with the stage manager in a maze of curtains. She wore a white French coif, tied under the chin, and a dress of Quaker gray. While much of the old man's story was comprehensible to a bright child, suddenly he had embarked upon ruminations and speculations, a passage where she could not follow him even if she had not been so nervous.

> The immeasurable value and meaning of that whole tragedy lies, to me, in senses finally dearest to a nation—the imaginative and artistic senses—the literary and dramatic ones. Not in any common or low meaning of those terms, but a meaning precious to the race, and to every age . . . Its sharp culmination, and as it were, solution of so many bloody and angry problems, illustrates those climax moments on the stage of universal Time, where the Historic Muse at one entrance, and the Tragic Muse at the other, suddenly ringing down the curtain, close an immense act in the long drama of creative thought, and give it radiation . . .

Caesar in the senate house. Napoleon perishing in the wild night storm at St. Helena. Socrates drinking the hemlock.

The final use of a heroic-eminent life—especially of a heroic-eminent death—is its indirect filtering into the nation and the race, and to give . . . age after age, color and fibre to the personalism of the youth and maturity of that age, and of mankind. Then there is a cement to the whole people, subtler, more underlying, than any thing in written constitution, or courts or armies—namely, the cement of a death identified thoroughly with that people, at its head, and for its sake . . .

A voice whispered in Laura's ear that *it is almost time*. The old gentleman was speaking of lilacs, saying that the perfume of lilacs was forever associated in his mind with the thought of Lincoln's death. Laura held the pyramidal clusters of fragrant purple lilacs, freshly clipped, overflowing the osier basket. She would carry them onstage when the old man had ceased talking. The basket with its braided wale handle and burden of blossoms was more than half the size of the girl.

The lovely voice maintained its steady rhythm, but now assumed the weight of finality and summation, as Whitman took his leave of Lincoln:

Dear to the Muse—thrice dear to Nationality—to the whole human race—precious to this Union—precious to Democracy—unspeakably and forever precious—their first great Martyr Chief.

The applause came, first in scattered bursts, then greater and greater waves. Someone in the balcony called for the poem as an encore, "O Captain! My Captain!" Now the poet's voice started up again, but it seemed that he was not speaking so much as singing, mournfully.

O Captain! my Captain! our fearful trip is done,
The ship has weathered every rack, the prize we sought is won,
The port is near, the bells I hear, the people all exulting,
While follow eyes the steady keel, the vessel grim and daring;
  But O heart! heart! heart!
    O the bleeding drops of red,
      Where on the deck my Captain lies . . .

The voice faltered . . . now the poet was not singing so much as weeping. Tears flowed down his red cheeks and glistened on his beard, and it did not seem as if he could continue. Now it was time for Laura Stedman to make her entrance.

As the basket of lilacs appeared from the wings, with the child beaming behind it, the crowd broke into the loudest ovation of the day, drowning out the verses of Whitman's well-known poem and the cracked voice that was too overcome with emotion to finish it. Laura moved into the spotlight.

"She walked to where he sat and held out her gift without a word," recalled the reporter from the *Times*. The old man's sadness had almost made her cry. "He stared, took them, and then took her. It was December frost and Maytime blossom at their prettiest contrast as the little pink cheeks shone against the snow-white beard, for the old man told his appreciation mutely by kissing her and kissing her again."

Many in the audience were weeping, and the tears that were shed in that space the poet had hallowed with his words were as much for the fallen President as for the grieving poet. In that moment the men were united.

SOURCES AND NOTES

Abbreviations and Short Titles Employed in the Notes

BARTON, AL & WW: William E. Barton. *Abraham Lincoln and Walt Whitman*.
Indianapolis: Bobbs-Merrill, 1928.

BROOKS, WASHINGTON: Noah Brooks. *Washington in Lincoln's Time*. New York:
Rinehart, 1958; reprint of 1895 edition.

CHRONOLOGY: Joann P. Krieg. *A Whitman Chronology*. Iowa City: University of
Iowa Press, 1998.

CORR: Whitman. *The Correspondence of Walt Whitman*. Ed. Edwin Haviland Miller. 5
vols. New York: New York University Press, 1961.

CW: Lincoln. *Collected Works of Abraham Lincoln*. Ed. Roy P. Basler. 8 vols. New
Brunswick: Rutgers University Press, 1953.

DAY BY DAY: Earl Schenck Miers, ed. *Lincoln Day by Day: A Chronology, 1809–1865*. 3
vols. Washington, D.C.: Lincoln Sesquicentennial Commission, 1960.

GLICKSBERG, WHITMAN: Whitman. *Walt Whitman and the Civil War*. Ed. Charles
I. Glicksberg. Philadelphia: University of Pennsylvania Press, 1933.

HAY, DIARY: Hay. *Inside Lincoln's White House: The Complete Civil War Diary of John
Hay*. Ed. Michael Burlingame and John R. Turner Ettlinger. Carbondale: Southern
Illinois University Press, 1997.

HERNDON, LINCOLN: William H. Herdon and Jesse W. Weik. *Herndon's Life of
Lincoln*. New York: Da Capo Press, 1983; reprint.

LV, 1856: Whitman. *Leaves of Grass*. New York: Fowler & Wells, 1856.

LV, 1860–1861: Whitman. *Leaves of Grass*. Boston: Thayer & Eldridge, 1860–1861.

MEMORANDA: Whitman. *Memoranda During the War.* Camden, N.J.: 1875.

NUPM: Whitman. *Notebooks and Unpublished Prose Manuscripts.* Vol. 2, Washington. Ed. Edward F. Grier. New York: New York University Press, 1984.

NYT: *The New York Times.*

OATES, WMTN: Stephen B. Oates. *With Malice Toward None: The Life of Abraham Lincoln.* New York: Harper & Row, 1977.

SANDBURG, LINCOLN: Carl Sandburg. *Abraham Lincoln: The Prairie Years and The War Years.* New York: Galahad Books, 1993; reprint.

SANDBURG, PRAIRIE YEARS: Carl Sandburg. *Abraham Lincoln: The Prairie Years.* 2 vols. New York: Harcourt, Brace, 1926.

SANDBURG, WAR YEARS: Carl Sandburg. *Abraham Lincoln: The War Years.* 4 Vols. New York: Harcourt, Brace, 1939.

WWC: Horace Traubel. *With Walt Whitman in Camden.* Vols. 1–3, New York: Rowman & Littlefield, 1961; Vol. 4, Philadelphia: University of Pennsylvania Press, 1953; Vols. 5–9, Carbondale: Southern Illinois University Press, 1964–1996.

Sources clearly cited in the text are not listed below. Block quotations are noted by first words; quotations within paragraphs are noted by final words, or first through last words with ellipses.

As of 1990, historian James M. McPherson estimated that there were more than fifty thousand books on the Civil War. The details of the War's progress that I have included are so numerous, elementary, and well established, that—except in the case of newspaper accounts—I have not annotated them. I have reserved the limited space for citations on quotes and data less familiar to readers.

Preface

xii *"Blood Money":* Jerome Loving, "The Political Roots of *Leaves of Grass,*" in *A Historical Guide to Walt Whitman,* ed. David S. Reynolds (New York: Oxford University Press, 2000), pp. 102–103.

xiv *"thunderstruck and stunned": CW* 2:282.

xv *"betrayal of precious rights":* David Herbert Donald, *Lincoln* (New York: Simon & Schuster, 1995), p. 168.

xv *"as it is in right":* Oates, *WMTN,* p. 112.

xvi *The men wrecked . . . looted some shops:* Kenneth M. Stamp, *America in 1857: A Nation on the Brink* (New York: Oxford University Press, 1990), p. 146.

xvi *"harlot slavery":* Sandburg, *Lincoln,* p. 121.

Chapter 1: Springfield, 1857

3 *his own accounting . . . four thousand dollars:* David Herbert Donald, *Lincoln's Herndon* (New York: Alfred A. Knopf, 1948), p. 54.

3 *His favorite philosopher-poet . . . Emerson:* Herndon, *Lincoln,* p. xxiv.

3 *"Some Hints on the Mind" . . . "if not its law":* Donald, *Lincoln's Herndon,* p. 56.

4 *"has yet contributed":* Corr, vol. 1, p. 41, Emerson's letter to Whitman, July 21, 1855. Without Emerson's permission, Whitman used this private letter of praise to promote *Leaves of Grass.* He permitted Charles Dana to print the letter in the *New-York Tribune,* and then included it in the 1856 edition of *Leaves.*

4 *the second edition of Whitman's* Leaves of Grass: Herndon's ownership of *Leaves of Grass* is recalled by Henry B. Rankin in his *Personal Recollections of Abraham Lincoln* (New York: G. P. Putnam's Sons, 1916), pp. 125–127, and confirmed by William E. Barton, in his *Abraham Lincoln and Walt Whitman,* p. 92. Barton writes: "Herndon owned a copy of *Leaves of Grass* . . . At the time Herndon procured his copy of *Leaves of Grass,* about 1857, Lincoln was approaching his debate with Douglas . . ." Barton spoke with authority, having purchased Herndon's library. Emerson's endorsement of the 1856 edition, Barton's knowledge that the book was purchased "about 1857," and the nationwide distribution of the 1856 edition—as opposed to the regional sale of the first edition—all indicate that it was the 1856 rather than the 1855 edition that Herndon purchased. The Barton (and Herndon) Collection is at the University of Chicago Library. Herndon's copy of *Leaves of Grass* is lost.

4 *He laid it down . . . to explode:* Rankin, *Personal Recollections,* p. 125.

4 *"merits of Walt Whitman's poetry":* Donald, *Lincoln's Herndon,* p. 34; *vide* also Lincoln biographer Ida M. Tarbell, in her 1923 foreword to Henry B. Rankin's *Intimate Character Sketches of Abraham Lincoln, ut infra:* "To their table came all the leading journals of the South as well as North—to be read and discussed. Here, too, came Whitman's *Leaves of Grass,* pregnant lines arresting Lincoln, who as he read would often go over aloud to his companions something which had stirred his imagination or pricked his heart" (p. 12).

5 *Description of Lincoln's office:* Donald, *Lincoln's Herndon,* p. 32, and Herndon, *Lincoln,* p. 255.

5 *"I can remember it better":* Herndon, *Lincoln,* p. 268.

5–6 *nearly impossible to efface:* Ibid., p. 421.

6 *"employed without reserve":* Chronology, pp. 30–31.

6 *"this gathering of muck":* Ibid.

6 *"this glorious Native American":* Ibid.

6 *"its poetic merit":* Henry B. Rankin, *Personal Recollections,* p. 125; *vide* also Henry B. Rankin, *Intimate Character Sketches of Abraham Lincoln* (Philadelphia: J. B. Lippincott, 1924), p. 55.

6 *"I mind how we lay in June"*: LV, 1856, pp. 10–11.

6 *"I turn the bridegroom"*: Ibid., p. 63.

7 *"I am the hounded slave"*: Ibid., p. 64.

7 *"They do not know"*: Ibid., p. 20.

8 *"A woman waits for me"*: Ibid., p. 240.

8 *"free soil, free labor"*: Oates, *WMTN*, p. 129.

8 *"Walt Whitman, an American . . . counterpart of on the same terms"*: LV, 1856, p. 41.

9 *"Have you outstript the rest?"*: Ibid., p. 36.

9 *"Quite a surprise occurred"*: Rankin, *Personal Recollections*, p. 125.

9 *"I celebrate myself . . . my heart"*: LV, 1856, pp. 5–6.

10 *"in Whitman's versification"*: Rankin, *Personal Recollections*, p. 126.

10 *"and unique forms of expression"*: Ibid.

10–11 *"Time and again . . . he fancied"*: Ibid.

11 *"fire by the women"*: Ibid., p. 124.

11 *In 1928, a rival biographer*: Barton, *AL & WW*.

11 *"hostile spirit toward Whitman"*: Glicksberg, *Whitman*, pp. 4–5. Gay Wilson Allen's comment on Barton in *The Solitary Singer: A Critical Biography of Walt Whitman* (New York: Macmillan, 1955), p. 578, is that "his book is exceedingly biased [against Whitman]."

11 *unaware of Whitman's existence*: Glicksberg, *Whitman*, p. 138.

11 *One of the points . . . Rankin's account*: The proximate date of 1857 for Lincoln's reading of *Leaves*, based on Rankin's memoirs, was

logically corroborated by Thomas Bird Mosher in his introduction to a 1919 edition of *Leaves of Grass*. *Vide* Barton, *AL & WW*, p. 90.

13 *"the appropriateness of things"*: Herndon, *Lincoln*, pp. 478–479.

13 *"preacher happened to be present"*: Ibid., p. 479.

13 *"the hollow, and the sham"*: Ibid., pp. 475–476.

14 *"Only what nobody denies is so"*: LV, 1856, p. 51.

14 *"Trippers and askers surround me"*: Ibid., pp. 9–10.

15 *"the true and the good"*: Herndon, *Lincoln*, p. 480.

15 *"standpoint of reason and logic"*: Ibid., p. 481.

15–16 *"Equal justice . . . physical pain"*: CW 2:264.

17 *Poe's poetry . . . Oliver Wendell Holmes*: CW 1:377.

17 *"so fine a piece as I think that is"*: CW 1:378.

17–18 *"As distant mountains please"*: CW 1:368.

18 *"into harmless insanity"*: CW 1:384, letter to Andrew Johnson, September 6, 1846.

18 *"But here's an object more of dread"*: CW 1:385.

19 *"in that direction"*: Herndon, *Lincoln*, p. 257.

20 *Others have told it often*: *Vide* Richard Hofstadter, *The American Political Tradition and the Men Who Made It* (reprint, New York: Vintage Books, 1974); Carl Sandburg, *Abraham Lincoln: The Prairie Years*; Donald, *Lincoln*; et al.

20   *Whitman's earliest mention of Lincoln:* Justin Kaplan, *Walt Whitman: A Life* (New York: Simon and Schuster, 1980), p. 259.

20   *"half* slave *and half* free": *CW* 2:461.

22   *"variety of the genus, Democrat": CW* 2:400.

22   *"In those days": CW* 2:404.

22–23 *"They have him":* Ibid.

23   *"to the last plank": CW* 2:405.

23   *"Now I protest":* Ibid.

24   *"black slaves and white masters": CW* 2:408.

24   *"female slave": CW* 2:409.

24   *"There are white men enough": CW* 2:407–408.

24   *"The plainest print": CW* 2:409–410.

25   *"Now I am curious": LV,* 1856, p. 218.

25   *belated honeymoon:* Donald, *Lincoln,* p. 197.

25   *"Hunger is a sharp thorn":* Sandburg, *Prairie,* vol. 2, p. 106.

25   *"Burn high your fires": LV,* 1856, p. 221.

26   *"Crowds of men and women":* Ibid., p. 211.

26   *"Who was to know":* Ibid., p. 218.

26   *"Consider, you who peruse":* Ibid., p. 220.

27   *"the prairie, the hillside":* Kaplan, *Walt Whitman,* p. 259.

27   *"poverty was my position":* Oates, *WMTN,* p. 135.

27   *"shall be rich":* Ibid.

28   *"bill-jumper": WWC* 3:237–238; Kaplan, *Walt Whitman,* 224 ff.

28   *"like a satyr, and rank":* Amos Bronson Alcott, *The Journals of Bronson Alcott,* ed. Odell Shepard (Boston: Little, Brown, 1938), pp. 286–287.

29   *"If you meet some stranger": LV,* 1856, p. 123.

29   *"What is more subtle than this":* Ibid., p. 219.

29–30 *"You will hardly know"* Ibid., p. 100.

30   *"in the U.S. Senate": Day by Day,* vol. 2, p. 211.

31   *it was received coolly:* As published in Lincoln's *Collected Works,* volume 2, the April 6, 1858, "First Lecture on Discoveries and Inventions" has the following footnote: "The manuscript ends abruptly at the top of a page. Probably there was more to the lecture which Lincoln utilized in his revised version (q.v., February 11, 1859, *infra*)." I have treated the "revised version" as the natural conclusion of the April 6, 1858, speech.

31   *"emancipation of the mind":* J. G. Randall, *Lincoln the President* (New York: Dodd, Mead, 1945), vol. 1, p. 19.

31   *"nomination to the presidency":* Ibid., p. 44.

31–32 *"All creation is a mine": CW* 2:437.

32   *"How could the 'gopher wood' . . . wagons and boats": CW* 2:438–442.

32   *"exurge from you": LV,* 1856, p. 129.

32–33 *"Manufactures, commerce . . . lamps in the darkness":* Ibid., pp. 131–133.

33   *"We shall find": CW* 3:359.

33   *"with which it works":* Ibid.

33   *"distances of time and of space": CW* 3:360.

34 *"civilization and the arts"*: *CW* 3:363.

34 *"America, curious"*: *LV*, 1856, p. 182.

34–35 *"Language-using controls"*: Ibid., p. 191.

35 *"Great are the myths"*: Ibid., p. 161.

35 *"Great is language"*: Ibid., p. 164.

36 *"It avails not"*: Ibid., p. 212.

37 *"a revolution . . . American soul"*: Kaplan, *Walt Whitman*, p. 232.

38 *"receptacle, his hat"*: Herndon, *Lincoln*, p. 324.

38 *"What is prudence, is indivisible"*: *LV*, 1856, p. 260.

39 *"Towering genius . . . utmost stretch"*: *CW* 1:114.

39–40 *"Great is justice! . . . exact tribunal"*: *LV*, 1856, p. 165.

40–41 *"Let the crust of hell . . . under his heel!"*: Ibid., pp. 319–320.

41 *"If we could first know"*: *CW* 2:461.

42 *"was kicked to the winds"*: *CW* 2:464.

43 *"The house-builder at work"*: *LV*, 1856, p. 143.

43 *"understood one another from the beginning"*: *CW* 2:465–466.

43 *"care nothing about it"*: *CW* 2:467.

43 *"politic to say so?"*: Herndon, *Lincoln*, p. 325.

44 Lincoln replied: Ibid.

44 Lincoln invited a dozen friends: Ibid., p. 326.

44 *"damned fool utterance"* . . . *"make you President"*: Ibid.

Chapter 2: New York, 1861

45 *"Everything appertaining . . . raised arm, and upright hand"*: *NUPM*, p. 472.

46 *"study within itself"*: *CW* 3:480.

46 *"left his father"*: Kaplan, *Walt Whitman*, p. 183.

46 *"Stevenson's Carriage factory"*: *NUPM*, p. 454.

47 *"Slept with me Sept 3ʳᵈ"*: Ibid., pp. 487–488.

47 *"a show as 'candy butcher'"*: Ibid., p. 490.

47 *"on brotherly terms"*: *LV*, 1860–1861, p. 66.

47 Whitman house on Classon Avenue: Charley Shively, ed., *Calamus Lovers: Walt Whitman's Working-Class Camerados* (San Francisco: Gay Sunshine Press, 1987), pp. 36–50.

48 *"something or other was wrong"*: *WWC* 1: 151.

48 *"the expurgated book"*: *WWC* 1:124.

48 *"large number of copies"*: Kaplan, *Walt Whitman*, p. 247.

48 *"among the mass public"*: Ibid., p. 254.

49 *"O darkness!"*: *LV*, 1860–1861, pp. 274–275.

50 *"slough"* or *"stagnation"*: Corr., p. 61, letter to Emerson.

50 *"Nothing is sure"*: *NUPM*, pp. 517–518.

51 *"weighed two hundred and ten pounds"*: *WWC* 4:378.

52 *"rather rude, but noble"*: All quotes from Dr. John Roosa, and details about Whitman in New York Hospital, are from *NUPM*, pp. 525–528, an appendix from Richard Henry Stoddard's "The World of Letters," originally published in the New York *Mail and Express*, June 20, 1893.

52 *"men and women beat him . . . romance*

of surgery and medicine": *NUPM*, p. 484.

53 *Charley Pfaff*: Background information about Pfaff's Cellar as well as quotes in this section come from Christine Stansell, "Whitman at Pfaff's," *Whitman Quarterly Review* 10 (winter 1993), pp. 107–123.

56 *"sexual predator . . . stock breeder"*: Kaplan, *Walt Whitman*, p. 242.

56 *"no other literary comparison"*: Stansell, *ut supra*.

56 *"fact of my experience"*: W. D. Howells, *Literary Friends and Acquaintance: A Personal Retrospect of American Authorship*, ed. David F. Hiatt and Edwin H. Cady (Bloomington: Indiana University Press, 1968), p. 67.

57 *"The vault at Pfaffs"*: *NUPM*, p. 454.

58 *"this Lincoln person"*: Sandburg, *Prairie*, p. 211.

59 *"killing off an enemy"*: Herndon quoted in Michael Burlingame, *The Inner World of Abraham Lincoln* (Urbana: University of Illinois Press, 1994), p. 149.

59 *"matter of human interest"*: Donn Piatt, quoted in Reinhard H. Luthin, *The Real Abraham Lincoln* (Englewood Cliffs, N.J.: Prentice-Hall, 1960), p. 385.

60 *"arising from its actual presence"*: *CW* 3:550.

60 *"thumb on his middle finger"*: Herndon letter quoted in James Mellon, comp. and ed. *The Face of Lincoln* (New York: Viking Press, 1979), p. 30.

60 *"with an inward fire"*: Brooks quoted by Sandburg, *Prairie*, p. 213.

60 *"like that of the dead"*: Ibid.

60 *"to a New York audience"*: Ibid., p. 214.

60 *"the overthrow of Douglas"*: Rankin, *Personal Recollections*, p. 249.

61 *"idle and starving workmen"*: *NYT*, February 20, 1861. Information about Lincoln's New York visit is from *NYT*, February 19 and 20, 1861, except where otherwise noted.

62 *"I see that you have provided"*: *CW* 4:227–229.

63 *"raising his hat and bowing"*: *Baltimore Sun*, February 21, 1861.

64 *"delighted with the spectacle"*: Ibid.

65 *"Fellow Citizens"*: *CW* 4:230.

65 *"a capital view"*: Walt Whitman, *Specimen Days; & Collect* (Glasgow: Wilson & McCormick, 1883), pp. 307–308 (quoting lecture first given in 1879).

66 *"Two or three shabby"*: Ibid.

68 *"break and riot came"*: Ibid., p. 308.

68 *His boys visited . . . serenade them*: *Baltimore Sun*, February 21, 1861.

69 *Lincoln would stand back-to-back*: *NYT*, February 20, 1861.

69 *"They mutually surpassed each other"*: New York *World*, February 21, 1861.

69 *"people is prepossessing . . . Western"*: *Baltimore Sun*, February 21, 1861.

69 *"Union itself was made"*: *NYT*, February 21, 1861.

70 *"force it on The States"*: Walt Whitman, "The Eighteenth Presidency!" in *Complete Poetry and Collected Prose*, Library of America,

(New York: Literary Classics of the
United States, dist. by Viking Press,
1982), p. 1310.

70 *"breast and arms":* Ibid., p. 1308.

70 *"WW and 'President elect' ": NUPM,*
p. 436.

70–71 *"Who are you": LV,* 1856,
pp. 191–192.

Chapter 3: *The Federal City, New Year's
Day,* 1863

My main source of information
about the architecture, institutions,
and flora and fauna of Washington,
D.C., in the period 1861–1865 is
William D. Haley, ed., *Philp's
Washington Described* (New York:
Rudd & Carleton, 1861). I have used
the city map published by Casimir
Bohn in Washington, D.C., circa
1860. Richard M. Lee's *Mr. Lincoln's
City: An Illustrated Guide to the Civil
War Sites of Washington* (McLean,
Virginia: EPM Publications, 1981)
is useful both for its many period
photographs and for its compendious
text. J. G. Randall, *Lincoln the
President,* vol. 2, provides rich
background information on the
Emancipation Proclamation.

75 *At midnight all around* . . . Morning
Chronicle observed: This is a
paraphrase of "New Year's Day in
Washington," in the *Chronicle* of
January 2, 1863.

76 *"suffered terribly this morning":*
Anson Stager's "Second Dispatch,"

December 31, 1862, *Washington
Chronicle,* January 3, 1863.

76 *"rebels in the center": Washington
Chronicle,* January 2, 1863.

76 *"greatest carnage . . . has occurred":
Washington Chronicle,* January 3,
1863; Stager's "Third Dispatch,"
ibid., January 2, 1863.

76 *"If there is a worse place than Hell,
I am in it":* Sandburg, *Lincoln,*
pp. 328–329, quoting T. J. Barnet
quoting Lincoln.

76 *"known in the earth's wars":* Kaplan,
Walt Whitman, p. 268.

77 *"since the world began":* Oates,
WMTN, p. 327.

77 *"believes in him any more":* Ibid.

77 *All evening . . . of New Year's Day:*
John G. Nicolay and John Hay,
Abraham Lincoln: A History, 10 vols.
(New York: Century, 1890), vol. 6,
p. 421.

78 *"a servile insurrection":* Oates,
WMTN, p. 321.

79 *"paid by the proprietor":* Lee, *Mr.
Lincoln's City,* p. 58.

79 *"to take boarders": CW* 6:33. All
Lincoln quotes concerning the lady
are from this source.

80 *"What can I do for you?":* Lincoln and
the Civil War: A Profile and a History,
ed. Courtlandt Canby (New York:
George Braziller, 1960), p. 232.

81 *"the waves of this conflict":* Jim
Bishop, *The Day Lincoln Was
Shot* (New York: Harper, 1955),
p. 17.

82 *"favor of Almighty God": CW* 6:30.

82 *Lincoln went to fetch Mary:* Details of

the New Year's levee come from newspaper accounts and Brooks, *Washington*, pp. 48, 69.

85 *"gathered to that mad focus"*: *WWC* 2:26.

85 *"the gallant, handsome . . . in love with him"*: Roy Morris Jr., *The Better Angel: Walt Whitman in the Civil War* (New York: Oxford University Press, 2000), pp. 72–73.

86 *Whitman studied . . . brother:* *Memoranda*, p. 6.

86 *"brown woolen blanket"*: Corr., vol. 1, p. 58.

86–87 *"fixed eyes in the morning"*: Glicksberg, *Whitman*, p. 70; and *NUPM*, p. 504.

87 *whiskey-spiked coffee:* Glicksberg, *Whitman*, p. 68.

87 *lying on the battlefield:* Allen, *Solitary Singer*, p. 284.

87 *"if they couldn't grumble"*: *NUPM*, p. 509.

87 *"of elderly men"*: Ibid., p. 510.

87 *"if he wishes it"*: Allen, *Solitary Singer*, p. 285.

87 *"quite romantic"*: Corr., vol. 1, p. 81.

87 *"created to do"*: Allen, *Solitary Singer*, p. 287.

89 *"in her fair youth"*: Corr., vol. 1: p. 69.

89 *"of the contemporary"*: Kaplan, *Walt Whitman*, p. 150.

89 *"invisible electric fluid"*: Ibid. For Whitman's actions, *vide* Kaplan, *Walt Whitman*, pp. 149–151.

90 *"melancholy saturating all"*: *Memoranda*, p. 4.

90 *"rooted in the same ground"*: Barton, *AL & WW*, p. 170.

92 *"our greeting was cordial"*: The meeting of the Piatts and Whitman is described in a letter from J. J. Piatt to Charles N. Elliott printed in Clara Barrus, *Whitman and Burroughs, Comrades* (Boston: Houghton Mifflin, 1931), p. 10. All Piatt quotes are from Barrus.

92 *"a little in their profession"*: *CW* 8:337.

93 *"the space of three hours"*: Nicolay and Hay, *Abraham Lincoln*, vol. 6, p. 429.

93 *the pen steady:* Randall, *Lincoln the President*, p. 168.

93 *"it will be for this act"*: Charles M. Segal, ed., *Conversations with Lincoln* (New York: G. P. Putnam's Sons, 1961), pp. 234–235. The original source of this statement is probably Governor Oliver Morton, who made it in introducing Lincoln to an audience in 1865. *Vide Washington Star*, March 18, 1865.

93 *" 'he had some compunctions' "*: Frederick W. Seward, *Reminiscences of a War-Time Statesman and Diplomat, 1830–1915* (New York: G. P. Putnam's Sons, 1916), p. 227.

93 *"at his apprehension"*: Ibid.

94 *"a new life"*: Quotes *passim* from the *Washington Chronicle:* January 2, 1863.

94 *"hug him to death"*: Oates, *WMTN*, p. 333.

94 *"where people most do congregate"*: *NUPM*, p. 545.

95 *"I come across"*: William C. Davis, *Lincoln's Men: How President Lincoln Became Father to an Army and a*

Nation (New York: Touchstone, 2000), p. 100.

Chapter 4: February 1863

96 *"snow-white kid gloves"*: Details of Stratton and Warren's visit are from the *Washington Chronicle*, February 13, 1863, and the *Washington Star*, February 14, 1863.

96 *"the long and short of it"*: Carol Easton, "Charles S. Stratton (1838–1883)," in *The People's Almanac*, ed. David Wallechinsky and Irving Wallace (Garden City, N.Y.: Doubleday, 1975), p. 110.

97 *"completely in the shade"*: "Movements of Gen. Tom Thumb and Lady," *Washington Star*, February 14, 1863.

97 *"the whole of its existence"*: John Nicolay quoted in Helen Nicolay, *Lincoln's Secretary: A Biography of John Nicolay* (New York: Longmans, Green, 1949), p. 166.

97 *"yellow-reddish halo"*: NUPM, p. 555.

97 *"on the Maryland side"*: Ibid.

98 *"on the continent"*: Ibid., pp. 555–556.

98 *a dead horse*: *Washington Chronicle*, January 2, 1863.

98 *"foot of North Capitol Street"*: *Washington Chronicle*, February 13, 1863.

99 *"At this writing . . . rottenness of its streets"*: Brooks's description of D.C. is in the *Sacramento Union*, February 28, 1863, and June 27, 1864, and in Brooks, *Washington*, pp. 294–295.

99 *"uncomfortably laid out"*: Charles

Augustus Murray quoted in John W. Reps, *Washington on View: The Nation's Capital since 1790* (Chapel Hill: University of North Carolina Press, 1991), p. 82.

99 *"a diseased project"*: Dickens quoted in Reps, *Washington on View*, p. 108.

100 *"sparks in the distance"*: NUPM, p. 556.

100 *"scribbling for the papers"*: Corr., vol. 1, p. 83.

100 *"a comforting word to them"*: Ibid., p. 63.

101 *"began to cry"*: Ibid., p. 64.

102 *"when you look upon it"*: LV, 1856, p. 129.

102 *"blue, white, brownish, yellow . . . vestments of majesty"*: All quotes concerning the Capitol are from NUPM, pp. 563–567.

103 *"I fetch up here"*: Corr., vol. 1, p. 61.

104 *"America has yet contributed"*: Ibid., p. 41.

104 *"a nasty book"*: NUPM, p. 488.

104–105 *"I shall conquer my object"*: Corr., vol. 1, p. 61.

105 *"To hold men together"*: LV, 1856, p. 188.

106 *"Permit me to say"*: Corr., vol. 1, p. 65.

106 *"than in the Departments"*: Ibid., p. 66.

107 *"half full of sadness"*: Anna Laurens Dawes, *Charles Sumner* (New York: Dodd, Mead, 1892), p. 222.

108 *"his chair in the Senate"*: Brooks, *Washington*, p. 33.

108 *Sumner took pride . . . crossed knees*: Dawes, *Charles Sumner*, p. 224.

109 *"nothing but itself"*: Henry Adams,

The Education of Henry Adams: An Autobiography (1907; New York: Time, 1964), vol. 2, p. 18.

109 *"obliged to lie down":* Charles Sumner, *Selected Letters of Charles Sumner*, vol. 2, ed. Beverly Wilson Palmer (Boston: Northeastern University Press, 1990), p. 142, Sumner letter to Samuel Gridley Howe, February 1, 1863.

109 *"beyond any thing I could tell":* Corr., vol. 1, p. 75.

111 *"white as Sumner's hands":* Dawes, *Charles Sumner*, p. 224.

112 *"American original genius":* LeRoy H. Fischer, *Lincoln's Gadfly, Adam Gurowski* (Norman: University of Oklahoma Press, 1964), p. 260.

113 *"Everything here . . . fate of the rest":* Corr., vol. 1, p. 73.

114 *"He did not know me":* NUPM, p. 552.

114 *"Why, how can I . . . Virginia planter":* Corr., vol. 1, p. 74.

115 *"recollection of something":* NUPM, p. 552.

115 *"as I supposed":* Corr., vol. 1, p. 74.

115 *"to get something":* Ibid., p. 73.

115 *"a sort of general letter . . . another to Gen. Meigs . . . a sort of gelding—no good":* Corr., vol. 1, p. 74.

115 *The poet's instincts . . . source of the rumor:* David Herbert Donald, *Charles Sumner and the Rights of Man* (New York: Alfred A. Knopf, 1970), pp. 314–315.

116 *"It is very amusing . . . personal introduction of some big bug":* Corr., vol. 1, p. 73.

116 *"backing me from the State of New York":* Ibid.

116 *"giving me a boost? . . . Yes, I will, if I can":* NUPM, p. 564.

117 *"the loneliest man in Washington":* Donald, *Lincoln*, p. 426. According to Michael Burlingame, *Inner World of Abraham Lincoln*, p. 105, Lincoln is supposed to have told Bishop Charles Gordon Ames, "I am the loneliest man in America."

117 *inconsolable grief:* My sources for Mary Todd Lincoln are Jean H. Baker, *Mary Todd Lincoln: A Biography* (New York: W. W. Norton, 1987); Elizabeth Keckley, *Behind the Scenes: Thirty Years a Slave, and Four Years in the White House* (New York: G. W. Carlton, 1868); and Justin G. Turner and Linda Levitt Turner, *Mary Todd Lincoln: Her Life and Letters* (New York: Alfred A. Knopf, 1972).

117 *"scarcely tell she was there":* Baker, *Mary Todd Lincoln*, p. 214.

118 *"they are very near":* Turner and Turner, *Mary Todd Lincoln*, p. 256.

119 *"Eddie is sometimes with him":* Baker, *Mary Todd Lincoln*, p. 220.

119 *"make everything seem wrong":* Moncure Daniel Conway, *Autobiography: Memories and Experiences* (Boston: Houghton, Mifflin, 1904), vol. 1, p. 379.

120 *"poor drunken imbecile":* Donald, *Lincoln*, p. 409.

120 *"cheery as a boy":* Brooks, *Washington*, p. 56.

120 *"imbecile . . . sooner the better":* Donald, *Lincoln*, p. 411.

120 *"risk the dictatorship":* CW 6:78–79.

120 "first safe opportunity": Donald, *Lincoln*, p. 424.

120 "It does not exist": Ibid.

120 "worn and haggard . . . never tells a joke now": Ibid., p. 426.

121 "to rub it out": Herndon, *Lincoln*, p. 421.

121 "Have you considered": *LV,* 1856, p. 192.

122 "Meanwhile, corpses lie": Ibid., p. 253.

Chapter 5: *The Soldier's Missionary*

124 "people who comprehend him": *WWC* 3:525.

124 "What all the yelling was about": Morris, *Better Angel*, p. 88.

124 "Upon a few of these hospitals": Dispatch to *NYT*, February 26, 1863, in Walt Whitman, *Walt Whitman's Civil War*, ed. Walter Lowenfels (New York: Alfred A. Knopf, 1960), p. 85.

124 "pavilion style" ff.: Whitman, *Walt Whitman's Civil War*, pp. 85–86.

125 compound called Campbell Hospital: Description of Campbell Hospital, and "are demonstration enough": *Memoranda*, p. 11.

125 Whitman wore . . . black morocco boots: Corr., vol. 1, p. 103.

125 " 'false faces'?": This story comes from Ellen M. Calder (Nellie O'Connor), "Personal Recollections of Walt Whitman," *Atlantic Monthly*, June 1907.

125 "coach bag": The bag is in the collection of the Library of Congress, where I inspected it.

126 wide-brimmed hat: Morris, *Better Angel*, p. 104.

126 "never begin to produce": NUPM, p. 591.

126 "bad diarrhea also . . . live a week on one": NUPM, p. 593.

127 "feel funny enough": Corr., vol. 1, p. 81.

127 "showing our humanity": Ibid.

127 "under the knife": Corr., p. 82.

127 "Not a cholera patient": *LG,* 1855, p. 39.

127 "I am the man": Ibid., p. 39.

127 "I had known . . . the remaining hand": *Memoranda*, p. 12.

127 "pair of suspenders": NUPM, p. 592.

128 "sweet crackers, figs": *Memoranda*, p. 8.

128 "little comforts they have brought": NUPM, pp. 583–584.

128 "Chester H. Lilly . . . franked by Mr. Sumner" and passim: NUPM, pp. 572–604.

130 "with much hair": Corr., vol. 1, p. 89.

130 "cities and the east": Ibid.

130 "a strange influence here": Ibid., p. 102.

131 "machine or invention": *Memoranda*, p. 10.

131 "in various degrees": Ibid.

131 "relieve particular cases": Ibid.

131 "unmanly fear": Corr., vol. 1, p. 82.

131 "need of consolation": Ibid., p. 112.

132 "have seen many die here": NUPM, p. 681.

132 "I will have none": Geoffrey C. Ward, *The Civil War: An Illustrated History*

(New York: Alfred A. Knopf, 1990), p. 202.

133 *"as if for their lives"*: Corr., vol. 1, p. 77.

133 *"from heaven"*: Ibid., p. 83.

133 *"I think well of the President . . . doughnut complexion . . . menacing and high as ever . . . court dress or court decorums"*: Ibid., pp. 82–83.

134 *"the true and ideal" . . . "I wish I knew you" and passim*: Calder, "Personal Recollections."

135 *"but face pale"*: Corr., vol. 1, p. 81.

135 *"for the New York Bowery"*: Ibid.

135 *He who goes*: New York Times dispatch, quoted in Whitman, *Walt Whitman's Civil War*, p. 104.

135 *"clots of blood"*: NUPM, p. 670.

135 *"Poor fellows"*: Quoted in Whitman, *Walt Whitman's Civil War*, pp. 104–105.

136 *Sergeant Thomas P. Sawyer*: Background for the story of Thomas Sawyer and Lewis Brown comes from Morris, *Better Angel*, p. 132–136, and Jerome Loving, *Walt Whitman: The Song of Himself* (Berkeley: University of California Press, 1999), pp. 269–270, 277.

137 *"something from me . . . half a minute long . . . not for good . . . dear comrade"*: Corr, vol. 1, pp. 91–93.

138 *"there is great excitement . . . as blue about it as anybody"*: Ibid., 90–92 passim.

139 *"I succeed pretty well"*: Ibid., p. 90.

139 *"Congratulatory Order"*: Washington Evening Star, May 5, 1863, 2d ed.

140 *"completely disabled"*: Washington Morning Chronicle, Wednesday, May 6, 1863.

141 *"intuitive sagacity"*: Gideon Welles, *Diary of Gideon Welles, Secretary of the Navy Under Lincoln and Johnson* (New York: Houghton, Mifflin, 1911), vol. 1, p. 265.

141 *"he is overconfident"*: Brooks, Washington, p. 56.

142 *"anxiety to get facts"*: Welles, *Diary*, vol. 1, p. 266.

142 *"Is that so?"*: Day by Day, vol. 3, p. 182.

142 *"sad to see them"*: Corr., vol. 1, 97–98.

142 *"According to Noah Brooks . . . 'What will the country say!' " passim*: Brooks, *Washington*, pp. 60–61.

143 *might commit suicide*: Burlingame, *Inner World of Abraham Lincoln*, p. 105.

144 *"the poor pale helpless soldiers . . . into the ambulance" ff*: Memoranda, p. 13.

145 *"cool, clear and satisfied"*: Donald, *Lincoln*, p. 438.

145 *"fire the first time"*: Oates, *WMTN*, p. 348.

145 *"previous act of the war"*: George Gordon Meade, *The Life and Letters of George Gordon Meade* (New York: Charles Scribner's Sons, 1913), vol. 1, p. 372.

145 *"was to be is not"*: Randall, *Lincoln the President*, vol. 2, p. 269.

146 *"ruinous, if true"*: CW 6:241.

147 *"well nigh established?"*: Frémont to Sumner, June 9, 1863, quoted in CW 6:243.

Chapter 6: *The Looking Glass*

148 *"Will the whole come back"*: *LV*, 1856,
     p. 130. This was titled in the 1856
     edition "Poem of the Daily Work of
     the Workmen and Workwomen of
     These States."

149 *"graceful, boyish figure"*: John Russell
     Young quoted by Burlingame and
     Ettlinger in their introduction to
     Hay, *Diary*, p. xii. Background
     information on Hay also comes from
     Howard I. Kushner and Anne
     Hummel Sherrill, *John Milton Hay:
     the Union of Poetry and Politics*
     (Boston: Twayne, 1977).

149 *"turneth away wrath"*: Young, quoted
     ut supra.

149 *"Hellcat"*: Baker, *Mary Todd Lincoln*,
     p. 191.

150 *"less than a year"*: Ibid., p. 187.

150 *"having an affair"*: Ibid., p. 184.
     Baker's exact phrase is "Mary Lincoln
     and William Wood had become
     friends and possibly more," and she
     quotes John Nicolay's letter to
     Schuyler Colfax recalling "the war
     [Mary Lincoln] had with Mr. Lincoln
     about the Commissioner? They
     scarcely spoke together for several
     days."

150 *"new material for a dress"*: Ibid.,
     p. 202.

151 *"consort of her husband"*: Ibid.,
     pp. 228–229.

151 *"now Tad evoked memories of Willie"*:
     Ibid., p. 213.

151 *"made known their claims"*: Ibid.,
     p. 201.

151 *position in the Interior Department*:
     Ibid., p. 220.

151 *"have to send you there"*: Keckley,
     Behind the Scenes, pp. 104–105.

151 *"all to me"*: Baker, *Mary Todd
     Lincoln*, p. 226.

152 *Excepting a séance*: *Day by Day*,
     vol. 1, p. 181.

152 *Heintzelman's* Journal: Papers of
     Samuel Peter Heintzelman, Library
     of Congress.

152 *"when you went away"*: *CW* 6:283.

154 *"that won't kill him"*: Ward Hill
     Lamon, *Recollections of Abraham
     Lincoln, 1847–1865*, ed. Dorothy
     Lamon Teillard (Washington, D.C.,
     D. L. Teillard, 1911; facsimile,
     University of Nebraska Press, 1994),
     p. 131–132. Lamon tells this story of
     an "officer of the peace," on terms of
     intimacy with the President, who
     killed a man in the line of duty.
     Lamon does not name himself, but it
     is clear he is the officer.

154 *"someone taking my life"*: Ibid.,
     pp. 193–194.

155 *"guards and escorts"*: Sandburg, *War
     Years*, vol. 2, pp. 209–210.

155 *"trying to be, an emperor"*: Ibid.

155 *"determined upon it"*: Ibid.

155 *"dying all the while"*: Rufus Rockwell
     Wilson, ed., *Intimate Memories of
     Lincoln* (Elmira, New York:
     Primavera Press, 1945), p. 475.

155 *"President shall surely be buried"*: *LV*,
     1856, p. 334.

156 *"to the Soldiers' Home"*: Rufus
     Wilson, *Intimate Memories of
     Lincoln*.

156 *"to do such a thing":* Lamon, *Recollections of Abraham Lincoln,* p. 274.

156 *As the Count appeared:* The main sources of information on Count Gurowski are LeRoy H. Fischer, *Lincoln's Gadfly,* and the diaries: Adam Gurowski, *Diary from March 4, 1861, to November 12, 1862* (Boston: Lee & Shepard, 1862); *Diary from November 18, 1862, to October 18, 1863* (New York: Carlton, 1864); and *Diary: 1863–'64–'65* (Washington: W. H. and O. H. Morrison, 1866).

157 *"great keenness"* . . . *"splendid intellect":* *WWC,* 3:78.

157 *"a beast"* . . . *"a clever charlatan":* Fischer, *Lincoln's Gadfly,* p. 5.

158 *Adams Hill in the* Tribune *office:* Hay, *Diary,* p. 94.

158 *"looks worse than it was":* *WWC* 3:339.

159 *"And in looking . . . than the other":* Brooks tells the story in *Washington,* pp. 198–199.

159 *"authors and artists":* Nicolay quoted in Hay, *Diary,* p. 273 n.

159 *"because I was there":* Hay, *Diary,* p. 200.

161 *Sergeant Smith Stimmel passim:* Smith Stimmel, *Personal Reminiscences of Abraham Lincoln* (Minneapolis: W.H.M. Adams, 1928), pp. 15–36.

161 *"curious looking man, very sad": ff. Corr.,* vol. 1, p. 113.

163 *"sympathies and affinities":* Burroughs quoted in Clara Barrus, *Whitman and Burroughs,* p. 8.

163 *"and eye set and fixed":* Burroughs quoted in Ibid., p. 15.

164 *"Harrisburg in Imminent Danger"* . . . *"Sacked and burned":* Philip Shaw Palludan, *The Presidency of Abraham Lincoln* (Lawrence: University Press of Kansas, 1994), p. 203.

165 *"thin as a shad"* . . . *"Count Peeper":* Hay, *Diary,* p. 76.

165–66 *"I never knew . . . let somebody run that knows how!":* Paul F. Boller Jr., ed. *Presidential Anecdotes* (New York: Oxford University Press, 1981), p. 140.

166 *"must be a heathen":* Donald, *Lincoln,* p. 439.

166 *"neglected pyramid":* Orpheus Kerr quoted in Sandburg, *Lincoln,* p. 572.

167 *"Abraham is joking":* Kerr quoted in Ibid., p. 573.

167 *took her to the White House:* Mary Lincoln's carriage accident is reported in the *Washington Star,* July 2, 1863.

167 *"duty at this hour":* Ward, *Civil War,* p. 225.

167 *"catch it full":* Ibid., p. 224.

168 *"in a man's lifetime":* Ibid., 225.

168 *"totters to its destruction":* Randall, *Lincoln the President,* vol. 2, p. 286.

168 *"It was all my fault":* Ward, *Civil War,* p. 235.

168 *"with the highest honor":* *CW* 6:314.

169 *"whipped them myself":* Hay, *Diary,* p. 63.

169 *"distressed immeasurably because of it":* *CW* 6:328.

169 *"from pillar to post": Corr.,* vol. 1, pp. 114–115.

170 *"again before me"*: Ibid., p. 157.

170 *One evening . . . "must be made and met"*: Calder, "Personal Recollections."

170 *"—he [Lincoln] was not"*: Welles, *Diary*, vol. 1, p. 370.

171 *"even in the hospitals"*: Corr., vol. 1, p. 117.

171 *"for self-preservation"*: Ibid., p. 118.

171 *"quite a Japanee"*: Ibid., p. 105.

172 *"full of illusion"*: Memoranda, p. 11.

172 *"whichever way you move"*: Ibid.

172 *"I see the President . . . sadness in the expression" passim*: Memoranda, pp. 22–23.

172 met with Frederick Douglass: *Washington Chronicle*, August 12, 1863.

173 *"Five . . . Dollars $5/00. A. Lincoln"*: Day by Day, vol. 3, p. 201.

173 *"hard upon poor families"*: CW 6:384.

173 *"very cordial ones"*: Memoranda, p. 23. *Vide* p. 24, "his look, though abstracted, happen'd to be directed steadily in my eye. He bow'd and smiled."

Chapter 7: Halloween

Information about Albert Marshman Palmer and Hiram Barney comes from Hay, *Diary;* John Niven, *Salmon P. Chase: A Biography* (New York: Oxford University Press; 1995) and the entry on Albert Gallatin Palmer in Appleton's 1886 *Encyclopedia*.

176 *Whitman had gotten*: On Whitman's haircut and shirt, *vide NUPM*, pp. 538–539.

176 *"go about wringing their hands"*: Corr., vol. 1, p. 159.

177 *"production of 'Beautiful Pictures' "*: *Washington Chronicle*, August 4, 1863.

177 *"has to steer through"*: Corr., vol. 1, pp. 163–164.

179 *"holding his hand"*: This is from an 1863 diary/calendar in the Library of Congress, Thomas Biggs Harned Collection. I believe it has been inaccurately deciphered by Grier and others. It should read: "his face & manner have an expression + were inexpressibly sweet."

180 *"I love the President personally"*: Ibid.

180 *"Over the carnage"*: Walt Whitman, *Walt Whitman's Drum-Taps (1865); and Sequel to Drum-Taps (1865–6): A Reproduction*, Facsimile ed. F. DeWolfe Miller (Gainesville, Fla.: Scholars' Facsimiles & Reprints, 1959), p. 49.

Chapter 8: The Great Chase

The main sources of background information for this chapter are Niven, *Salmon P. Chase;* Robert B. Warden, *An Account of the Private Life and Public Services of Salmon Portland Chase* (Cincinnati: Wilstach, Baldwin, 1874); Hay, *Diary;* and John Townsend Trowbridge, "Reminiscences of Walt Whitman," *Atlantic Monthly*, February 1902.

184 *"any other man I ever knew"*: Albert Bushnell Hart, *Salmon Portland*

Chase (Boston: Houghton, Mifflin, 1899), p. 435.

184 *"does not see men":* Warden, *Account*, p. 582.

184 *The upper crust:* The source for the description of the wedding is Niven, *Salmon P. Chase*, pp. 340–344.

186 *"horsefly on the neck of a plowhorse":* Hay, *Diary*, p. 78.

187 *"will never do worse":* Ibid., p. 103.

187 *"refusing what he asks":* Ibid.

187 *"laying pipe":* Hay, *Diary*, p. 120.

187 *Pomeroy owned stock:* Niven, *Salmon P. Chase*, p. 357.

188 *financier Jay Cooke:* Ellis Paxson Oberholtzer, *Jay Cooke, Financier of the Civil War* (Philadelphia: George W. Jacobs, 1907), vol. 1, p. 364.

189 *"manly and loving soul":* Corr., vol. 1, p. 187.

189 *"active and cheerful":* Ibid., p. 183.

189 *"greater part of the time":* Ibid., p. 185.

189 *"very much with her":* Ibid., p. 183.

190 *"Jeffy got sick":* Ibid., p. 189 n.

190 *"than I will stand":* Ibid., p. 189.

190 *"shot him dead on the spot":* Morris, *Better Angel*, p. 159.

190 *"put along side of Andrew":* Ibid.

190 *"restless for the other":* Whitman, *Walt Whitman's Civil War*, p. 14.

190 *"religion with me":* Ibid.

191 *"sun shines in all day":* Corr., vol. 1, p. 168.

191 *"then swiftly descend":* Ibid., p. 185.

191 *"bring out* Drum Taps*":* Ibid.

191–92 *"to the man himself"* . . . *"feeling so much"* . . . *"the Secretary's door":* Trowbridge, "Reminiscences of Walt Whitman."

192 *Trowbridge was . . . tinged with envy:* John Townsend Trowbridge, *My Own Story: With Recollections of Noted Persons* (Boston: Houghton, Mifflin, 1904), pp. 52–54.

193 *"my own freezing feet":* All quotes *passim* from Trowbridge, "Reminiscences of Walt Whitman."

194 *"cut its throat":* Corr., vol. 1, p. 174.

194 *"unprovided with a latch key":* Trowbridge, "Reminiscences of Walt Whitman."

195 *"an honorable poverty"* . . . *"a younger brother's love":* Ibid.

195 *Trowbridge found Whitman:* The story of Trowbridge's breakfast with Whitman: Ibid.

196 *"First, O songs, for a prelude":* Whitman, *Drum-Taps*, p. 5.

198 *"but not resonant tones":* Trowbridge, "Reminiscences of Walt Whitman."

198 *"A SIGHT in the daybreak":* Whitman, *Drum-Taps*, p. 46.

199 *"never would have had* Leaves of Grass*":* Whitman, *Walt Whitman's Civil War*, p. 15.

199 *"Come up from the fields, father":* Drum-Taps, p. 39.

200 *"Bearing the bandages":* Ibid., p. 32.

202 *"assistance from the government":* Trowbridge, "Reminiscences of Walt Whitman."

203 *"in so good a cause":* Ibid.

203 *"this nasty book here?":* Quoted in NUPM, p. 488.

203 *to the House and Senate: Washington Star*, December 9, 1863.

203 *lavish editorial praise: Washington Star* and *Washington Chronicle*, December 11, 1863.

203 *"on entering this house"* . . . *"mentioning* Leaves of Grass*":* Quotes *passim* from Trowbridge, "Reminiscences of Walt Whitman."

206 *Jay Cooke paid $2,000:* Oberholtzer, *Jay Cooke*, vol. 1, p. 18.

206 *President's monthly salary* . . . $2,022.34: *Day by Day*, p. 226.

206 *Whitelaw Reid on the committee:* Niven, *Salmon P. Chase*, pp. 358–360.

206 *"the support of Ohio":* Salmon Chase quoted in John C. Waugh, *Reelecting Lincoln: The Battle for the 1864 Presidency* (New York: Crown, 1997), p. 114.

207 *"destruction of the rebellion":* Pamphlet is quoted and discussed in Donald, *Lincoln*, p. 481.

207 *"abusive pamphlet":* Ibid.

208 *"your honor as a gentleman":* Ibid.

208 *"honor of the nation":* Second anti-Lincoln pamphlet quoted in Oates, *WMTN*, p. 382.

208 *"available candidate":* Pomeroy Circular quoted in Donald, *Lincoln*, p. 482.

208 *"occasion for a change":* CW 7:213.

209 *"of every honorable mind":* Donald, *Lincoln*, p. 483.

Chapter 9: *Wilderness*

210 *"florid-tawny":* Trowbridge, "Reminiscences of Walt Whitman."

210 *his friend A. Van Rensellaer:* The source of the Van Rensellaer story is William O'Connor's *The Good Gray*

Poet: A Vindication (New York, Bunce & Huntington, 1866), p. 5, and a photostatic copy of the holograph letter itself reproduced in Barton, *AL & WW*.

211 *"so we went off":* A. Van Rensellaer to Walt Whitman, July 30, 1865.

211 *arguing that Van Rensellaer did not exist:* Barton, *AL & WW*, pp. 95–105. Whitman biographer Gay Wilson Allen's comment on Barton's effort is, "He has questioned the authenticity of the letter, but his book is exceedingly biased and this specific argument is not convincing." Allen, *Solitary Singer*, p. 578.

212 *"just as it is told":* Barton, *AL & WW*, p. 100.

212 *"live to see the end":* Day by Day, p. 238.

213 *"first class battle":* Corr., vol. 1, p. 193.

213 *"the best cause":* Ibid., p. 225.

214 *"while the war lasts":* Ibid., p. 197.

214 *"affected by the weather":* Ibid., p. 207.

214 *"could be but 18":* Ibid., p. 205.

214 *"in the hospitals & c.":* Ibid., p. 204.

214 *"callous & indifferent":* Ibid., p. 205.

215 *"noble manner and talk.":* Ibid., p. 218.

215 *"swollen out of shape":* Glicksberg, *Whitman*, p. 150.

215 *"I can tell you":* Corr., vol. 1, p. 216.

216 *"standing with others on a balcony":* Ibid., pp. 211–213.

217 *"& always will be":* Ibid.

217 *"gorgeous and showy":* Hay, *Diary*, p. 189.

217 *"as they passed by":* Corr., vol. 1, p. 212.

218 *"results so much":* Ibid., p. 213.

218 *"show them this letter":* Ibid., p. 215.

218 "*miracle in itself*": Ibid.

218 "*the hole after him*": Horace Porter, *Campaigning with Grant* (New York: Century, 1897), p. 98.

218 *hardly look at him without weeping:* Francis B. Carpenter, *Six Months at the White House with Abraham Lincoln* (New York: Hurd & Houghton, 1866), p. 30.

219 "*in his shirt to find us*": Hay, *Diary*, p. 194.

219 "*or it will kill me*": Schuyler Colfax, *Life and Principles of Abraham Lincoln* (Philadelphia: J. B. Rogers, 1865), p. 11–12.

219 "*communing with himself*": Oates, *WMTN*, p. 386.

219 *The "Wilderness" was aptly named:* Data on the Battle of the Wilderness comes from John S. Bowman, ed., *Encyclopedia of the Civil War* (North Dighton, MA: JG Press, 1992) pp. 182–183; and Morris, *Better Angel*.

220 "*usurped the place of earth*": Morris, *Better Angel*, p. 176.

220 "*if it takes all summer*": Oates, *WMTN*, p. 387.

220 "*unusual portion mortified*": Whitman, *Walt Whitman's Civil War*, p. 103.

221 "*cannot last many hours*": Corr., vol. 1, p. 217.

221 "*like getting well*": Ibid., p. 219.

221 "*tending a poor fellow*": Ibid., p. 221.

221 "*from being in too much*": Ibid., p. 223.

221 "*if he could only die*": Ibid., p. 227.

222 "*out of their senses*": Ibid., p. 231.

222 "*not felt first rate myself*": Ibid.

222 "*rather too much with*": Corr., vol. 1, p. 229.

222 "*fifty years old*": Ibid., p. 229.

222 "*absorbing the pus*": Ibid., p. 231.

222 "*virus in my system*": Ibid., p. 233.

222 "*change of air, & c.*": Ibid., p. 234.

Chapter 10: *Why Lincoln Laughed*

224 The item that provoked Lincoln's amusement can be found in *The Choice Works of Thomas Hood, in Prose and Verse* (New York: Lovell, n.d.). Bibliophiles estimate that this edition was published in the 1860s. In the absence of copyright laws, after Hood's death in 1845 dozens of editions of his works were published in England and America, from *Prose and Verse* (New York: Wiley & Putnam, 1845) to *Hood's Own; or, Laughter from Year to Year* (London: E. Moxon, 1862). Many used Hood's illustrations.

226 "*must not cry; that is all*": Boller, *Presidential Anecdotes*, p. 123.

228 "*no regard for life*": Keckley, *Behind the Scenes*, pp. 133–134.

228 "*conduct of the war*": Donald, *Lincoln*, pp. 502–503.

228 "*the damnedest fool*": Hay, *Diary*, pp. 197–198.

229 "*all for his re election*" . . . "*not even interesting*": Donald, *Lincoln*, pp. 502–504.

230 "*or longer sustained*": *CW* 7:419.

230 *the Wade-Davis Bill:* Waugh, *Reelecting Lincoln*, p. 226.

231 "*constitutionally by Congress*": Hay, *Diary*, p. 218.

231 *"I am inconsolable"*: Donald, *Lincoln*, p. 512.

231 *"fixed within myself"*: Hay, *Diary*, p. 219.

231 *"To the Supporters of the Government"* . . . *"the country's gone too"* passim: Waugh, *Reelecting Lincoln*, pp. 259–267.

233 *"that can befall a man"*: Brooks, *Washington*, p. 156.

233 *"It reminds me"* . . . *"can stand it if they can"*: Carpenter, *Six Months at the White House*, p. 145.

233 *"wild for Peace"*: *CW* 7:515, footnote letter from Weed to Seward, August 22, 1864.

234 *"setting strongly against us"*: *CW* 7:518, footnote letter from Raymond to Lincoln, August 22, 1864.

234 *"Madame Lincoln"*: Oates, *WMTN*, p. 400.

234 *"bills will be sent to him"*: Keckley, *Behind the Scenes*, p. 150.

234–35 *"This morning, as for some days"*: *CW* 7:514.

235 *"peace platform"* . . . *"the Chicago Surrender"*: Donald, *Lincoln*, p. 530.

235 *"war on a peace platform"*: Welles, *Diary*, vol. 2, p. 136.

235 *"vanity, or ambition"*: *CW* 7:506, from Diary of Joseph T. Mills.

235 *"for all future ages"*: *CW* 8:96.

236 *"much rather walk"*: Boller, *Presidential Anecdotes*, p. 127.

236 *"and fairly won"*: Waugh, *Reelecting Lincoln*, p. 297.

236 *"& prostitution gangrened"* and quotes passim: Corr., vol. 1, pp. 240–242.

238 *"provender with them"*: John S.

Bowman, ed., *Who Was Who in the Civil War* (North Dighton, MA: World Communications, 1998), p. 188.

238 near *Election Day:* Lincoln's election eve speech is in *CW* 8:58.

239 *"She is more anxious than I"*: Hay, *Diary*, p. 244.

239 *"all evening in fact"*: Ibid., p. 246.

239 *"rights of humanity"*: *CW* 8:96.

240 *"dumb fidelity"*: Hay, *Diary*, p. 246.

Chapter 11: Spring, 1865

242 *"nineteen enemies"*: Carpenter, *Six Months at the White House*, p. 276.

242 *"to your poems, &c."*: Corr., vol. 1, p. 246, footnote letter from O'Connor to Whitman, December 30, 1864.

242 *"I shall get so this spring"*: Ibid., p. 250.

243 *"with Major-General Butler"*: Whitman, *Walt Whitman's Civil War*, p. 206.

243 *"now in theirs"*: Ibid., p. 206.

243 *"the trial myself"*: Corr., vol. 1, p. 252.

243 *"when I come home"*: Corr., vol. 1, p. 250.

244 *"guard against trouble"*: Ibid.

244 *"presence of death"*: *WWC* 3:538.

244 *"I never knew"*: *Memoranda*, p. 43.

244 *"a great storm"*: Ibid.

244 *"suffused the soul"*: Ibid., p. 44.

245 *"comforts me somehow"*: Ibid., p. 42.

245 *"Come, so Come!"*: Barrus, *Whitman and Burroughs*, p. 20.

246 *The conductor:* The essential biography of Peter Doyle is Martin

Murray, "Pete the Great," *Walt Whitman Quarterly Review* 12 (summer 1994), pp. 1–50, available online at www.iath.virginia.edu/whitman/archive 1 /biography/supplementary/doyle/doyle.htm

246 *"The storm was awful":* Allen, *Solitary Singer*, p. 363.

246–247 *"One flitting glimpse":* LV, 1860–1861, p. 371.

247 *Doyle was Irish:* Doyle's history comes from Murray, "Pete the Great."

249 *"a mute inglorious Whitman":* Barrus, *Whitman and Burroughs*, p. 82.

249 *"type of mentality":* Dr. William Tindall, "Beginnings of Street Railways," in *Records of the Columbia Historical Society*, ed. Francis Coleman Rosenberger (Washington, D.C.: Columbia Historical Society, 1918), vol. 21, pp. 49–50.

250 *"the hour of closing came":* Walt Whitman, *Calamus: A Series of Letters Written During the Years 1868–1880 by Walt Whitman to a Young Friend (Peter Doyle)*, ed. Richard Maurice Bucke (Boston: Small, Maynard, 1897), pp. 24–25.

250 *"shout in the woods":* Ibid., p. 21.

250 *"all is love":* Shively, *Calamus Lovers*, p. 101.

250 *"church of the world":* Swinburne quoted in Barrus, *Whitman and Burroughs*, p. 206.

251 *On the main thoroughfares:* Description of Washington on March 3 is from the Washington *Evening Star*, March 4, 1865.

252 *"all made a mark'd combination":* "The Last Hours of Congress," from an Occasional Correspondent [Whitman], March 6, 1865, *NYT*, March 12, 1865.

252 *"shock did it good":* Ibid.

252 *"inches deep with it:* Ibid. Quotes *passim* are from Whitman's March 6 *NYT* dispatch, with details from the *Washington Star*, and the *Daily Morning Chronicle*, March 4, 1865.

254 *"around the Capitol building":* Brooks, *Washington*, p. 212.

255 *"right over him":* Whitman, *NYT*, ut supra.

255 *"by the sun of prosperity":* Brooks, Washington, p. 213.

255 *"All dreaded it . . . we be not judged":* CW 8:333.

255 *"a sacred effort":* Oates, *WMTN*, p. 412.

256 *"With malice toward none":* CW 8:333.

256 *"before they were due":* Whitman, *NYT, ut supra.*

256 *"equality with the occasion":* Sandburg, *War Years*, vol. 4, p. 96.

256 *"It made my heart jump":* Brooks, *Washington*, p. 195.

257 *"sadness and canny shrewdness":* Whitman, *NYT, ut supra.*

257 *"rudest forms of manliness":* Ibid.

258 *"thought he would die":* Morris, *Better Angel*, p. 205.

258 *"to the spacious sidewalks":* Whitman, *NYT, ut supra.*

258 *"to be somewhere else": Memoranda,* p. 43.

259 *"and much for Surgeon.)":* Whitman, *NYT, ut supra.*

259 *preparations for the ball:* Description
of the inaugural preparations in the
Patent Office building is from the
Washington *Morning Chronicle*,
March 7, 1865.

260 *"two short winters since":* Whitman,
NYT, ut supra.

260 *"hearth they would steam":* Donald,
Lincoln, p. 568.

261 *"through the next four years":* Keckley,
Behind the Scenes, p. 157.

261 *"the tired spot":* Brooks, *Washington*,
p. 55.

261 *"complete exhaustion":* Bishop, *Day
Lincoln Was Shot*, p. 38.

261 at Grover's Theatre: *Day by Day*,
vol. 3, p. 320.

261 *March 17, St. Patrick's day . . . Oliver
Morton: Washington Star*, March 18,
1865.

261 *occupied room 231:* Poore, *ut infra*,
vol. 1, p. 231.

261 *"his valuable services":* Ibid.

262 *Booth was taking:* Background on
John Wilkes Booth comes from
Francis Wilson, *John Wilkes Booth:
Fact and Fiction of Lincoln's
Assassination* (Boston: Houghton,
Mifflin, 1929); Lloyd Lewis, *The
Assassination of Lincoln: History and
Myth* (Lincoln: University of
Nebraska Press, 1994; reprint of 1929
ed.); and *The Conspiracy Trial for the
Murder of the President*, ed. by
Benjamin Perley Poore, 3 vols.
(Boston: J. E. Tilton, 1865).

262 *"Tara's Harp" . . . "Hail to the
Chief": Washington Star*, March 18,
1865.

263 *Whitman looked at the President:*

Allen Thorndike Rice, ed.
*Reminiscences of Abraham Lincoln by
Distinguished Men of His Time* (New
York: North American Review,
1888); also reprinted in Walt
Whitman, *Complete Poetry and
Collected Prose*, ed. Justin Kaplan
(New York: Library of America,
dist. by Viking Press, 1982), p. 1197.

263–266 *Lincoln then stepped . . . left the
balcony:* Atmospheric details of
Lincoln's speech, as well as the text,
come from the *Washington Star*,
March 18, 1865.

264 *"beyond, disembodied,":* WWC
3:22–23.

266 *John Wilkes Booth opened at Ford's
Theatre:* William Hanchett, *The
Lincoln Murder Conspiracies* (Urbana:
University of Illinois Press, 1983),
p. 125 ff.

267 *"life from out his heart?":* Ibid., p. 125.

267 *"without losing his own":* Rufus
Wilson, *Intimate Memories of
Lincoln*, p. 475.

267 *President dreamed of his own
assassination:* Bishop, *Day Lincoln
Was Shot*, p. 56. This is the famous
dream reported in Lamon's
Recollections of Abraham Lincoln, in
which Lincoln recalls waking in the
White House to the sound of
weeping, coming downstairs, and
viewing a corpse laid out in the East
Room. "Who is dead?" he asks.
"The President," a soldier replies,
"killed by an assassin." Scholars such
as Don E. Fehrenbacher have
discredited Lamon's story, partly on
the basis of Lincoln's dating of the

dream in early April, when the President was at the front. Bishop's footnote reads: "It is commonly agreed that Lincoln is wrong about the time of the dream. Lamon, who remembered this dialogue almost word for word, believed that the dream occurred on March 19, the night after the Lincolns saw *Faust*."

267 *seventeen known references:* F. DeWolfe Miller, introduction to Whitman, *Walt Whitman's Drum-Taps . . . and Sequel to Drum-Taps*, pp. xxvii ff. Data *passim* concerning the printing of the book are from this source, except as indicated.

268 *"continually bringing out poems":* Corr., vol. 1, p. 185.

268 *"able to go around":* Ibid., p. 236.

268 *"print my books myself ":* Ibid., p. 244.

269 *"faith & triumph":* Ibid., pp. 246–247.

269 *On April 4:* Day by Day, vol. 3, p. 325.

269 *"Glory, glory!":* Oates, *WMTN*, p. 421.

270 *"nightmare is gone":* Shelby Foote, *The Civil War: A Narrative* (New York: Random House, 1958–1974), vol. 3, p. 896.

270 *"between April 1 and 15 ":* F. DeWolfe Miller, *ut supra*, p. xxxvi.

270 *best clothes:* Studio photograph of Doyle by Moses P. Rice, John Rylands Library, Manchester, England.

270 *"cheerful—almost joyous":* Donald, *Lincoln*, p. 593.

271 *"my mind to go":* Whitman, *Calamus*, ed. Bucke, pp. 25–26.

272 *conductor tapped his baton:* Details of the evening come from Oates, *With*

Malice Toward None, pp. 430–432, and Bishop, *Day Lincoln Was Shot*, *passim*.

273 *"If that is so I'll get out!":* All Doyle quotes are from Whitman, *Calamus*, ed. Bucke, pp. 25–26.

Chapter 12: When Lilacs Last in the Dooryard Bloom'd

274 *"definite purport and idea)":* Corr., vol. 1, p. 246.

274 *"silently to each other":* Whitman, *Specimen Days; & Collect*, p. 26.

275 *"in the public ways":* NUPM, p. 765.

275 *"stirring wonder brewing":* Ibid., p. 762.

275 *"& gas lanterns":* Ibid., p. 764.

275 *"blood of Abraham Lincoln has":* Ibid., p. 765.

276 *"than Abraham Lincoln's death":* Whitman, *Specimen Days; & Collect*, p. 315.

276 *On Monday, April* 17: F. DeWolfe Miller's study: *Vide* his introduction to *Walt Whitman's Drum-Taps . . . and Sequel to Drum-Taps*.

279 *"such a triumphal march":* Sandburg, *War Years*, vol. 4, pp. 398–399.

279 *"in private chambers":* NUPM, p. 768.

279 *"No mourning drape hang":* Ibid., p. 769.

280 *"Sorrow grieve sad":* Ibid., p. 767.

280 *"Hermit Thrush":* Ibid., p. 766.

281 *"one of his principal poems":* Barrus, *Whitman and Burroughs*, p. 24.

281 *"the finest souls may know":* John

Burroughs, quoted in Neltje
Blanchan, *Bird Neighbors* (New York,
Doubleday & McClure, 1897), p. 125.

282 *"I give you my sprig of lilac":* The
extracts and the entire text of "When
Lilacs Last in the Door-Yard
Bloom'd" are taken from the first
publication of the poem in *Walt
Whitman's Drum-Taps . . . and Sequel
to Drumtaps;* pp. 3–12 in *Sequel.*

293 *ideal of the democratic nation:* My
reading of the poem here owes a debt
to Kenneth Burke's 1955 essay,
"When Lilacs Last in the Dooryard
Bloom'd," reprinted in *A Century of
Whitman Criticism,* ed. Edwin
Haviland Miller (Bloomington:
Indiana University Press, 1969),
pp. 292–302.

295 *"dwells on these bearded lips":*
Whitman, *Drum-Taps,* p. 34.

296 *subjugate his own voice:* Some post-
Foucaultian readers deconstruct the
poem as an allegory of Whitman's
sexual renunciation, e.g., the broken
lilac stem as castration symbol.

296 *"as a social force":* Allen, *Solitary
Singer,* p. 339.

298 *"long into the night":* NUPM, p. 779.

298 *his New York regiment: Corr.,* vol. 1,
pp. 260–263.

298 *"hope in life almost crushed":* Baker,
Mary Todd Lincoln, p. 254.

299 *"some sort of notices appeared":*
F. DeWolfe Miller, *ut supra,* p. xxi.

300 *"O Captain! my captain!":* Whitman,
Sequel to Drum-taps, p. 13.

301 *jointly reviewed with* Leaves of Grass:
Kaplan, *Walt Whitman,* p. 195.

301 *"with some sweet passages":* Ibid.

301 *memorized and recited his verses:* Allen,
Solitary Singer, p. 476.

302 *"Till all my widow'd race be run":*
Alfred, Lord Tennyson, *In
Memoriam,* IX.

302 *"not for thee the glow, the bloom":*
Ibid., II.

302 *"sorrow drowning song":* Ibid., XIX.

303 *"ever wrote the poem":* WWC 2:304.

303 *"from and after this date":* Chronology,
p. 69.

303 *out for persecution:* Allen, *Solitary
Singer,* pp. 345–346.

304 *to the departmental library:* Kaplan,
Walt Whitman, p. 306.

304 *October* 28, 1865: F. DeWolfe Miller,
ut supra, p. xlix.

305 *"cannot be called a true poet":* Allen,
Solitary Singer, p. 360.

305 *"be got at a bookstore":* F. DeWolfe
Miller, *ut supra,* p. li.

305 *the hermit thrush:* The copy described
is in the Rare Book Collection of the
Library of Congress.

Chapter 13: *Madison Square Theatre: New
York, April 14, 1887*

Background on the history of New
York, population, immigration, etc.,
comes from Kenneth T. Jackson, ed.,
The Encyclopedia of New York City,
(New Haven: Yale University Press,
1995), and E. Robinson & R. H.
Pidgeon, *Robinson's Atlas of the City
of New York* (New York: E.
Robinson, 1885).

311 *MADISON SQUARE THEATRE:*
Display ad, *NYT,* April 14, 1887.

312 *"cloud of my life"*: Corr., vol. 2, pp. 222–223.

313 *"a mere physical wreck"*: Allen, *Solitary Singer*, p. 453.

313 *"It was past belief"*: S. Weir Mitchell, *When All the Woods Are Green: A Novel* (New York: Century, 1894; 1910), p. 274.

314 *"overturned fruit stall"*: David S. Reynolds, *Walt Whitman's America: A Cultural Biography* (New York: Alfred A. Knopf, 1995), p. 565.

314 *"modern times"*: Ibid., p. 517.

314 get on with his life: Corr., vol. 2, p. 334.

314 was assuaged: Information on Harry Stafford and William Duckett comes from Shively, *Calamus Lovers*, pp. 138–147, 173–181.

315 horse and buggy: Allen, *Solitary Singer*, p. 523.

316 *"regarded in the future"*: WWC 4:142.

316 *"misunderstood Jesus"*: Barrus, *Whitman and Burroughs*, p. 201.

316 *"I do not deserve it."*: Corr., vol. 4, p. 56.

317 *"as that of a god"*: John Burroughs, *Whitman, A Study* (Boston: Houghton, Mifflin, 1896), pp. 52–53.

317 *"attractiveness of the man"*: Richard Maurice Bucke, *Cosmic Consciousness: A Study in the Evolution of the Human Mind* (New York: E. P. Dutton, 1923), p. 217.

317 confessing to accepting bribes: Niven, *Salmon P. Chase*, p. 513, n. 28.

318 the successful Madison Square Theatre: Information about the Madison Square Theatre is from J. A. Sokalski, "The Madison Square Theatre: Stage Practice and

Technology in Transition," *Theatre History Studies* 21 (June 2001); Wayne S. Turney, "Madison Square Theatre," online; and E. J. Phillips, 1880s Letters, "Madison Square Theatre Company," online.

319 companion William Duckett: Details of travel, Corr., vol. 4, pp. 82–83.

319 *"Personal Intelligence"*: NYT, April 14, 1887.

319 The body of Abraham Lincoln was being exhumed: NYT, ibid. The story of the attempt to rob Lincoln's grave is told in Lewis, *Assassination of Lincoln*, pp. 281–282.

320 end of the labyrinth: Lewis, *Assassination of Lincoln*, pp. 283–284.

321 From the porte-cochere . . . corner of Twenty-second: Robinson's Atlas.

322 stood at 48 degrees: NYT, April 15, 1887.

322 had a toothache: This and many other details of the day come from the New York *Evening Sun*, April 15, 1887, "An Old Poet's Reception," which took up thirty-eight column inches in the paper.

322 all pasted up: Whitman's "makeshift book" pasted on *The Bride of Gettysburg* is in the Charles E. Feinberg Collection, Library of Congress.

322 *"to lecture upon Lincoln"*: Letter from John Burroughs to Walt Whitman, February 3, 1878, reprinted in Barton, *AL & WW*, pp. 192–193.

323 *"and Literary Entertainments"*: Reynolds, *Walt Whitman's America*, p. 555.

323 *production of* The Taming of the Shrew: "Lucentio's Banquet Outdone," *NYT,* April 14, 1887.

324 *"so far in at last":* Ibid.

326 *for desecrating the Sabbath:* Kenton J. Clymer, *John Hay: The Gentleman as Diplomat* (Ann Arbor: University of Michigan Press, 1975), p. 9.

326 *Hay had held:* On Hay's career, *vide* Kushner and Sherrill, John Milton Hay.

326 *how many celebrities:* "Walt Whitman on Lincoln," *Critic* 173 (April 23, 1887); *NYT,* April 15, 1887; *Evening Sun, ut supra.* The *Critic* review, unsigned, is almost certainly by Jeannette Gilder.

326 *Mark Twain knew most: Vide* R. Kent Rasmussen, *Mark Twain A to Z,* (New York, Oxford: Oxford University Press, Facts on File, 1995), *passim.*

327 *copy of* The Prince and the Pauper: Justin Kaplan, *Mr. Clemens and Mark Twain: A Biography* (Simon & Schuster, 1966), p. 239.

327 *Carnegie . . . greatest poet in America:* Allen, *Solitary Singer,* p. 525.

327 *stove molders' strike:* "A Big Struggle" *NYT,* April 15, 1887.

327–28 *high in the air: NYT,* April 14, 1887; "Lynched in a Court Room."

328 *"had a genesis":* Reynolds, *ut supra,* p. 305.

329 *edging of lace: Evening Sun, ut supra.*

329 *Suppé's "The Poet's Dream," etc.:* Lecture programs in the Charles E. Feinberg Collection, Library of Congress.

329 *"to slowly improvise":* Barton, *AL & WW,* p. 211.

330 *"How often since":* Whitman's speech is taken from the *New York Times* and from the text of his speech "The Death of Abraham Lincoln" as preserved in the Charles E. Feinberg Collection, Library of Congress.

333 *lead of the casket:* Lewis, *Assassination of Lincoln,* p. 286.

333 *"easily recognizable":* "Abraham Lincoln's Body," *NYT,* April 15, 1887.

333 *slightly tilted back:* Philip B. Kunhardt, *Lincoln: An Illustrated Biography* (New York: Alfred A. Knopf, 1994), p. 399.

334 *faint white powder:* Ibid., pp. 372, 383.

335 *Now they laughed:* "Walt Whitman on Lincoln," *Critic* 173, p. 206.

336 *"tragedies of Eschylus":* Merrill quoted in Barton, *Abraham Lincoln and Walt Whitman,* p. 211.

337 *Laura made her way:* "Walt Whitman on Lincoln," *Critic* 173, p. 206.

339 *Laura moved into the spotlight: NYT,* April 15, 1887.

339 *The voice faltered:* Merrill's pamphlet memoir of this occasion, published in Toronto in 1922, and quoted at length in Barton, *Abraham Lincoln and Walt Whitman,* pp. 211–212, reports this sequence of events. "The voice died away in the noise of the applause, which appeared to me an outrage to the grief of the poet."

ACKNOWLEDGMENTS

First, I want to record my gratitude to my agent, Neil Olson, and my editor, Elisabeth Kallick Dyssegaard, for their faith in this project from its inception, and their encouragement and advice as the book evolved.

Next I would like to thank Dr. Alice Birney, the literary manuscript historian at the Library of Congress, for guiding me through the voluminous Whitman Collections there. Dr. Birney made it possible for me to view manuscripts and artifacts—including Whitman's haversack—not currently on display.

I want to thank all the staff at the Library of Congress who helped me, in the Map Room and the Periodicals Collection, and especially librarians Fred W. Bauman Jr., Jeffrey M. Flannery, and Bruce Kirby in the Manuscript Division, for their assistance in locating documents and microfilm. In the Rare Book and Special Collections Division, Gerald Wager, Head of Reference and Reader Services, and Clark Evans, Reference Specialist, saw to it that I got hands-on experience with the early editions of Whitman's *Leaves of Grass* and *Drum-Taps,* and other books. Dr. John Sellers, Civil War Specialist of the Manuscript Division, helped answer many of my questions about Lincoln. Dr. Sellers also put me in touch with other scholars in the field.

Historian Michael Burlingame helped me to solve research problems, as did Tom Schwartz, the Illinois State Historian, and my friend Neil Grauer of Baltimore. Lincoln biographer Stephen B. Oates cautioned me about relying upon Ward Hill Lamon's account of "Lincoln's Dream," and Whitman biographer Jerome Loving contributed insights about Whitman's speaking voice and other matters. Author Eric Foner offered helpful advice concerning Stephen Douglas.

Sometimes it seemed that everywhere I went in this book, the historian David Herbert Donald had preceded me: his biographies of Herndon, Sumner, and Lincoln are invaluable works of scholarship. So are Justin Kaplan's biographies of Whitman and Twain, which I have cited often in my notes; I am especially grateful to Mr. Kaplan for his personal encouragement.

Thanks to Richard Moe, Civil War historian and president of the National Trust for Historic Preservation, for his gracious hospitality in allowing a tour of the Soldiers' Home, and to his assistant Sophie Lynn, for guiding the tour. Ms. Lynn also provided me with a map of Lincoln's route from the White House to the Soldiers' Home. I am also indebted to Richard Coates, Curator of the Treasury Building, for his personal guided tour of the building where Whitman and his friends worked. Mary Edwards made available to me the Treasury's large photograph collection. I also want to thank architectural historian Laurie Ossman of the Maryland Historical Society for helping to arrange both of those tours.

At the Milton S. Eisenhower Library of the Johns Hopkins University, librarians Nancy Darovanitch and Amy Kimball in Special Collections were helpful in arranging for me to use, and photocopy, the huge *Robinson's Atlas of the City of New York,* and James Gillispie of the maps division provided the map of New York drawn by M. Dripps in 1866.

Jay Satterfield, Head of Reader Services, Special Collections Research Center of the University of Chicago Library, diligently searched the Barton Collection there for William Herndon's copy of *Leaves of Grass*. Determining that Herndon's book was not in that collection was important. Betty K. Koed, Assistant Senate Historian, United States Senate, answered my questions about Whitman's meetings with Charles Sumner and Preston King.

In writing this book I was fortunate in having two astute readers, Rosemary Knower and David Bergman, study the manuscript in early drafts and suggest numerous changes in style and structure. I owe them an enormous debt of gratitude for their insights into the persons and events in the book. And I am also grateful to Janet Fletcher for her meticulous fact-checking and copyediting and to Julia Cheiffetz for her kind editorial assistance.

I was born in Washington, D.C. Half a century ago I walked the streets that Whitman and Lincoln knew, when many of the blocks looked much as they did when these heroes were alive. My father, and his father before him, owned an amusement arcade and shooting gallery at 413 Ninth Street N.W., dead center of the action described in this book. I worked there in my youth, and I can still smell the gunpowder. To my father, and mother, and grandparents, I owe the sense of place.

INDEX

MAP AND ILLUSTRATION CREDITS

Page